Cerebral Abyss

Paradigms, Ignorance, and Our Imperiled Future

Frank Camelio

Current Edition: First
Date: October 2020

Registration Number: TXu002195496

Library of Congress Control Number: Pending

ISBN: Print (Paperback) 9798552893850

Dedication

To Humanity:

May you develop the wisdom to continue your journey to the only paradise possible, the one you construct here on Earth and integrate with every other living thing.

Other Books by Frank Camelio

Savior
(Fiction)

One Last Hope: Strategies to Prevent Imminent National Decline and Create a Better Future
(Nonfiction)

Foreword

Hold on. Things are about to get a bit strange for most readers. You're about to look at yourself and your world through unique lenses—and they won't be rose-tinted. You will learn to see and dissect the world through your own paradigms and grasp the paradigms of others. If you don't know what a paradigm is, don't worry. For now, think of it as a system of belief—a personal or collective worldview—but there's more to paradigms than simply believing or not believing in commonplace or arbitrary ideas. You will come to appreciate the connection between your worldviews and your ignorance. You will look at history differently and discover that human events unfolded the way they did largely due to the paradigms that dominated human thinking during the march of history. We begin this journey with a brief overview of times past and present.

Historians have classified numerous periods of the past to provide a retrospective—overarching, simplifying themes that characterize the various eras of human history. They have given us the Dark Ages, the Age of Discovery, the Scientific Revolution, the Enlightenment, and many others. More recently, historians and media pundits have labeled the ages in which they live, such as the Atomic Age, Space Age, and Computer Age (or Information Age). These latest designations are often premature and lack the perspective of hindsight. By waiting, these present-day seers would eventually come to see the events, decisions, outcomes, ideologies, and values of their era crystallize with thematic clarity. Yet patience is not a stalwart human trait.

And I am impatient and eager to explain the flow of history through the paradigms that occupied the thoughts and steered the behaviors of our ancestors. I portray the causes of human ignorance through unconventional but convincing historical, scientific, economic, political, and sociological perspectives or paradigms, of both the past and present. I cannot predict with complete certainty how future historians will view our current era, but I am confident that they will claim that we have descended into a truly ignominious Age of Ignorance (my term for the present state of our individual and collective awareness).

In the Dark Ages (approximately 476 to 1000 C.E. or Common Era), humanity did not have widespread access to reliable, scientifically vetted information. Literacy was rare, and people relied largely on orally transmitted knowledge, which was often imbued with irrational opinionating of mystical and mythical qualities. Stated simply, most people told stories and accepted what respected individuals or those in power said, such as a king, noble, or the clergy. A plethora of fictions helped to define the worldviews of social groups. People believed what they did because of stories and because of their interpretations of their sensory environment. We might judge them to be highly ignorant. Yet, are we any better today?

In the present, the Age of Ignorance exists largely because of one significant pervasive phenomenon: we act contrary to facts and substantiated trends. We do this even though the data at our disposal is acquired through disciplined and controlled methods and despite overwhelming evidence of their veracity or plausibility. One need only to read, listen, or view distributed media to observe the extent of our individual and collective ignorance. Sensationalized storylines, misinformation, opinion-laced tweets, fake, trivial, or distracting social media posts, and poorly researched and analyzed information flood the internet and broadcast and print media daily. Sadly, some scientists and pseudo-scientists of questionable integrity also disseminate false or misleading information. The shared data becomes infused into the noösphere[1] - the collective consciousness of humanity. The noösphere is the sum total of all the stored data (knowledge) available for recall, whether in the minds of persons, physical records, or analog or digital storage devices. Destroyed media from the past and present (scrolls, books, film, etc.), the memories and uniquely known information humans have taken to their graves, and displaced or vanished cultures represent a loss of knowledge from the noösphere. The twenty-first century noösphere has become immense, nigh overwhelming, due to the significant growth of population and the technological advances in data storage and retrieval.

In the present, the data deluge serves to contaminate the noösphere, with minutia and diversions. Often, the knowledge that drifts to the forefront lends too much credence to the untrue and the irrelevant. The contamination can be spectacular, as government entities, businesses, NGOs (non-governmental organizations), and individuals frequently neglect a spectrum of evidentiary data concerning environmental degradation, socioeconomic disparities, decaying infrastructure, wasteful utilization of public resources, health

[1] Teilhard de Chardin, 180-184.

information, and much more. Consider, for example, how the tobacco industry promoted its profits over the health of consumers, once countering claims of scientific research that indicated a definitive link between cigarette usage and lung cancer.

Within the fog of ignorance permeating the noösphere, political, economic, cultural, technological, and religious forces are moving the modern era toward potential and real disasters on a planetary scale. These forces stem directly from the paradigms or perspectives through which we see the world.[2] We are our own worst enemies because our paradigms steer us to think and behave ignorantly. To help lift the fog, I decided to assess the historical impact of paradigms that recurred from era to era. As my analysis congealed, it led me to one persuasively simple reality: Humans are collectively as ignorant today as in any era of the past. While I cannot prove this statement with the scientific rigidity I'd prefer, the body of evidence is convincing. History is my ally. However, we cannot evaluate history through the standard lens of historians, archaeologists, and other researchers who delve into our past. We must examine history in terms of the dominant paradigms that prevailed during specific periods of human development. These paradigms have largely dictated how history has unfolded. The most dominant paradigms in each era led to the specific outcomes by which we have characterized the past. They provide us compelling arguments for explaining the course of human events up to the present.

Of note, many past paradigms persist whether they are credible and beneficial or not. Some paradigms have shifted. Others have vanished. As if suffering from amnesia, we either forget or pay little heed to the negative impact of past and present-day paradigms. We fail to recognize how the collective set of paradigms that dominate in our present is leading us to a perilous future. We have learned little from history because we have failed to adequately uncover the linkage between our paradigms and the course of history—until now.

While I believe that "troubles" lie ahead for humanity if we persist in our ignorant ways, the challenges do not necessarily equate to doom and gloom. My primary aims are to expose the dangers of our

---

[2] Certainly, greed and malfeasance are behind many of the misdeeds and propaganda causing people to make imprudent decisions and create misguided policies. Yet, as we shall see, these corruptions stem directly from the paradigms through which we see the world.

continued paradigm paralysis and to present sufficient evidence that our current dominant paradigms are driving fundamental flaws in our thinking and behaviors. As a result, a significant segment of humanity faces an irrepressible bleakness. My outlook is tempered by the knowledge that we can minimize most of the negative outcomes for humanity through incremental and step shifts in our paradigms.

The trends, however, are disturbing. Rather than solving problems, Moderns (you and I) are exacerbating them. Sociopolitical dramas are playing out throughout the world to establish a direction for humanity, often without regard for facts and verifiable rationales. Amplifying the negative effects of our ignorant ways is a war of paradigms. The paradigms are global in scope and include mega-corporate imperialism, [3] technocratic capitalism, divine purpose, ecological absolutism, and rampant globalization, among others. These and other paradigms are vying for dominance. Most of these paradigms do little to promote the general, long-term human welfare. Which paradigms will survive is a matter of conjecture, but we can predict with high certainty that as long as the paradigms responsible for our current Age of Ignorance persist, a significant portion of humanity will live in appalling misery.

We may not be able to eliminate the despair and wretchedness of all of the world's population, but, as Plato envisioned, we may be able to remove the shackles binding us to our caves, open our eyes to enlightenment, and find pathways to a greater good.[4]

---

[3] I developed this term to describe the way multinational corporate conglomerates are gradually replacing nation-states in their influence over the direction of humanity. With the exception of large nation-states, these mega-companies have accumulated wealth (assets) beyond that of a majority of nations. I call it imperialism because these global entities attempt to wield control over most of humanity. They tap the resources and siphon wealth toward their domains, much as Old World colonial imperialists did in the New World, Africa, and Asia. These entities create paradigms of a "better world" through advertising and other media to shape our perspectives. They differ only in means and methods of past power brokers to expound their narratives and sculpt the paradigms of society. We will revisit this topic in greater depth when we discuss dominant paradigms.

[4] The reference to Plato, shackles, and caves refers to the Parable or Allegory of the Cave in Plato's *Republic*, further discussed in this book. The true source of the allegory may be Socrates whose dialogues Plato used to describe the characteristics of a hypothetical cave-world. I give all credit to Plato, however, for his thoughtful efforts in writing the allegory down for posterity. We will have much more to say about this parable in the pages that follow.

Acknowledgements

When I retired from active service in the U.S. Navy, I decided to broaden myself and step out of my comfort zone to learn the fundamental principles of political science, history, and sociology at the University of Hawaii (UH), West Oahu. Due to my previous studies in physics, mathematics, and engineering, my natural inclination is to view systems as an integrated whole—in this case, the human-ecological system. This scientific approach helped me to apply holistic methods to formulate Big Picture assessments of human development. My studies expanded and advanced my understanding of the political, cultural, sociological, economic, and religious forces and systems that have shaped the present. I accordingly acknowledge the positive influences of Dr. Monique Mironesco, Dr. Louis Herman, Dr. Jayson Chun, Dr. James Turner, Dr. Michael Delucchi, Dr. Dayna Minatodani, Dr. Alan Rosenfeld, and Dr. Sailiemanu Lilomaiava-Doktor. Your courses in American, global, and comparative politics, political philosophy, constitutional law, mass media and politics, world history, cultural anthropology, the history of terrorism, and more, provided me a robust knowledge of who we are and how we got here. Thank you all for stimulating and stirring me to think with freshened perspectives and for helping me to acquire the intellectual tools to develop meaningful hypotheses to explain the human condition.

There is one other very special collection of people to thank. Every day, I see, hear, or read about the efforts of individuals and groups to counter the forces that are preventing us from breaking free of our collective ignorance and transcending to a New Enlightenment. Their endeavors indicate we can change and elevate ourselves above much of the fray of our own ignorance. It requires that we not only conscientiously analyze past facts and trends, but also evaluate where our paradigms and ignorance are leading us. Many are already combating ignorance in local, national, and global arenas by writing about and acting upon alternative perspectives, meanwhile educating others. Though the challenges facing these individuals and groups are daunting, their actions and efforts speak volumes of their humanity. You know who you are even if others don't. I acknowledge and applaud your steadfastness and wisdom.

Frank Camelio
October 2020

Table of Contents

Table of Figures (Paradigm Funnels)

Table of Paradigm Filters

Table of Ignorance Determinations

Chapter 1: Introduction

"Humankind, We Have a Problem—a Big One."

"... humans are all too often willing to grasp at unrealistic promises of a better life and to believe that a better life can only be attained by clinging to intolerance and ignorance, by lessening the lives of others."
– Michael Shermer [5]

Since you started to read this book, I'm going to take a stab at what you're thinking right now: "Cerebral abyss ... paradigms ... ignorance ... is the author trying to make something out of nothing and to conjure up yet another pseudo-, human-induced calamity?" My answer is a resounding "No!" This book is about the danger to "us" – you and me and nearly eight billion others. The topic is critical to our collective futures, both as individuals and as a species. I humbly and sincerely submit that this book could be one of the most important you ever read, not because you will learn specific knowledge about the human condition but because you will become more conscious of yourself, others, and your surroundings—what makes you *you* and others themselves, and why circumstances play out the way they do. Greater awareness also means less ignorance and better informed decision-making. Most importantly, you will learn that by thoughtfully

---

[5] Shermer, 278.

interacting with others, you can stimulate the necessary paradigm shifts to create a better future for all humanity.

I realize that given the seemingly unglamorous nature of the topic, I need to keep you reading and must convince you quickly about the severity of the problems we face. Let's get to it.

What exactly is the problem? We are adrift in a sea of largely self-generated ignorance, caught in a riptide of competing paradigms that control our thoughts and behaviors. As a result, our decision-making is impaired, both as individuals and groups (e.g., nations, races, political entities, socioeconomic classes, etc.). All this will become clearer in Chapter 2 as we delve into the factors that create our paradigms and imperil our decision-making. For now, let me illustrate the problem by examining a common phenomenon that links our paradigms to our ignorance.

Consider cell phones and other handheld, internet-connected devices. These are true marvels of human ingenuity. People love their cell phones and similar gadgets. Most would feel lost, perhaps even empty, without them. Yet few consumers understand how cell phones work. That in itself doesn't make these users grossly ignorant. However, how the cell phone influences us, and simultaneously, fails to diminish our ignorance, led me to an undeniable conclusion: human thoughts and behaviors are grossly uninformed despite the technological wonders at our disposal. I assert my conclusion confidently because I have observed firsthand the derision and disparagement held by a large segment of the population regarding scientific matters. Their perspectives (or paradigms)—their mental models—of science are rooted in disdain and disbelief, without logical foundation. The reasons are many—ideology, ego, religion, lack of education, and group-think, among others. Ignorance is the result.

It's perplexing. On the one hand, we recognize that over four hundred years of study, research, experimentation, and disciplined methodologies have placed cell phones in our hands. Yet a large segment of humanity refuses to accept the validity of the sciences that have created these devices and shaped our modern society. Additionally, only a small fraction of users leverage their devices' capabilities to improve their knowledge of anything and everything.[6] It's mind-numbing to watch. With cell phones in hand, we are literally overdosing on excess, inconsequential, and often false information and opinions—checking texts and e-mail incessantly, updating social media websites addictively, and trolling mindlessly to access the latest and greatest ways to attain instant gratification or recognition. These behaviors often occur as we go about our daily activities, including at the dinner table, in classrooms, while driving, and during business meetings. Rather than engaging with information to improve our knowledge and to examine the true and relevant, we produce and consume data haphazardly and communicate ideas and information with little substantive content. As we do, we're multitasking our way to greater ignorance by making it harder to separate the important from the mundane and irrelevant.

Worse yet are the power brokers, who, with cell phones in hand, find fault with scientific endeavors and mock the conclusions of trustworthy and sincere scientists. The know-it-alls have convinced themselves that they have a greater understanding of the universe than the innovators who placed cell phones in their hands, dismissing hundreds of years of progressive scientific endeavor. They disingenuously prize their cell phones as an integral part of their lives while finding ways to minimize the efforts of scientists who seek to find truths about our existence and our surroundings.[7] They deny geological, climatological, biological, medical, and anthropological data and research, discounting many of the ideas generated in these fields, often solely based on religious, cultural, and/or ideological "reasoning" or financial benefit. Some of these charlatans prefer the

---

[6] This statement generally does not apply to the developing world, with historically poor information infrastructure, where cell phones play an integral role in the lives of people—everything from finding work to accessing vital services. These people use cell phones to gain functional knowledge and to better thrive in their societies. This in no way implies the cell phone is a cure for their ignorance. The reason for this will become clear later as we link our ignorance to our paradigms.

[7] The same is true of most technological innovations. For example, the thermodynamics behind the science and technology of refrigeration also applies to the analysis of weather and climate. Yet, climate change deniers, who claim climate science is a hoax or otherwise incorrect, hypocritically utilize refrigerators and air conditioners to serve their own comforts.

miraculous and metaphysical to proven principles. They refute the reasonable and coherent explanations derived from the scientific method or by logical argument. To many of them, evolution and human-induced climate change are scams.

In the extreme are the religious and ideological fanatics who use cell phones to carry out nefarious deeds, such as detonating bombs to promote their paradigms. They justify their actions through twisted theological and ideological interpretations and beliefs, contradicting well-vetted historical and scientific findings. Yet they employ the products of the very science they detest for a singular purpose: to elevate their worldview or paradigms to supremacy.

The preceding examples capture the essence of the problems addressed in this book, but for us to appreciate their significance we must delve into the details. Despite the large volume of confusing and contradictory content to which we are exposed, humanity still possesses the tools to lift the shroud of ignorance and to function intelligently in the increasingly complex world we've created. Unlike our ancestors, we have access to abundant, well-scrutinized knowledge about our surroundings and ourselves—an understanding acquired through deliberate and disciplined systems of analysis. That knowledge has dramatically expanded and continues to be refined, a quantum leap over our comprehension of the world several hundred years ago. Unfortunately, we have largely chosen ignorance over enlightenment as if we aspire to live in a Cognitive Dark Age. We do what humanity has always done—act and think according to a set of paradigms—a largely inflexible interpretation of the world around us. We may know more than our forebears on an absolute scale, but there's also much, much more to know to function successfully in modern society. One simple reason for this phenomenon is that we can only grasp a small volume of the noösphere[8] or the sum total of human knowledge today; however, as we shall see, there's more to the story than Big Data effects.

Some might claim that our present-day ignorance is unavoidable. Using Pascal's idea that "*Knowledge is like a sphere, the*

[8] This term is explained in the Foreword. Please refer to that section if you skipped over it.

greater its volume, the larger its contact with the unknown,"[9] a fallibilist might argue that the knowledge held by any individual cannot keep pace with the explosion of new information. Humans have finite mental capacity; thus, the fraction of total knowledge we know decreases—meaning as information amasses, individual ignorance increases. And if that's not enough, by injecting inconsequential and dubious information into the equation, we are artificially inflating our sphere of knowledge with nonsense—a true corruption of the noösphere. We haphazardly introduce errors that diminish what is known while simultaneously increasing what is unknown.

In everyday life, however, there is a way to deflate the sphere. Pascal's line of thinking fails to recognize that information is reducible to "Big Picture" elements—facts, themes, and concepts that are proven, verifiable, highly probable, logically rooted, and/or communally holistic and synergistic. Thus, to provide a qualitative and quantitative assessment of ignorance through the ages, this book considers past and present Big Picture content. We shall distill these elements in each era of history. For example, human conflict has occurred for a plethora of reasons throughout our history. If we catalogued the causes of war, we would understand that most wars were fought for one or more of the following reasons: resources, religion, control (power), and ideology. Sure, there may be many more esoteric reasons for waging wars but not with sufficient frequency to gain our attention. By focusing on these Big Picture elements, we avoid the quagmire of minutia. Sometimes the Big Picture is obvious; other times not. However, before we claim to understand the Big Picture, we must validate that the information that went into its determination is both true and relevant.

As mentioned previously, we currently have relatively easy access to well-tested and evaluated evidentiary data to make these critical assessments. Thus, we should be better able to inform our decision-making, but we often squander the opportunity, failing to

---

[9] See Witte in bibliography for Blaise Pascal quote. Also, note that if the radius of a sphere doubles, its volume increases by a factor of eight and its surface area by a factor of four. Using the Pascal analogy, then, if what we *can* know increases eight-fold (what's inside the sphere), what we don't know (what's in contact with the sphere's surface) increases four-fold. The (known) unknowns (what we are ignorant of) are greater than in times past when our knowledge was limited. We shall return to the concept of knowns and unknowns and other sources of ignorance in Chapter 3.

seek and to utilize the knowledge necessary to escape the perspectives of our "caves."

To explain his ideas about truth and enlightenment, Plato conceived of a situation where adult prisoners, who were confined by chains in a cave from childhood, are only able to experience the world as fire-cast shadows. Their paradigm of the world became the dark and dreary two-dimensional shadow events cast on their cave walls. Their "picture" of the world was very narrow. Plato conjectured that if one or more of these prisoners escaped to see the light of day, take in the colors of the skies, lands, and waters, and experience the freedom of movement, they could not readily accept and understand their new paradigm of reality and would struggle to become enlightened. Eventually, the escapees might come to accept and understand their new world. If however, they returned to their caves, they could not see and perform as well in the darkness compared to their former comrades. If the escapees tried to educate the prisoners about the outside world, the prisoners would consider the escapees as blinded by the outside light and would scoff at the other-worldly (Big Picture) view in disbelief, unable to shift their paradigm to another reality.

In our metaphorical modern caves, we seem trapped in a cerebral abyss, where our paradigms block the light that would shift our perspectives, shrink our ignorance, and elevate our altruistic and public-spirited qualities.[10] If unchecked, our current Age of Ignorance portends a disappointing future for humanity. The remainder of this book is devoted to the development of ideas and methods to shed the veil or ignorance that is corrupting our decision-making today and darkening our tomorrows.

Before proceeding, I should note that the phenomenon of ignorance has recently become a field of study called agnotology. The academic approaches taken rightfully focus on causes and states of ignorance within a social context. While I coined the terms Age of Ignorance and Cognitive Dark Ages for use in this book, some agnotologists have come up with similar classifications about our current state of ignorance. For example, Rose and Bartoli speak of a "culture of ignorance" that has ushered in an "Age of Intellectual Darkness."[11] This book will continue to refer to the Age of Ignorance

---

[10] Note: It is particularly important that our public officials not be cave-dwellers!

[11] Rose and Bartoli, 184-189. This article is highly recommended.

and Socratic caves, the latter of which substitute for a culture of ignorance.

Additionally, the reader may already be assuming that my forecast for the future is pessimistic despite some notable evidence to the contrary. In his recent book, *Enlightenment Now: The Case for Reason, Science, Humanism, and Progress*, Steven Pinker paints a promising picture of a New Enlightenment and a better future based on numerous data-supported trends covering a gamut of sociological, economic, medical, foreign relations, and other data. I agree with and applaud his general prognosis. However, his perspectives are also paradigm-dependent. The fraction of the world living in poverty and starving may be declining as the food produced per arable acre is increasing, but the total suffering remains needlessly high. An optimist could cite as a reference point that the world once had seven billion people of whom one billion were living in wretched poverty. Then, statistically, the optimist could claim progress if the world now has eight billion in it and only one billion live in misery, meaning the percentage living in poverty has decreased. However, a critical question endures. Why should one in eight humans have to endure such hardship? Why do any humans have to endure abject lives? I maintain that our collective paradigms are the reason we accept less from ourselves and tolerate such widespread wretchedness.

Accordingly, this is not a book about pessimism or optimism about the future, but it is about elevating ourselves—finding ways to shift our thinking and behaviors to encourage the best possible outcomes for the greater human family.

Why Explore This Topic?

If you made it this far, you may still be wondering, "Why would anyone write or read a book on such a bizarre topic? Humans have existed in various states of ignorance since becoming consciously aware of themselves. People are ignorant of many aspects of life because of personal hardships, culture, education, religion, and more—they always have been and always will be ignorant about much of what goes on around them. And despite our scientific advances, the world remains a mystery to most. So, isn't ignorance simply an inevitable quality of the human condition?"

If you're thinking along these lines, you have great insight into this topic. Given that a person cannot know everything about his or her surroundings, you inherently understand that under the definition of ignorance we will use in this book, there are varying degrees of ignorance. You understand that ignorance is a lack of knowledge or information; however, in this book, ignorance has a broader meaning. Ignorance manifests itself in many other ways—such as when a person blindly accepts information as true, when a person cannot or will not distinguish among fact, fiction, and fancy, and most significantly, when a person persists with actions and promotes ideas as proper and true despite clear evidence to the contrary.

Also, one thing you may not appreciate is the connection between our perspectives—the paradigms we accept and live by—and our ignorance. Our worldviews determine how our minds filter information and interpret our observations and experiences. One's cumulative worldview stems from the integration of numerous paradigms or perspectives, some more dominant than others. Accordingly, our collective outlook on life dictates our level of ignorance. For example, due to ideological and/or religious perspectives, a person might reject valid medical information without sufficient rationale (e.g., decline vaccinations for ideological reasons), and whimsically discredit the opinions of others, even trained professionals. Such a person imposes limits upon himself, failing to acquire the knowledge necessary to think critically and make sound decisions. Under such circumstances, a person would always live with a high level of ignorance and impair his ability to successfully and harmoniously cooperate with others. If the same person is a parent, his or her children will come to accept the same or similar paradigms, much as the prisoners in Plato's cave, who lived from childhood under a restrictive worldview.

In the context in which this book approaches ignorance, the Buddhist perspective is relevant. In the Buddhist tradition, the inability to see the transitions and changes of life—the arising and passing away of phenomena—describes a state of ignorance.

> … not seeing arising and passing away is ignorance, while seeing all phenomena as impermanent is the doorway to all the stages of insight and awakening. [12]

---

[12] Goldstein: online article, cited in References.

Enlightenment and insight stem from the ability to see impermanence in nature and in our lives, including the inner self. Understanding that change can and does occur frees the mind to explore and possibly to shift one's paradigms through careful and deliberate consideration of all available and applicable information.[13] Accordingly, in the Buddhist view, closed-mindedness opens the door to suffering.

And so, armed with the expanded definition of ignorance described previously and an introductory awareness of paradigms, you still undoubtedly have questions. You might add, "Some people don't know what they don't know and live in a state of bliss for not knowing. If they become less ignorant, will their lives be any better?" Perhaps not, but the lives of nearly eight billion others and their descendants would certainly improve.

Further, if you're an academic type, you might ask, "Despite our scientific and technological advances, the human brain and nervous system is effectively the same as our hunter-gatherer forebears, with similar emotional, cognitive, and instinctive characteristics. Why should we expect our behaviors and perspectives to change or our minds to accept paradigm shifts that lead us toward enlightenment? We may have access to greater and more accurate knowledge, but our cognitive and emotional skill sets are no different than our distant ancestors. We are who we are. After all, how many of us show true concern for our own ignorance?"

These are great comments and questions, which I will address in the pages to follow. You will learn that ignorance and the paradigms that drive them are complex phenomena. To illustrate, some geneticists speculate that natural selection may progressively "program" a genetically induced ignorance[14] into many species. (Note: A Glossary of paradigm and ignorance terms follows the Epilogue. They

---

[13] The Buddhist notion of ignorance differs from theological perspectives on ignorance, where any lack of faith implies ignorance of the true nature of the divine. Divinity-based religions require devoted adherence to their tenets and historical narratives even if there are questionable elements within their foundational belief structures.

[14] Underlined (print version) or hyperlinked (eBook version) words appear in a Glossary of notable ignorance and paradigm terminology. With the eBook, you can return to your place in the book by clicking on the same hyperlinked term in the glossary.

are accessible by following links in the eBook version of this book (return link provided). In the print version, the terms remain underlined to facilitate use of the Glossary.) Areas in which genetically induced ignorance may occur are the senses. A level of sensory ignorance could improve the species' chances of survival—behaviors which cause the organism to selectively ignore certain sensory data. In some cases, the neural network of one sense (e.g., visual) may override the neural input of another sense (e.g., auditory).[15] For example, a wild cat hunting prey must have razor-sharp focus on its target and filter out (ignore) other sensory data that do not pose a threat (e.g., background noises and odors). Does this mean humans also inherit some level of ignorance—sensory or cognitive filters that serve the group or individual?[16] If so, do those inherited traits still manifest themselves in the modern era? We shall therefore examine some of the subtle complexities associated with ignorance—historically, economically, scientifically, ideologically, religiously, culturally, and socially.

One critical question will emerge from the analysis, "How good are our decisions when we individually or collectively live in varying states of ignorance?" The answers to this and related questions will prove useful in assessing the effects our ignorance is having on the present and future of human affairs and the well-being of our species. A survey of ignorance research will assist us in this endeavor (Chapter 5).

By obtaining a broader understanding of the paradigms that drive our ignorance, we can develop methods to improve our awareness of ourselves, each other, and the world we inhabit and to reduce ignorance worldwide. To this end, we begin.

---

[15] Mejias, Jorge. *Sensory competition (1): A clash of odors*, posted online at mappingignorance.org.

[16] Evolutionary forces have established differing levels of ignorance in most species. For example, humans do not hear very low and very high frequencies, and our sight remains confined to a narrow "visible" spectrum of electromagnetic radiation. We can't see infrared radiation without special equipment. Our physical limitations create a state of ignorance about the world around us—though we've certainly circumvented many limitations through our use of tools (technology).

Chapter 2: Paradigm-Ignorance Relationships

Paradigms and Ignorance

Paradigm is a part of the conditioning of the mind, our conditioning thought patterns.
– Bob Proctor [17]

To have a meaningful discussion about ignorance, we must first understand the term "paradigm," which we previously introduced as a worldview or perspectives. More broadly, however, a paradigm is a system of thoughts and beliefs about the world and human existence. Dictionaries may include the terms "pattern" and "model" in the definition of paradigm. These align with this book's definition. Our systems of thoughts and beliefs stem from mental patterns that ultimately stimulate personal and group behaviors. We will find that the physiological substance of an individual's patterns resides in his or her neural networks. At any given point in time, our system of thoughts and beliefs also represents a model—what we believe human life was, is, and should be and what we believe motivated, motivates, and should motivate human behavior.

---

[17] See "Official Bob Proctor" Facebook page post for April 10, 2017: https://www.facebook.com/OfficialBobProctor/posts/10155208924229421:0.

From where do paradigms originate and how do they develop? The answers to these questions appear in detail on the pages to follow, but a brief overview will assist in understanding the complexities associated with paradigms and their development. The starting point is the human nervous system which includes the brain. From birth, sensory stimuli and instinctive responses slowly bring clarity to a befuddling environment within which every individual finds himself or herself. Patterns begin to emerge—periods of dark and light, feeding sessions, and cycles of comfort and discomfort. The brain formulates crude models of the world. Much later, as the individual acquires language skills, his nervous system develops the ability to process sensory inputs through natural and symbolic formats.[18] Over time, the patterns refine and embed themselves in memory centers. These are the substance of the paradigms that steer our lives and shape our thoughts and behaviors. Our outlooks or perspectives on just about everything have their roots in our experiences (e.g., our political views).

The significance of paradigms cannot be overstated. For example, paradigms steer the everyday routines of our political environment, not just for the individual but society at large. In the United States, consider the high-intensity attention paid to Supreme Court nominees. Groups and individuals with politically conservative perspectives or paradigms want to stop liberal-minded justices from being appointed and vice-versa. One side is trying to prevent certain paradigms from penetrating the legal principles of the nation through the decisions rendered by the Supreme Court; the other side is trying to incorporate them into our nation's laws. The paradigms integrated into our legal system can have profound social consequences and lay the foundation for the future course of the nation.

At their core, paradigms represent human mental constructs (MCs) of our world.[19] MCs include myths, stories, the impact of our experiences, scientific theory, and all types of abstractions, including mathematics. They stem from a highly active human imagination—a

---

[18] An example of natural format is when one person observes another screaming, indicating excitement, danger, pain, or similar situational causes. Symbolic formats usually take the form of visual and auditory inputs—such as the sight of a national flag or symbol (e.g., the Christian cross) or the way a person interprets the meaning of written or spoken words.

[19] Harari, *Sapiens*, 20-25; 31-32.

product of the socialization process among group members and of the human brain's ability to develop symbolic representations of real-world stimuli. The imagination draws upon basic and complex cognitive abilities, such as memorization, classification, analysis, and synthesis. Our brains evolved to make connections between and among the sea of stimuli in which they find themselves. Our survival depends on these innate abilities of our brains.

The random and recurring stimuli in our surroundings shape our imagination. So do our individual and species genetics. If our sensory or mental functions are genetically compromised, we may formulate incomplete or inadequate MCs of our environment (e.g., the impact of poor vision or hearing). In addition, memories and symbolic triggers in our surroundings can kindle our imagination and elicit specific or general thoughts and behaviors. Of note, it does not matter whether our memories are accurate or selective. What we manage to remember helps us to form paradigms and to apply them. Language is a symbolic trigger that provides a virtually endless source of emblematic content, both written and oral. Physical symbols, such as flags, animals (e.g., the eagle), geometric shapes (e.g., the swastika[20]), and alphanumeric characters, similarly offer a plethora of representations and meanings, which evolve into MCs.

As the brain experiences the world, it develops rules and pieces together physical and mental relationships. The mind then interprets the world based on its experiences. These cognitive interpretations or MCs cannot be real in an objective sense.[21] Rivers, land, clouds, flora, and fauna are examples of the real. Thoughts are energetic processes stemming from brain activity, creating a highly subjective depiction of the exterior world. Thoughts integrate mental representations of our world based on sensory input and cognitive and emotional memories. Thoughts exist only in the brain, however. There is nothing tangible in a thought other than the neural-electrochemical impulses in the nerve cells that created it. But thoughts are a catalyst for much more. Memories and experience eventually coalesce within our brain matter to form neural networks, the bio-electrochemical substance of our paradigms. As these neural networks integrate with each other, they

---

[20] The reader is encouraged to research the origins and meanings of the (reversed) swastika symbol in Buddhism and Eastern religions.

[21] Harari, *Sapiens*, 31-32.

create organized neural impulses, which form a systematic, symbolic representation of our world—a virtual reality existing only within the mind.

The reader should not misinterpret the preceding. Though we consciously connect to the real world through an intangible mind-world, the products of our cerebral machinations are clearly tangible and conspicuous. We affect our surroundings. Thoughts and stimuli lead to actions and reactions—muscular movements, vocalizations, and other deliberate responses. Cerebral activity steers our behaviors—over seven billion of us. Our MCs of the world impel us to build or destroy, to cooperate with or battle each other, and to explore or disregard our surroundings. Our impact on the world stems directly from the intricate mental processes in our brains. Imagine the impact if the entire world's population were to operate under the same paradigms. The effect on our planet might produce highly good outcomes or devastatingly bad ones or somewhere in between, depending upon the nature of the paradigms.[22]

Good outcome paradigms have a shared utility, such as those mental models or rules that provide liberties and help sustain social order.[23] We develop legal and other social systems to minimize the disorder in our lives. Consider the chaos on our roadways if drivers did not understand or abide by agreed upon rules of the road for the safe operation of motor vehicles. Most people understand they have a high probability of making it safely from point A to point B if their paradigm for driving aligns with those of other drivers. They have mentally internalized the "good driver paradigm" and think and act accordingly, such as obeying traffic signals and signaling and looking before making lane changes.

---

[22] An example of a "good outcome" paradigm: We all subscribe to the perspective that we must act nonviolently toward each other and respect all of Earth's ecosystems. The reader should be able to come up with numerous, devastatingly "bad outcome" examples.

[23] We must tread lightly here. The notions that good and bad exist are paradigms themselves. Outcomes and consequences are neither good nor bad, neither lucky nor unlucky; they just follow from our actions and external forces. However, since life's focus is species survival, we can assign the label "good" to those paradigms that foster ecosystem balance for most species, and "bad" to those that promote ecosystem imbalance and destruction. Alternately stated, good refers to paradigms that put the least species (and/or individuals in a species) at risk and bad to paradigms that put a significant number at risk.

Bad outcome paradigms have negative consequences, if not for all, at least for many. Most of us have grown up with MCs about social and economic class. We apply (learned) rules to individual classes. We may consider the rich (or upper) class elite and successful. The middle class represents the hardworking backbone of society. Members of the lower class tend to be indolent, uneducated, poor, and/or simply unlucky. The preceding class assignations are overly simplified for illustrative purposes, but such paradigms of class structure have developed over the millennia. Those in power have dictated the narrative that most of us have internalized. Our "class structure paradigm" shapes our thoughts and behaviors toward other members of society. The present class perspective represents a win-lose situation. Notably, our society accepts poverty as the inevitable destiny of a large segment of the population. Our Economic paradigm, to be discussed later, guarantees winner and loser outcomes. If you're a winner, you live in relative or obscene comfort. You may donate to charities for the poor and downtrodden or even physically support altruistic efforts, such as food banks. However, the collective set of paradigms you live by defines what you think and how you act. Your paradigms are actually ensuring the status quo for the impoverished and most of their descendants.

Culture, religion, race, and ethnicity contribute to our paradigms, including the when and what of eating and the clothes we wear. For example, breakfasts vary by region, country, and hemisphere. Consider also the variation in headwear based on ethnicity and religion. Cultural, ethnic, and religious norms have imbedded themselves in our neural networks as paradigms or rules to follow.

The preceding paragraph includes a hidden "chicken or egg" enigma. Does our culture and spiritual outlook create our paradigms or do our paradigms create our culture and religion. History suggests the latter. One can imagine how hunter-gatherers developed paradigms of the world based on their fears, senses, wonderment of their surroundings, and tribal narratives. In time, the paradigms formed the foundations of social cohesion. Culture was born. Divine interventions were used to explain the unknown. As human social units coalesced into civilizations, conflicts and communication between and among individuals and groups eventually spurred paradigm shifts. A multitude of cultures and religions evolved and their associated paradigms passed on to future generations.

Note that I have refrained from including posited psychological theories or phenomena to explain mental activity since they tend to be untestable scientifically (e.g., Freud's reliance on human drives [sex, hunger, etc.] to explain behavior). Neuroscience has altered psychology to bring data-driven perspectives into the forefront. As such, I describe mental processes as neurobiological events in the brain rather than psychological states of a nebulous mind. While neurobiology is in its infancy, it has begun to reshape our understanding of mental activity and thought patterns, particularly through advances in brain scanning technology.

To illustrate the distinction between a traditional psychological approach and instrumented neurological methods, consider the source of an erotic dream. One could interpret the mental event to stem from a sexual repression in the individual (Freudian interpretation); however, without establishing a physical link between brain function and sexual repression, we have little hope of ever being able to test this hypothesis. The dream more likely represents a form of biophysical and biochemical "house-cleaning" or a "do over" event during sleep. In the former, lower-priority[24] memories are cleared from neurons and synapses to make room for higher-priority content. In the latter case, high priority content stored in neural networks infiltrate the dream state. Such physical processes should eventually become measurably clarified as we further refine the tools of neuroscience. Thus, when we discuss the development of paradigms within the human brain, think in terms of the neurological processes (bioelectrical and biochemical) that have repetitively occurred to form them. While psychologists may be able to piece together a set or series of psychological triggers to explain the actions of an individual or group, this book explains those actions as a direct result of the neural networks and physiological circumstances (e.g., illness, fatigue) existing in individuals immediately preceding the actions.

Scientifically obtained evidentiary data support our approach. For example, we know that biochemical changes in the brain can affect behavior and drives, such as nicotine's addictive effects and, in the extreme, the impact of hallucinogenic drugs on inhibition. Thus, natural (e.g., as found in foods) or synthetic (e.g., as produced in laboratories or industrial facilities) biochemical substances can

---

[24] Higher and lower priorities depend upon the scope and intensity of an individual's experiences.

influence paradigm development, even changing or shifting them, at least temporarily. For example, those who suffer from bipolar disorder may obtain relief through lithium drugs. When a bipolar person's mood stabilizes, his or her paradigms (neural networks) also attain equilibrium.

So as not to introduce too many variables into the discussions that follow, we will primarily focus on the MCs that develop through commonplace processes. Ordinary or mainstream activities, such as minimal-to-moderate alcohol consumption, cigarette smoking, taking over-the-counter and prescribed, non-addictive medications, and ingesting marijuana also qualify as natural even though they may distort perspectives temporarily.[25] Abnormal development of MCs includes those affected by significant biochemical imbalances or neurological disorders. Some may occur as a result of highly addictive medications and drugs; others may result due to rare infections or genetic diseases. Other anomalous MCs may arise due to physiological impediments such as those caused by injury (e.g., concussion). None of these uncommon circumstances qualifies as mainstream.

Although certain paradigms can develop as a result of neurological dependencies, they may only be prominent during the period of dependency. The dependency (and paradigm) could linger or even be replaced by a newer, stronger dependency or a more dominant paradigm.[26] Note that dependencies are not a necessary ingredient for paradigm development, however. Whether dependencies are formed or not, all normal activities of life—attending school and church, playing games and sports, reading, working, interacting with family, friends, and strangers, and more—will influence the development of a person's paradigms. We will consider all these influences upon a person's neural networks as natural or normal.

---

[25] The nicotine within tobacco products certainly qualifies as "mind altering" because of its addictive properties, but for our purposes in this book, the effects on neural networks are minimal and integrated into an individual's Self paradigm (discussed in Chapter 3).

[26] People can and do overcome dependencies, most often with the assistance of professionals and/or self-help organizations. When they succeed, a new or revised (shifted) paradigm forms. The old neural networks are suppressed or restructured. The main focus of alcohol and drug rehabilitation programs is shifting the paradigms of affected individuals.

To reiterate, paradigms never exist tangibly outside the human brain since they represent an imbedded neural network of neurons and synapses within the mind. This biophysical circuitry generates thoughts and stimulates actions. As a result, our MCs of the world give rise to an objective reality through the physical activities they stimulate. This sentence is worth repeating: Our MCs of the world give rise to an objective reality through the physical activities they stimulate. Whatever the resulting acts and activities,—waging war, giving to charities, farming, stealing, writing laws, building homes, enslaving others, et al—they profoundly affect the lives of all humans, other living things, and the local and even distant environs.[27]

Of all the objective realities created by humanity throughout its history, only one consists of disciplined methodologies to uncover the truth about the world. Scientific endeavor is the singular, human mental and physical activity that attempts to accurately distill the world outside and inside the mind into its constituent parts and to determine accurate relationships among events and phenomena. Scientific pursuits include tool-making that expands the reach of our senses, the strength of our bodies, and the communicative abilities of our nervous system, the last of which includes developing the cognitive tools of oral and written language. We gain purpose through these efforts, which is "to identify phenomena and develop agreement regarding the description of the whole from glimpses or partial fragments. Truth is achieved through reasoning rather than pure observation because only the *results* of causal forces may be observed rather than the causal forces themselves."[28] Interestingly, since we can only search for the truth about reality through the paradigms held in our minds, the opportunity for error is extremely high—unless we are strictly faithful to established, rigid methodologies. We will address this opportunity for error in the pages to follow.

Whether one labels MCs as real or virtual is irrelevant. Whether one accepts reality as a set of reasoned truths or negotiated truths is equally immaterial.[29] The outcomes derived from a person's

---

[27] This paragraph itself represents the philosophical paradigm of critical realism (part of the Ideological paradigm discussed later in this book). Relativist ontology is an opposing view. For additional discussion, see Goldstein.

[28] Levers, 2.

[29] Ibid.

or group's MCs are what matter. Outcomes equate to reality. Restated alternately, human-induced outcomes can trace their origins to paradigms because paradigms drive the behaviors and thoughts that lead to real-world actions with real-world consequences. Consequences apply even if the sources of the MCs are mythological, mystical, or hypothetical. Yes, I've intentionally repeated myself (yet again) to drive home this point.

Consider life in ancient Egypt, which, in retrospect, was based largely on mythology, mysticism, and immature science. Power (authority hierarchies), religion, class structure, and the local environment and climate shaped the mental models held by Egyptians. Wars were fought, gods and pharaohs worshipped, pyramids and dwellings constructed, tools forged and utilized, animals domesticated and hunted, and food grown and stored. The paradigms existing then had a profound effect on the lives of all Egyptians and their local environment. Through a collection of interrelated dominant paradigms, many Egyptians found meaning in their lives—whether they served in the army, worked the fields, or labored in building the pharaohs' shrines.[30] As it occurred then and still occurs now, blended or composite paradigms provide(d) the cognitive wherewithal for us to interpret the world around us and assign meaning to our actions.

We could re-state the preceding as: Paradigms determine (1) our biases and interpretations of the world and (2) our actions and reactions to the happenings around us. Since our paradigms encompass every facet of life—personal, social, economic, political, religious, cultural, ideological, symbolic, and more,—they impel us, individually or collectively, to live our lives in specific ways. Our social, religious, and cultural laws and traditions stem from our collective paradigms. In fact, social cohesion depends upon what Yuval Harari refers to as imagined orders.[31] Imagined orders include subjective reality—what an individual accepts about himself and his environment, and an intersubjective reality—what a group of individuals accepts about themselves and their environment.[32] As long as group members

---

[30] Victims of slavery and then-existing slave paradigms likely failed to find meaning in their lives.

[31] Harari, *Homo Deus*, 167. As we shall see, these imagined orders are effectively a combination of two or more dominant paradigms.

[32] Ibid, 167-175.

believe in certain rules, they will cooperate with each other and multiply their efforts accordingly.[33] Money, divinities, and laws add meaning and utility to life when they become part of a collective intersubjective reality or imagined orders.

Similarly, self-perception establishes a person's own subjective reality, often bringing meaning and utility to life. A negative self-perception could create a sense of desperation and dysfunction. And we should not dismiss the possibility of an individualized imagined order—an intersubjective reality held by a person with multiple personalities. Whatever their origin, both subjective and intersubjective realities are rooted in paradigms, many of which have proven historically powerful in both scope and magnitude. We presented an example from ancient Egypt. We turn now to modern history.

A gruesome case of the power of paradigms in influencing human thought and behavior occurred last century on Saipan during World War II.[34] Japanese citizens there feared for their lives as American forces assaulted and gained control of their island. They lived under a paradigm that perceived U.S. Marines as barbarians, who would torture, kill, maim, and rape civilians. Their intersubjective reality convinced them it would be better to die honorably by committing suicide and killing their own children in the name of the emperor. Their neural networks had assembled these paradigms from experiences and rituals. Emperor Hirohito fortified this socio-cultural paradigm by adding a spiritual (religious) component: those who committed suicide rather than be captured would acquire the equivalent status of a warrior in the afterlife. Japan's leaders feared that the surrender of civilians on Saipan and other islands, especially in light of the humane treatment they would likely receive, would ultimately unravel the will of the people on the Japanese mainland to sustain the war effort. Thousands of Japanese inhabitants of Saipan believed the honorable-path paradigm decreed by the emperor and his agents.[35] They ended their and their children's lives, many by jumping

---

[33] Of course, some of the cooperation can lead to negative consequences, such as the class structure paradigm embedded into our culture.

[34] See Goldberg, Chapter Fourteen, Toland, Chapter 20, and Hughes.

[35] Civilian casualties on Saipan were over twenty thousand (two out of every three), including those killed by U.S. Marines, those killed by Japanese forces (to prevent civilian capture), and those committing suicide and murder-suicide.

off cliffs to their deaths or huddling around grenades and detonating them. This was not the first time in history that humans had chosen mass suicide, but it is the most recent of such scale that was unambiguously driven by a collective composite paradigm. Strikingly, the paradigms that drive the human mind to suicidal actions can easily overwhelm a person's survival instinct.[36]

So how do paradigms wield such power over us? Consider the framework within which the brain functions.[37] As advances in neuroscience have determined, the human brain responds to internal and sensory inputs in a series of electrochemical processes and transitions that we refer to as states of mental activity. The states or modes of activity integrate varied brain functions (sight, hearing, memory, motor control, etc.). The resulting amalgamation of brain processes combine into sets and patterns of thoughts and behaviors. Memory plays a significant role in crystallizing the thematic character of thoughts and behaviors. As we've discussed previously, when mental patterns progressively solidify over time, paradigms form as a neural network or integrated neural networks. The collective set of integrated networks (paradigms) embodies an individual's personality. The paradigmatic circuitry acts as filters in accessing memory and in processing inputs to determine what stimuli are most important and relevant at a given time.

In effect, survival depends upon paradigm development. Once solidified, paradigms help to eliminate internal self-debates to accelerate the decision-making process. In nature, for example, birds take flight as predators approach—a largely instinctive paradigm moderated or intensified by experience.[38] Human paradigm development is not as straightforward since some paradigms may form in conflict with others, hampering decision-making. Generally, however, our life experiences stimulate bioelectrical activity that form

---

[36] For those Japanese who chose suicide, their individual subjective reality either aligned with or was weaker than the group intersubjective reality. Alternately stated, the Group paradigm was more dominant than each person's Self paradigm. (The next chapter discusses Self and Group paradigms in detail.)

[37] Levitin, 39-53. The neurological content of this paragraph is drawn from these pages.

[38] Some animals, such as many that inhabit the Galapagos Islands, have yet to develop a fear of humans.

neural patterns that eventually evolve into well-defined neural networks. Note, however, that as paradigms form, they may do so with little opportunity to validate their veracity, significance, or utility. Our worldviews could be highly skewed and unrepresentative of reality.

How can we identify what paradigms a person's neural networks contain? The paradigms manifest themselves as mental and physical responses to stimuli. In principle, it's similar to the situation wherein a person doesn't stick his finger into a flame because he remembers the pain it will cause or how Pavlov's dogs would salivate at the ringing of a bell given the repeated association of bell-ringing with feeding. Thus, for example, a person who develops intolerance of others' religious beliefs or racial and ethnic traditions as a child may as an adult openly criticize people of different religions, races, or ethnicities because of stories she had internalized from youth. Still another person may, without coercion, don a vest bomb because he believes in a religious cause. People can conceal some of their paradigms from others for quite some time, but eventually their behaviors provide clues or direct evidence to the workings of their neural networks.

Thus, from a biophysical perspective, paradigms are the neural networks that serve as processing filters for developing and recalling memories and for taking action. The actions may consist of motor responses, well-considered or snap decisions, or emotional reactions. Examples include forming a fist to strike someone, expressing an opinion orally or in writing, complimenting an acquaintance, voting on a ballot, painting a picture, composing music, neglecting someone in need, talking to one's self, and a host of similar activities. The actions, reactions, and decisions that result often reflect a specific paradigm or a combination of paradigms. For the Japanese who chose suicide on Saipan, fear of brutalities at the hands of the Americans and the belief in duty to the emperor and in his promise of an honorable afterlife influenced their decisions. Memory and thematic thought patterns served as a catalyst in their decision-making. All normal brains function this way. Paradigm development and the ensuing responses are inescapable attributes of the human condition. The specific paradigms that develop, however, are not necessarily predetermined.

To illustrate the paradigmatic filtering process, consider a person with racial or ethnic biases who would normally not choose to eat at a restaurant where certain races or ethnicities congregate. If, however, she was with a group from work who spontaneously chose to eat at a restaurant patronized by groups she disliked, she may, contrary to her paradigm, reluctantly go along with the group to prevent embarrassment or ridicule (and possibly to conceal her biases). The dramas that play out in the individual mind because of paradigms are difficult, nigh impossible, to grasp. However, over time, patterns of thoughts and behaviors develop into personality traits and values.[39] These traits will eventually reveal the depth of an individual's ignorance and the integrity of his decisions and actions.

And yes—our paradigms are the primary reason for our ignorance. One need only examine the mindset of Southerners in the United States during the nineteenth century to understand the real and potential perils of paradigm-induced ignorance. Most Southerners held the perspective that African-Americans were intellectually and culturally inferior. The collective Southern paradigm justified slavery and supported an illogical premise that Black Americans could never attain mental and social equality.[40] The paradigm helped to shape Southern society. The paradigms of North and South clashed, resulting in hundreds of thousands of casualties.

Economic paradigms have also created strong beliefs among the populous. Capitalism and communism are two economic paradigms determining the way societies manage and distribute wealth. They were the two most dominant economic paradigms of the twentieth century.[41] The capitalistic West, led by the United States, engaged in numerous conflicts and supported a plethora of policies to contain and minimize communism. Subsequently, through globalization initiatives, capitalism became the dominant economic paradigm by outspending Soviet bloc nations, effectively "breaking the communist bank" and exposing flaws in the communist

---

[39] People demonstrate their values through their actions and not their words. A person may claim to be an art lover; however, if he never visits an art museum, thumbs through art books, purchases art, draws, paints, or pursues any artistic enterprises, the person clearly does not value art. We might say the person is "just blowing smoke."

[40] Through the gradual shifting of paradigms, I have confidence that, in the future, race-based discrimination will fade away in the United States—however, not during my lifetime.

[41] In practice, twentieth-century communism barely qualified as communism because of the way government, at all levels, dictated outcomes whether they were feasible or not.

socioeconomic systems. During this period known as the Cold War, these opposing paradigms created significant states of ignorance within and among the nations involved.

Globalization is a combined economic-ideological paradigm of its own. The globalization ideology has its roots in ancient times—the idea that a group must extend beyond its geographic base to improve its chances of survival or its quality of life. Trade was one option, but empire building and colonizing efforts often offered greater benefits. In time, globalization merged with capitalism to connect the nations of the world financially and materially. Globalization has allowed the creation of the super-corporations described earlier, entities with more financial clout than a majority of nations. Is the capitalistic paradigm the best one for humanity or do capitalistic principles of financial engagement fuel ignorance and flawed decision-making? Would a blended approach of capitalism and socialism better serve the citizens of the world?

We will briefly evaluate the capitalistic paradigm in a later section of this book, but for now, we can reframe the posed questions: Does one economic paradigm sow a greater number of the seeds of ignorance compared to another? Does one economic paradigm put ecosystems and a larger number of species at risk? An understanding of the workings of paradigms can help answer these questions and avoid blindly promoting one economic paradigm over another. For example, in modern times in the U.S., the word "socialism" often generates negative reactions—as if the term represents an evil. Political rhetoric and the fear of communism helped to establish this widespread perspective in the American public. Like ignorance, paradigms can defy logic. Ironically, many older Americans with anti-socialist perspectives collect Social Security and/or other government-financed pensions and acquire medical insurance through Medicare. Thanks to socialistic policies enacted during the Great Depression, the United States survived as a nation and a vast number of its citizens, particularly the elderly, have the ability to eke out a tolerable existence. The problem with anti-socialist dogma, which has persisted for decades in the United States, is that we may fail to consider alternative solutions to socioeconomic problems such as poverty. The same is true of an anti-capitalist paradigm, which, if enacted, might overly constrain large and small businesses and reduce their ability to invest in products and services that would serve the greater human good.

The history of human economic interactions illustrates that paradigms or worldviews can change over time. Economic systems evolve. Capitalism replaced mercantilism, which had succeeded feudalism. Some changes occurred due to forceful intervention. For example, the victors in war oftentimes forced paradigms upon the vanquished. European colonialism effectively did this to the native societies of North, South, and Central America, Africa, and Oceania.

Consider also the paradigms associated with poverty. The poor and homeless see the world differently than the upper and middle economic classes. Their focus is survival. They have few opportunities to improve their financial status and to alter their lifestyles. The poverty paradigm, for those living it, differs markedly from those seeing it from the outside. The poor generally confine their perspectives to their immediate needs and surroundings. For the wealthy, the poverty paradigm can range from empathetic support to contempt for those perceived as unable or unwilling to lift themselves from their financial woes.

Paradigms encompass non-social perspectives as well. Ancient humans largely believed the Sun, planets, and stars revolved around the Earth (geocentric perspective). Their eyes told them so. Religious and cultural traditions emerged from this paradigm, serving as a catalyst for anthropocentrism. As knowledge accumulated, the paradigm of our place in the universe eventually evolved to a heliocentric view. Even today, with our advanced instrumentation and satellites, our views of the cosmos continue to shift, sometimes slowly and incrementally, and sometimes rapidly and significantly. The cosmological paradigm today, which, unfortunately, only a small percent of humanity can describe, has Earth orbiting the Sun, which is rotating within the Milky Way galaxy, which in turn is on a trajectory away from some mysterious point in space where the Big Bang established the universe. The Earth is hurtling through the cosmos along a complex path to some other place than where we just were.

The current cosmological paradigm provides us a perspective that can overwhelm us. Our significance becomes trivial. We live on an infinitesimally small planet for an infinitesimally small amount of time on an astronomical scale. Still, the cosmological perspective broadens our understanding of our local universe and our origins. The cosmological worldview can assist in clarifying and refining religious and spiritual paradigms, many of which seem entrenched in past perspectives and are no longer sustainable given our updated knowledge and scientific methods of analysis. As we shall see, however, entrenched paradigms resist change.

Those opposing change could pose the following: "Even though today's cosmological paradigm is more accurate, what's wrong with holding a more ignorant view, such as a static model of the universe containing a heliocentric solar system? Doesn't it provide sufficient knowledge and perspective from which we can govern human affairs?" The mindset expressed by this question is critical to understanding how paradigms and ignorance influence human decision-making. Sure, we could stick our heads in the sand and ignore the added complexity of a more accurate cosmological model, but at what cost? If we readily dismiss complex and broader perspectives, will we oversimplify and narrow our outlook and sustain prejudices that serve the few vice the many. Danger lurks in sustaining paradigms that lack evidentiary data or oversimplify our world. We create paradigm conflicts when we skirt the truth or misrepresent reality. The simple inference: paradigmatic stagnation equates to greater ignorance.

If we accept the world our parents or guardians presented to us as children, we might never shift our paradigms. We could easily lose sight of validated truths, and equally importantly, the Big Picture that provides a template for our interconnectedness to each other and our surroundings. We could easily fail to cope with shifting paradigms, even minor ones. For example, technological advances have changed the way we live and communicate. New information and concepts constantly challenge our present paradigms (e.g., same-sex marriage), often introducing confusing and unsettling complexities that rattle our worldview. Is the average human mind even capable of understanding the significance of more developed and complex paradigms? More importantly, how can we recognize whether a shifting paradigm will actually improve our lives and/or our worldview?

To answer these questions, one must realize that paradigms are rarely stagnant despite the human propensity to avert change. Paradigms tend to shift, sometimes slowly, sometimes abruptly. The shift may not always be to ones with greater validity and with greater benefit to humanity. Consider the rapid rise of paradigms associated with fascism and Nazism in the twentieth century and the suffering they caused. Typically, however, paradigms slowly and naturally evolve to expose a clearer and truer perspective of our world and ourselves. It took well over a century for the greater part of humanity to accept that the Earth revolves around the sun.

The good news is that we don't need to understand all of the details of highly complex paradigms. For example, regarding scientific matters, it is unrealistic that every citizen will understand the details of the theory and engineering behind the safe operation of a nuclear power plant. We should expect a considerable level of ignorance by the public on the topic. However, those who design and operate the plants bear the responsibility to keep the public safe, and explain, in simple terms, why the safety features work. Through proper communications, the public's perspective of nuclear power could shift to a less ignorant perspective. In practice, enlightening the public is more difficult than it may seem. The steps and processes taking the public to a less ignorant state require a requisite level of functional knowledge, a topic we will examine in detail in Chapter 5.

The synopsis of paradigms and their development in this section provide a solid foundation for understanding the relationship between paradigms and ignorance and between paradigms and human history. From our discussion, we can reasonably postulate the following: (1) paradigms shape history, in large part by influencing human decision-making and actions, and (2) paradigms play a significant role in determining the level of personal and collective ignorance. We will further develop these ideas and confirm their validity. Additionally, we will demonstrate how systematically and logically developed Big Picture paradigms can facilitate the reduction of ignorance.

Earlier, we provided examples to illustrate how paradigms shape history (e.g., the Civil War and Saipan). Numerous others exist, familiar to anyone with a cursory knowledge of history. Religious and ethnic paradigms created the Crusades. In the past five hundred years, Western European nations fabricated a colonization paradigm to restructure New World "heathen" societies under Western religious, cultural, and economic norms. Twentieth century "crusades" included the attempted genocide of Armenians by Turks and of Holocaust victims by the Nazis. Nazi Germany also promoted the paradigm of a Master Race. Hindu culture promoted caste systems. Capitalists, socialists, and communists continue to tweak and advance contrasting ways of life and worldviews, many with destructive ecological consequences. The paradigm of royalty persists in many cultures and societies, sustaining social class distinctions by setting aside groups of privileged individuals. The effects of paradigms go beyond history, however. Paradigms have altered the human family tree through actual or near genocides. The reader should examine the plight of native Tasmanians and other peoples to learn how certain groups attempted to eradicate or minimize the existence of other groups.[42]

The list of impactful paradigms is voluminous so in the next chapter we will focus on the dominant paradigms that have affected the course of history.

Paradigm Special Focus: Nuclear Weapons

Political paradigms have varied significantly over the course of civilized history. Two subsets of political paradigms have persistently been foreign policy and military power—the established mindset of how to deal with those outside one's group and what posture of force to take against outsiders. What applied in the past to hunter-gatherer tribes and to ancient civilizations still applies today. We fight or come to terms with outsiders. However, in the modern era, technology has made weaponry extraordinarily destructive, particularly nuclear weapons. Thus, numerous paradigms have emerged regarding the production and use of nuclear weapons that deal with us-versus-them scenarios.

Many view nuclear weapons as a self-inflicted scourge upon humankind and call for their destruction. They believe that the major powers will eventually use their large existing arsenals in suicidal conflicts, killing a large fraction of the human population directly or, in the aftermath, indirectly through residual radiation or a nuclear winter.

Others believe nuclear weapons serve as a deterrent to the kind of global warfare experienced in the twentieth century. They support the notion that it would be mad to pursue MAD (Mutually Assured Destruction) by engaging in nuclear warfare. MAD is the major nuclear weapons paradigm that endures in a spectrum of negotiations, treaties, and policies, including limitations on the proliferation of nuclear weapons.

These two opposing perspective still exist today although each has undergone refinements with the end of the Cold War. While nuclear arsenals have diminished from their peak, the dominant paradigm favors the status quo where a limited number of nations retain large arsenals of nuclear weapons. However, a few nations are

---

[42] Diamond, *Third Chimpanzee*, 276-309.

still trying to join the nuclear club. It's conceivable that nations with small nuclear arsenals may not accept the notion of MAD. Their ignorance could lead to serious consequences for humanity. We'd then have to ask, "What paradigms would foster sufficient ignorance that would allow any person or group to consider the plausibility of a good outcome from a limited or all-out nuclear war?"

To answer this question, in part, we must recognize that paradigms create beliefs and perspectives that restrict our ability to accept facts and the truths around us. They also bias the way we assess our surroundings and interact with others, shrouding us in ignorance. For example, during the 1962 Cuban Missile Crisis, which brought the United States and the Soviet Union to the brink of all-out nuclear warfare, U.S. military leadership favored an assault on Cuba to forcibly remove the missiles, warheads, and launchers the Soviet Union had secretly installed there. The Soviets had knowingly crossed a U.S. policy line (effectively, the Monroe Doctrine) and were attempting to gain a nuclear edge, a shorter response time to reach key U.S. targets. U.S. military leaders recommended an aggressive response that could have spiraled into a major conflict. Key members of the military leadership seemed ignorant of the available options and had a superficial understanding of the enemy. Their paradigm was one of military might, leveraging our tactical and strategic advantages. The top brass therefore recommended forceful removal of Soviet weaponry.

To reiterate, the dominant paradigms to which we subscribe can increase the scope of our ignorance and by doing so shape our personal and collective futures. The paradigm of military might (a subset of the Power paradigm discussed in Chapter 3) has needlessly killed millions over the course of history. The body count in the twentieth century alone attests to the gruesomeness of this ignominious perspective. The mindless battlefield tactics employed in the first few years of World War I exemplify the ignorance paradigms can create. There were many a foolhardy general during the Great War who thought masses of men could defeat a storm of bullets, a maze of barbed wire and trenches, and heavily concentrated artillery. Although the battlefield circumstances differed, the Eastern Front of World War II proved equally brutal.

Fortunately, during the Cuban Missile Crisis, President John F. Kennedy considered an alternate paradigm and pursued diplomatic options, averting certain disaster for both nations and undoubtedly the world. Although Kennedy had served in the military and attained hero status, he never accepted the traditional military mindset. Kennedy adhered to a political paradigm where give-and-take leads to mutually beneficial outcomes. Nikita Khrushchev, the Soviet Premier, reached out to Kennedy in an attempt to avert a disastrous confrontation.[43] Kennedy did not default to a paradigm rooted in "swinging a Big Stick" and found a win-win solution that effectively diffused the crisis (no military action against Cuba and the removal of U.S. medium-range missiles from Turkey and Russian missiles from Cuba). Whatever one's opinion of Kennedy, we should applaud his actions and his ability to recognize the ignorance around him—at least during the Cuban Missile Crisis.

[43] Levitin, 155.

Chapter 3: A Brief History of Paradigms and Ignorance

History as the Evolution and Confluence of Dominant Paradigms [44]

"The greatest scientific discovery was the discovery of ignorance." – Yuval Harari [45]

One could easily examine the numerous eras that define human history—the Ancient Era (e.g., Bronze and Iron Ages), the Dark Ages, the Age of Discovery (or Exploration), the Protestant Reformation, the Enlightenment, the Scientific and Industrial Revolutions, and more—and conclude that there's a developmental

---

[44] Author's note: By paying little attention to New World civilizations in the following, it is not my intent to characterize their history as insignificant. They are the unfortunate inheritors of geographical and climatological disadvantages compared to the Old World. As a result, New World technology matured more slowly than their Old World counterparts, placing these societies at a competitive disadvantage with those of the Old. As we shall learn, technology enables paradigm shifts that can alter the course of history. History is what it is, but I view with disdain how the then-existing dominant paradigms of Old World colonial powers led to the purposeful decimation, dehumanization, and dominance of New World societies.

[45] Harari, *Homo Deus*, 248.

progression to human knowledge and humanity's awareness of its place in the universe. However, there's a significant oversight in this line of thinking. The ancient Greeks, Romans, and Chinese had sparks of enlightenment only to see their worlds collapse into dark ages of seemingly incalculable ignorance. Chaos reigned well beyond the Dark Ages as Mongol hordes, nomadic raiders, Vikings, and other legions of destruction prevented humanity from collaboratively pursuing knowledge. Aggression against others wasn't always the rule. For centuries, China withdrew from the world stage and adopted isolationism. In Europe, after the Dark Ages, societies eventually stabilized despite seemingly perpetual warfare. Human knowledge progressively and steadily blossomed until the present era. Yet here we are, saddled by ignorance. How did this happen?

The simple answer: Our current Age of Ignorance stems from the evolution and confluence of dominant paradigms throughout human history. While we have expanded our understanding of the Earth, our universe, our own beginnings, and ourselves, many "old school" paradigms persist in the present and dominate our thinking and behavior. While most of the dominant paradigms of the past have undergone shifts, their underlying constructs remain founded in myth, legend, and story. As a result, humanity is collectively bound by paradigmatic chains to faulty mental models. In our self-created cognitive caves, human thoughts, behaviors, and decisions have proven highly corruptible.

In prior historical periods, humans could only experience the world with their raw senses; thus, they pursued the truths about their world with immature scientific knowledge and methods. Physical and mental tool development, such as stone implements, fire, and language, provided a means to illuminate these experiences. Much later, technological improvements such as the telescope and microscope greatly extended what humans could perceive with their senses. Accordingly, compared to the wealth of knowledge we have today, our forebears had limited ability to develop a cohesive and supportable Big Picture view of their universe. Beliefs rather than well-evaluated and verified facts governed individual and group paradigms. Beliefs generated stories that brought paradigms to life. Individuals from past eras certainly pondered many of the same existential questions Moderns ask, but many factors conspired against them, preventing them from compiling an experiential base to pursue the truth.

Religious and cultural belief systems prevented poorly developed scientific methodologies from budding. Meaningful knowledge could not accumulate sufficiently. Truth seekers such as Galileo Galilei faced severe backlash from and imprisonment by religious leaders because of his pioneering work in astronomy and physics. Galileo had ridden the tide of technological advances, such as writing instruments, lens crafting, and even linguistic developments, such as alphanumeric symbols, to alter the model of the world held in his lifetime. Advances in tools stimulated his and others' curiosity.[46] Abstract (symbolic) thinking matured, providing a means to distinguish between the objective and subjective—albeit crudely at first. Credit also goes to the hierarchal nature of ancient and Middle Age societies where a division of labor freed many to pursue the abstract without the benefit of structured educational systems.

Through most of human history, the challenges of survival provided the stimulus for an informal education system, such as occurred among hunter-gatherer, pastoral, and agricultural societies. Parenthood, mentorship, and apprenticeships allowed sophisticated cognitive processes to mature. The old taught the young survival skills. The chores necessary to sustain life took priority among tribal members. Humankind drew upon the capacity and capability of their evolved brain functions. Hunting, gathering, farming (primitive agriculture), tool-making, fabricating, and construction skills, along with refinements to oral and written languages, contributed to the relatively rapid cognitive development of our species. The cultural evolution of these early humans spurred the cognitive advances, resulting in a Cognitive Revolution that commenced well in advance of the Agricultural Revolution.[47] The foci of most of these cerebral and corporal pursuits were firstly survival and secondly easier access to food and other resources. Understandably, survival always took precedence over the pursuit of truths. Human societies progressively acquired functional understanding—knowledge of what it takes to

---

[46] As mentioned previously, oral and written language and mathematics are treated as cognitive tools in this book. They are part of the larger advances in technology resulting from human social progression. Computer programming or machine language is one example of the evolution and marriage of language and mathematics tools.

[47] Harari, *Sapiens*, 1-74. Harari places the Cognitive Revolution circa 70,000 BCE.

thrive in one's environment. Most societies successfully adapted to the group's immediate surroundings. However, functional knowledge in the mountains and forests differed from the functional knowledge needed on the coastline. With scientific methods lacking, mystery and myth dominated the noösphere of early societies.

As informal agricultural societies transitioned into civilizations, an even greater division of labor allowed a small fraction of the populous greater time to expand the scope of tool-making and to focus on artistic, engineering, and intellectual endeavors. Civilized life also allowed for the broad dispersion of ideologies, mythologies, and theologies. Group living inevitably led to power and paradigm struggles. Both the right and the wrong of might prevailed. For civilized humans, power not only meant individual and collective physical strength but also included possessions—land, spouses, structures, jewels, tools, weaponry, agricultural and pastoral capacity, slaves, and the like—and, to some extent, knowledge. Eventually, ancient societies developed a means to symbolically leverage material and human assets by adopting a system of coinage or monetary exchange. A pecuniary paradigm (an early example of the soon-to-be-discussed Economic paradigm) arose from the practices of bartering and sharing.

Thus, in ancient societies, a confluence of paradigms dictated how humans lived and what they thought (e.g., ancient Egypt, previously discussed). The same holds true today. Seven major paradigms influenced the Ancient's actions and thoughts, and the same seven dominate our actions and thoughts today. These are the Self, Group, Power, Ideological, Economic, Religious, and Scientific paradigms (capitalized when specifically referring to their dominant status). To help remember the seven, you may find an acronym such as SPIGERS, SERPIGS, or GI PRESS useful.

As the reader will come to realize, the given delineation of dominant paradigms is somewhat arbitrary. For example, under the Economic paradigm, a belief in capitalistic principles may seem, to some, to be rooted in ideology. Why not then include economic perspectives within the Ideological paradigm? The rationale for classifying an Economic paradigm as a separate worldview resides in two simple historical truths. First and foremost, economics represents a form of communication about the perceived value of an object or service and how to integrate that valuation into social structures. Valuation schemes are fundamental to social interaction. Monetary systems work because they effectively communicate trust in what a monetary unit's value represents—a financial intersubjective reality (e.g., X dollars correspond to a Y amount of goods and services). At their core, the transactions that occur (bartering, exchanging, using coinage) satisfy wants and needs, rather than intellectually aligning with a grandiose system of financial principles. Second, economic systems pervade the very fabric of our societies. Economics equates to survival, enabling the acquisition of food, water, shelter, tools, and other necessities. Even primal societies relied on bartering with goods (e.g., food, hides, etc.) rather than coinage. Thus, we need to separate the Economic paradigm from any ideological foundations and give it special consideration. Accordingly, while the seven dominant paradigms may appear a capricious collection of perspectives, they are logically founded in their historical influence on and the ontological development of human thinking and behavior.

Ultimately, the way we live and the content of our thoughts and beliefs originate from a blended composite of the seven dominant paradigms. The resultant combination of these paradigms also help to establish what we call societal norms; however, individuals within a society can vary widely in their perspectives—meaning there are as many blended or composite paradigms as there are members of a society. Consider your own daily actions and thoughts in the normal course of your life—omitting those instances you find yourself in fight or flight mode or suffering due to sickness or injury. Reflect on today, the day you are reading this paragraph—why did you do what you did, say what you said, or think what you thought? If you traced each thought and action, you would find roots in one or more dominant neural networks—generally, a blended composite of your paradigms! Much more will follow on why this is true.

More will also be said about each dominant paradigm, but first we address how the seven dominant paradigms create a composite paradigm. Figure 1 represents conceptually how a composite or blended paradigm leads to individual thought and behavior (one model out of many possible variations). In this representation, we view the mind as a mixing funnel though which the brain's mental activity flows, including autonomic and sensory signals. Neural networks within the brain, process various inputs, such as triggered memories, internal stimuli from organs, and external stimuli. Organs send signals to the brain that provide the "background noise" of an individual's physiological state. In a healthy person, the noise is very low; however, in a person suffering from infection, muscular-skeletal inflammation, or electrochemical imbalance, the noise can attain significant levels, affecting the person's thoughts and behaviors. Added to an individual's active memories and physiological state are the external stimuli that prompt raw visual, auditory, tactile, olfactory, and taste signals to their respective regions of the brain. Neural networks process all these inputs. Some processes are autonomic, such as the normally universal detection of odors. Other inputs require interpretation, relying on paradigmatic neural pathways that are largely dependent upon the individual's life experiences.

What precisely do we mean by stimuli? A person's internal neural environment stems from physiological effects within the body, including those with originate within the brain. An internal stimulus could be anything from a headache, nausea, fatigue, memories, nerve activation, or similar physical or mental distractions that could affect thoughts or behaviors. Most internal stimuli above background agitate the brain, such as toothaches, a bone impinging on a nerve from an injury or aging, infections, tumors, imbalance in digestive processes, fatigue, and many more. These internal stimuli can affect the individual's state of mind, either minimizing or enhancing the influence of dominant paradigms. These stressors (or relievers) are omitted from the representation in Figure 1. To understand paradigm development historically, socially, and individually, we will primarily consider time-averaged circumstances where internal stimuli provide few distractions and extremes. Memory is the primary internal stimulus of concern.

An external stimulus generally refers to inputs from the human sensory system, including the symbolic stimuli within oral and written languages and other symbols such as geometric shapes. Voice intonation can agitate or calm. A symbol such as a flag can elicit greatly different responses depending on the individual's composite paradigm. A person whose Group and Ideological paradigms are highly aligned with national doctrine will have greatly different reactions (thoughts and behaviors) to the sight of a nation's flag than someone who has suffered under those doctrines. We need only consider the symbolic content of the flag of the Confederate States to understand how differently two people, a white supremacist and an African American might respond. We clearly assign meaning to symbols through our composite paradigms. As our paradigms change, so does the meaning, particularly as we pass through various stages of life from infant to adulthood.

As a child develops, he absorbs information, experiences pains and joys, and learns from individuals and groups. Elements of the seven dominant paradigms evolve within the child's neural networks. Neural patterns form, many of which coalesce into crude versions of the major paradigms. They start out as indistinct memories, either reinforced or diminished through external stimuli. While still quite young, a person's worldview emerges as a vaguely formulated composite paradigm. In time, the neural networks come to amalgamate into a mature composite paradigm composed of the seven dominant paradigms. These dominant paradigms serve as filters when processing memories and stimuli to steer thoughts and actions. The filters are more distinct in adults than in children since they have typically been reinforced through repetition and life events.

The filtering processes are what Figure 1 is modeling. The circular wedges at the top of the funnel represent the relative contribution of each dominant paradigm in forming the blended paradigm that appears at the bottom of the funnel. The blended or composite paradigm effectively stems from the mental filters through which an individual comes to interpret the world. They direct his or her thoughts and actions. A child's worldview or composite paradigm is obviously much different than an adult's since mental filters change gradually through the developmental years. In early childhood, the Self paradigm will dominate all others. His or her mental filters are strongly self-directed. When the child comes to realize he or she is a member of a family unit, the Group paradigm begins to slowly blossom. At this early stage of life, the top of a child's funnel diagram would consist of a very large Self paradigm "wedge" and a significantly smaller Group paradigm wedge. All other dominant paradigms would barely register.

Let's dissect what Figure 1 is portraying. First, note that a dotted box represents the mind's complete neural network, encompassing all regions of the brain. This composite network contains sub-networks or mental filters that are diagrammatically represented by a full set of dominant paradigm wedges, seven in all. Thus, Figure 1 clearly applies to an adult. As the brain processes inputs from memories, other internal stimuli, and external stimuli, it filters content and context, eventually creating thoughts and actions (funnel exit). Just as a blue filter only allows the blue range of the visible spectrum to pass through it, neural networks filter multiple stimuli to "recolor" them, aligning them to (a) specific paradigm(s) resident within the mind.

The "swirling" cyclic arrows at the top and bottom of the paradigm funnel of Figure 1 represent the flow and interaction of neural activity to create an aggregate composite paradigm. The (larger) downward arrow near the bottom of the funnel represents the resulting composite paradigm. The end-products of this neural activity exit the funnel as thoughts and behaviors. To summarize, the thoughts and actions that ensue largely depend on the composite paradigm that stems from the weighted combination of the dominant paradigms, represented by the wedges.

Consider, for example, the symbol of Judaism, the Star of David. To a member of the Jewish faith, the Star may generate a strong sense of satisfaction since the individual remembers that the Star represents an association with a people who have endured wide-ranging struggles to maintain their religious beliefs and way of life. To an Israeli, the Star may represent even more—unification and hope for the future. To an anti-Semite, the Star probably evokes hatred and disgust. To many others, the Star may be of little significance. An individual's composite paradigm in the present determines his reaction(s), both thoughts and actions. If over time the same individual's composite paradigm shifts, the reaction(s) could be slightly or dramatically different. A shift in the composite paradigm implies that the relative sizes of the wedges in Figure 1 would have changed.

For illustrative purposes only, the paradigm wedges in Figure 1 are equal (though it doesn't appear that way due to the perspective of the view). This means that the composite paradigm held by this hypothetical (adult) individual has equal contributions from each dominant paradigm. Equal wedges are an idealized, generic representation, which is highly improbable. Typically, an individual's composite paradigm would consist of one or more dominant paradigms that would vastly outweigh the others. Thus, a person most strongly influenced by his or her religion would have a larger wedge for the Religious paradigm and smaller-sized wedges for the other six paradigms. The composite paradigm would therefore reflect and align with the individual's strong religious beliefs, preferences, and perspectives—but not completely. Other dominant paradigms could create a range of reactions still strongly influenced by the person's

Religious paradigm. The thoughts and actions that result (i.e., exit the funnel) reflect the brain's processing of all accessible memories and other internal and external stimuli. In the case in question, the person's mental filters will show a strong religious bias. Alternately, we could say that the thoughts and actions that result are largely due to the individual's composite paradigm in which the Religious paradigm dominates all others. In comparing the previous two sentences, we can see that when we speak of mental filters, we are referring to mental activity (brain processing) in which Religious influences have strongly shaped neural network memory patterns and responses to certain internal and external stimuli.

It is worth pausing here to mention that certain stimuli can act as triggers to cause imbalances in an individual's composite paradigm. Thus, a situational composite paradigm shift can temporarily occur by elevating a lesser paradigm to dominance. For example, a person, David, has strong religious and ideological convictions against stealing, but he still may do so. Imagine David occasionally hangs out with a group or gang that has filled the emptiness in his life. The group, including David, decides to steal a car and take if for a joy ride. The Group paradigm has temporarily displaced the Religious and Ideological paradigms in dominance. In another scenario, David's family is starving and poor so he decides to shoplift at a supermarket, an action likely spurred by his Self and Group (family) paradigms. One can debate whether David's Religious and Ideological paradigms are truly dominant, but such a discussion would significantly detour us from our Big Picture focus. History has had many David's whose paradigms undergo short-term situational shifts, but the paradigms that have determined the course of history are deep-seeded and firmly rooted. To these we shortly turn our attention.

To review, in Figure 1, the funnel represents the workings of the brain's neural networks. As the brain processes internal signals (memories and organ feedback) and external (sensory) stimuli, the mind filters the information based on the relative dominance of the individual's paradigms. What exits the funnel bottom (reactions) represents the effects of a composite paradigm that characterizes the mental environment within the brain. A person's behavior is largely dictated by the most dominant paradigms in his or her cerebral environment (neural networks). The resulting thoughts and actions define a person's value system and/or mental and physical states. While we may wish otherwise, our impulses are largely dependent on the paradigmatic framework of our neural networks.

The funnel bottom in Figure 1 also provides an estimation of ignorance level, which we will use primarily for historical assessments of ignorance. However, what we think and how we act (e.g., what we say, write, and do) expose the nature and depth of our ignorance. For example, we shall shortly learn that ego is a constituent factor of a person's Self paradigm. One's ego may lead an individual to make bold, unsubstantiated statements or twist the truth or blatantly lie about a topic of discussion—even express opinion as fact. An egoist's actions serve the individual above others, dominating his composite paradigm. Accordingly, the actions that stem from an egoist's composite paradigm provide a basis for assessing the ignorance level of an individual, at least qualitatively.

The range of ignorance an individual may display as a result of her paradigms can vary from very low to very high, which is what is portrayed for the generic case in Figure 1 for illustrative purposes only. However, as we shall see after further discussion, we could actually pinpoint the level of ignorance more precisely for the instance where a person's dominant paradigms are equally weighted as shown in Figure 1. The resulting composite paradigm will generally lead to highly ignorant outcomes. One might assume that a person whose dominant paradigms are equally weighted would be a well-balanced individual. The reality is quite different. A person would be "all over the map" in his or her actions and thoughts under such circumstances. At first glance, this statement might appear counterintuitive, but a person whose Self paradigm matches the strength of his Group, Scientific, and other dominant paradigms will have difficulty functioning consistently within society. Conflicts will arise quickly. For example, an individual with a strong ego (Self) who equally identifies himself by his race or ethnicity (Group), and similarly believes physical prowess matters more than intellect (Power), and judges the role of government to be the advancement of his group's causes (Ideological), cannot rationally have Scientific, Economic, and Religious paradigms of equal weight. At least one or all three of these other dominant paradigms would be subdued in the real world.

Figure 1: Generic Composite Paradigm

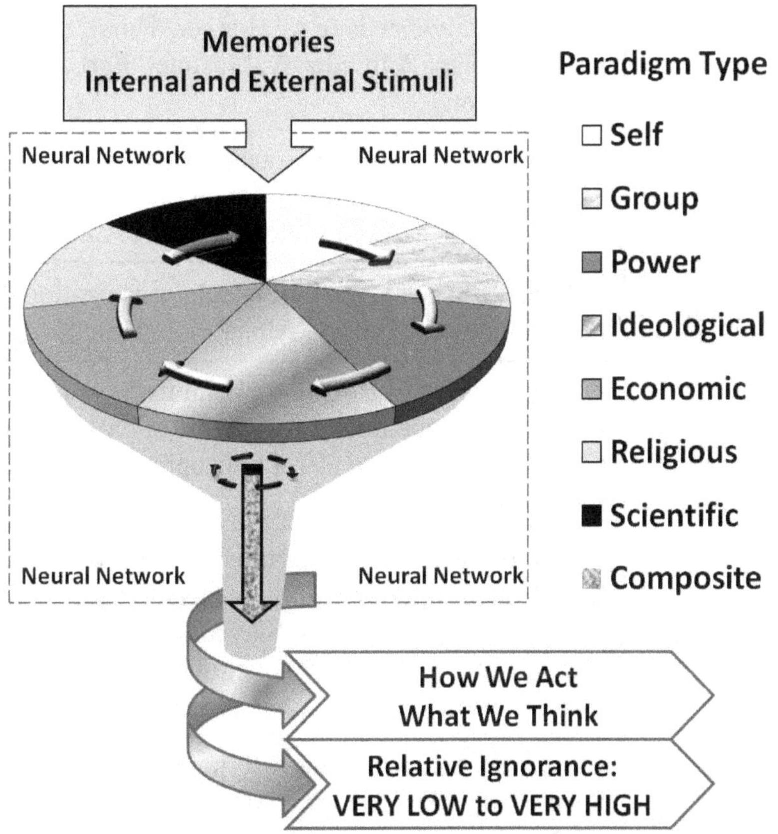

Table 1: Generic Dominant Paradigm Neural Filters

Dominant Paradigm	Major Filters Affecting Thoughts and Actions
Self	Neural/Bodily Needs (e.g., Hunger, Thirst, Sex), Gender, Fears, Pain, Survival Instinct, Ego, Introspection
Group	Ethnic, Cultural, Racial, Social, Tribal, Geographical, Climatic, Common Interests (clubs, sports, activities, etc.), Gender, Political
Power	Political, Physical, Psychological, Organizational (Bureaucratic), Military, Alpha Male/Female
Ideological	Non-Theological -isms (e.g., Feminism, Humanism, Secularism, Isolationism, Fascism, Globalism, Metaphysical, Philosophical (e.g. Existentialism)
Economic	Valuation Schemes, Bartering Systems, Monetary Exchange, Property/Wealth Ownership and Distribution, Entitlement, Slavery, Serfdom, Capitalism, Socialism, Mercantilism, Feudalism, Communism,
Religious	Divinities, Institutionalized Religions, Religious Sects, Cults, Agnosticism, Atheism
Scientific	Rigorous Observations, Data Collection, and Analytical Processes (e.g. Scientific Method, Analysis, Synthesis), Tool-Making (including symbolic tools such as oral and written language, number systems, mathematical equations, and algorithms)

To reiterate, our childhood and life experiences shape the seven dominant paradigms that make us who we are as adults. The paradigms fuse over time to create an individual's composite paradigm. Autonomic behavioral responses also play a role. Fear and pain can certainly affect one's perspectives. These contribute to a person's Self paradigm along with numerous other factors, such as the aforementioned ego. Table 1, a companion to Figure 1, shows many of the primary influencing filters of each dominant paradigm. Again, these are generic listings, which we will fine-tune as we examine each dominant paradigm within differing historical eras. The reader should become familiar with the influencing filters for each dominant paradigm as the list will expand to encompass specific perspectives that dominated during the historical period in question. A brief overview of Table 1 follows.

Self paradigm: The filters listed stem from nature and nurture—of genetic origin, upbringing, and experience. They integrate to provide a sense or awareness of self that define the individual irrespective of other paradigms. For example, a person with a strong gender-focused Self paradigm will see the world through his or her gender biases (e.g., the superiority of men over women).

Group paradigm: Gender and race filters will have strong genetic components, but the preponderance of filters will arise from experience and environment. Tribal and political influences provide a rich diversity of perspectives that typically manifest themselves as group paradigms. Common interests can also become the bases of paradigms, especially if they become strongly internalized. These include everything from the passive, such as stamp collecting, to the active and risky, such as skydiving. Criminal activity would fall into the risky category as well—for example, adopting a group's perspective that theft and violence are acceptable lifestyles.

Power paradigm: Alpha Males and Females utilize either innate or learned filters for physical and psychological intimidation. A similar phenomenon occurs with organizational power, where groups leverage the system (e.g., laws), technology (e.g., weaponry), or raw numbers to wield control over others.

Ideological paradigm: Myths, stories, facts, falsehoods, inspirations, motivations, and reasoned and spurious ideas provide a rich environment for the development of neural networks. Many such networks coalesce into ideologies. For example, justice and resource-sharing as ideals probably had their roots in hunter-gatherer societies.

These and early agricultural groups elevated those principles or ideals that improved individual and tribal survival. Failure to share the food of the hunt or of the fields threatened survival. The unwarranted murder of a fellow tribe or group member likewise meant there were fewer individuals to participate in hunts or manage the fields. These and similar taboos formed the early basis for the classification of right and wrong. The multitude of isms that developed eventually became thematic structures within neural networks. They evolved over time to become substantive ideologies involving our justice systems, ethics, philosophies, human rights, and more.

Economic paradigm: No one is born knowing the value of a dollar or any other bartering object or service. Neither is anyone born knowing he can enslave others for economic gain. Experience largely dictates the valuation systems that eventually become wired into our neural networks. Our inherent drive for survival overlays these valuation filters to color our thoughts and actions. We conclude that more is better because it improves our chances of survival (e.g., more food, water, domesticated animals, and land). Less is worse because it threatens survival. Everyone can't have more, so humans systematized financial operations both to accommodate large group dynamics and to satisfy our drives. As a result, economic paradigms gradually grew into complex isms (see Table 1), following an historical progression that effectively aligned with technological advances. Throughout history, individuals and groups have questioned "more-is-better" and "winner-and-loser" economics so they developed and promoted counter isms or systems as alternate Economic paradigms. The opposition isms are part of a much broader War of Paradigms, still in progress today.

Religious paradigm: Without language, most of the dominant paradigms would not exist, specifically, the Religious, Ideological, Scientific, and Economic. Language is a cognitive tool providing humans the ability to derive narratives, develop ideas and opinions, assess their surroundings, and build and quantify bartering systems. Language enabled humans to describe their divinities and to express what they mean by God, sometimes in the form of written texts. Groups later institutionalized their gods or God. Their goal was to establish, to the greatest extent possible, invariant descriptions of their divinities and the rules for worshipping them. Throughout history, societies have held a wide variety of Religious paradigms. Cults and sects emerged from Religious paradigm drift.

Scientific paradigm: Evolution armed humanity with the brains and bodies to explore their surroundings in unique ways. Brains, hands, and vocal cords provide humans the capability to develop cognitive and physical tools to improve our chances of survival. These tools can transform ecosystems, with both positive and/or negative consequences. The same tools permit humanity to explore their surroundings with rigor and certainty—to gain a truer representation of processes and events that make things happen the way they do. These depictions are the substance of Scientific paradigms. As tooling and methodological rigor improve, Scientific paradigms shift to more accurate versions.

Paradigms: An Evolutionary Perspective

Previously, we provided a neurological basis to explain why the brain creates and reacts to paradigms and why paradigms exercise significant control over thoughts and behavior. Here we examine an evolutionary foundation for these effects. Recall that the brain is a part of the body's vast neural network. The mammalian neural system developed over millions of years to improve each species chances of survival. The human nervous system vastly improves upon other mammalian species in its ability to construct symbolic representations of the physical world. Our ability to create MCs of the world in sensory and symbolic terms improves reaction times to threats and communication within social groups. The varied mental constructs that we develop usually advance the group's collective purposes. When humans were hunter-gatherers, tribal paradigms enabled both hunter and gatherer skill sets. Taboos (also paradigms) existed to minimize behaviors which would threaten the tribe. The paradigms helped to direct group efforts in securing food and shelter, in dealing with extremes in the elements, and in countering threats from other species and other humans. Thus, the development and application of paradigms is largely instinctive, assisting in individual and species survival.

As humans made the transition from hunter-gatherer to agriculture, they clustered together into larger groups. Population centers grew, and civilizations matured. People developed ethno-racial-cultural identities (e.g., the Persians and Chinese).The flourishing of civilizations also meant an affluence of paradigms, creating conflict within and among societies. Most early sociopolitical paradigms stemmed from survival instincts, an attempt to avoid a life of "...continual fear, and danger of violent death; and the life of man, solitary, poor, nasty, brutish and short." [48] Survival trumped enlightenment then and still does today. As we explore humanity's current dominant paradigms, we should keep in mind that they all ultimately developed to improve the survivability of individuals and groups. *We should also not blindly accept that the dominant paradigms of the present are the only ones that can enhance survivability.* This book will propose alternatives to the seven dominant paradigms that have persisted into the modern era. If the alternative dominant paradigms of the future truly improve human survivability, we should expect them to serve humanity at large and not select groups.

Self Paradigms

Self-perception and self-awareness influence an individual's thoughts and behavior. Together, they provide a foundation for a person's Self paradigm. Self-perception (or self-image) refers to "the idea one has of one's abilities, appearance, and personality" while self-awareness stems from the "conscious knowledge of one's own character, feelings, motives, and desires" (Oxford Dictionaries, Oxford University Press). Fear, pain, pleasure, hunger, thirst, instinctive love,[49] and ego also contribute to a person's Self paradigm. For this reason, Self paradigms are typically the most unpredictable of paradigms; they often rely on a person's emotional disposition at a given time. A person may be in a state of euphoric love, spiteful hate, grief, depression, sensually-motivated pleasures (sexual, tactile, flavorful, etc.), and others. In addition, because the human nervous system reacts to naturally occurring and manmade substances, a person's Self paradigm may vary due to exposure to foods, medications, illicit drugs, and atmospheric pollutants. Discomforts due to allergies and physiological abnormalities add distractions to the

[48] Hobbes, 64.

[49] Instinctive love refers to strong, natural affections between humans, such as parent and child. Love may also stem from paradigms conveyed in stories (fairy tales, mythologies, novels). Thus, love has both emotional and ideological components. Almost all instances of hate originate in paradigms, meaning hate is largely learned, such as occurs with racial, ethnic, and other biases.

mental states of individuals, influencing their thoughts and behaviors. A person with frequent headaches and muscular pain will likely shun social interaction. His Self paradigm, particularly the self-image component, and his Group paradigm, will often lack clarity due to the mental energy devoted to dealing with pain.

Ego serves largely as a self-survival mechanism. Notably, the stronger the ego, the more prominent the Self paradigm is among the other dominant paradigms. Ego can cloud judgment and force poor decisions, even afflicting those who are otherwise well-balanced, knowledgeable, and typically open-minded. When the paradigm of self dominates a person's perspectives, the individual will often descend into a self-generated fog of ignorance.

One of history's greatest cases of egomania was Adolf Hitler. He saw himself as a mythological heroic conqueror. His "view of self" led to many poor decisions. He rushed into war without careful consideration of the factors for success. He impatiently and aggressively moved forward—meaning Germany failed to consolidate its gains and improve its armaments and production capacities before proceeding to armed conflict.[50] Hitler's ego prevented him from internally debating the merits of aggression. When Hitler ordered an attack on the Soviet Union, he rushed again, and he (and his logisticians) neglected the need for cold weather clothing and footwear. The results for the German army were disastrous, and in the end, fortunate for the rest of humanity.

Hitler is but one of the many powerful leaders with strong egos who have dictated the course of history, more often plunging humanity into despair than elevating it to contentment. We have Napoleon, Genghis Khan, Stalin, and countless others, well-known and obscure. We can surmise with high confidence that their egos dramatically dominated their Self paradigms, leading to decisions based on the highest state of ignorance. Their ignorance stemmed from their decidedly narrow perspectives and blind spots for the truth. These conquerors, royals, tyrants, and wannabe divinities had their early life experiences strongly shape their egos, meaning their Self paradigm varied little over their lifetimes. The more ego-driven one's Self

[50] The Nazi ideologies that took hold of Germany from 1933-1945 provide many rich examples of the influence of paradigms in human history. These are included for illustrative purposes only and not to glorify in any way the horridly inhumane policies and actions perpetrated by the Nazis during this period.

paradigm is, the greater the probability that the person will fail to have any significant shifts in his Self paradigm over his lifetime.

Yet, among the dominant paradigms, the Self paradigm has, on average, been the most consistent in its characteristics over the course of human history—despite its day-to-day unpredictability due to internal and external stimuli acting on the mind. The reason is simple: the Self paradigm evolves from the inherent nature of the human nervous system, which, from best available evidence, has remained fixed over the millennia in which *Homo sapiens* have thrived. Archaeological evidence indicates the brains of Moderns are effectively indistinguishable from the brains of our hunter-gather non-Neanderthal forebears.

Species-defined sexuality plays a significant role in Self paradigm formation. To survive, early humans balanced cooperation with competition. Males, and to a lesser extent females, often competed aggressively to protect their family units, both in attaining food and fending off would-be competitors. The challengers could also kill the offspring of their opponents. Whether one attributes this behavior to a "selfish gene" phenomenon—the perpetuation of an individual's or group's DNA (deoxyribonucleic acid)—is immaterial. Inherently, parents protect their young to ensure the survival of their direct descendants. They endure hardships in order to sustain their ability to protect their family unit(s).

One appalling paradigmatic outcome of the inherited survive-and-protect predisposition is the lengths to which men have gone to ensure fidelity in their mates. They desired certainty in knowing they were protecting their descendants (genes) and not someone else's. This often led to drastic practices in limiting a woman's ability to enjoy or participate in intercourse while her male mate was absent—some practices which are still in existence today. This particular ego-and-survival-driven Self paradigm effectively morphed into a similar Group paradigm in some societies (e.g., laws governing sexuality in certain Middle Eastern societies), illustrating one mechanism by which one paradigm can integrate with or evolve into other paradigms.

While all paradigms are products of the human mind, the Self paradigm depends most strongly on the inherent genetic and physiological characteristics of an individual brain. The same cannot be claimed of the other dominant paradigms. Ideologies, economic and political systems, religious perspectives, scientific and technological (tool-making) knowledge, and even group composition and dynamics have changed significantly throughout human history. The changes arise due to stimuli in the local environment and due to interactions among individuals and groups, the latter reflected in various levels of competition, cooperation, and communication. To repeat, dominant paradigms can undergo significant shifts with one glaring exception: the Self paradigm. Ideas, knowledge, and tools have evolved significantly—but the human brain and the desires it generates have not.

The Self paradigm begins in infancy. The persistence of paradigms formulated in early childhood is both difficult to identify and to classify since the self is so weakly defined during the immediate years after birth. Still, researchers have developed techniques to assess the simplistic mental modeling done by infants. They designed a method to evaluate paradigm development by examining preverbal infant responses to caregivers (typically parents). As perceived by infants in one landmark study, researchers assigned caregivers to provide one set of infants a secure environment and another set insecure surroundings.[51] Secure environments consistently supported the infants' needs and comforts. They produced stronger infant attachments and responses to the caregivers. As the infants gained attachments to their caregivers, they gradually accepted certain realities about their environment. Primitive and simplistic paradigms formed about the infant's world, such as where certain events occur (e.g., feeding). The process of paradigm formation has nevertheless begun, albeit with limited cognition and self-awareness.

How can preverbal infants acquire paradigms? Some researchers attribute this ability to inherent biochemical processes in brain receptors. Oxytocin, a neuropeptide produced in the hypothalamus, is a primary enabler. Axons transmit the oxytocin into the amygdala where the receptor for oxytocin is located.[52] Researchers Johnson and Chen summarize their findings as follows:

> Infants are subjective individuals with their own personal perspectives and experiences of the world. Genotypic variations, not only in the oxytocin system, but surely in other neurotransmitter systems as well, impact the

---

[51] Johnson and Chen, 501-502.

[52] Johnson, Dweck, and Chen, 172-174.

> emotional weight and relevance of an individual's experiences from the very beginning of life, setting the stage for meaningful individual differences in not only personality, but also social and cognitive development.[53, 54]

While we've tied paradigms to neural networks, the notion that our paradigms are ultimately the product of numerous biochemical processes in the brain may see bizarre to most. In time, a better understanding of the processes involved will emerge. For now, we need only recognize that the set of influences responsible for the Self paradigm create dominant perspectives within the individual, which manifest themselves as thoughts and behaviors. As discussed in Chapter 2, we cannot neglect the role of biochemistry in the paradigm creation process. The physiological and psychological effects of addictive substances are considerable. Nicotine, heroin, opiates, caffeine, and even salty, fatty, or sugary foods taken in excess can influence the Self paradigm through biochemical processes, ultimately dictating thoughts (and desires) and behaviors. The addict's worldview represents mental models distorted by biochemical influences.

We should also not dismiss the powerful effects of biochemical processes in developing feelings of love and hate. These processes play a significant role in establishing short-lived and long-term paradigms that ultimately affect the decision-making process throughout an individual's life.[55]

The *non-addictive* scenarios in which the Self paradigm plays a significant role in affecting one's thoughts and behavior are too numerous to describe or catalogue in this book, but a hypothetical contemporary example in which a Self paradigm drives ignorance will prove illuminating. Imagine an individual named Joe, who is trying to decide how to vote on a referendum to allow the building of a state-of-the-art, coal-fired power plant ten miles from his home. He's been exposed to a spectrum of pro and con arguments, many of a technical

---

[53] Ibid, 176.

[54] One could assume the aforementioned processes help determine the variations in the strength of individual ego.

[55] Short-lived paradigms refer to those that emerge during emotional experiences (e.g., grief) and gradually fade over a relatively short interval of time, typically a few hours to a few weeks.

nature. Joe has a college degree, but lacks a technical (scientific) education. In fact, he often feels inadequately informed and inferior whenever scientific matters become the topic of discussion. His self-image is exceedingly low when confronted with technological information. Although he is capable of researching the details of both sides of the issues, he fears his own inadequacies. Joe opts not to research the proposal and not to participate in referendum voting. Using the generic influences on the Self paradigm from Table 1, we can assess that fears, a fragile ego, and weak introspective abilities strongly influence Joe's Self paradigm, at least on this and similar issues.

Joe's situational paradigm of self became the tipping force for his actions (his decision not to vote and not to explore a deeper understanding of the issues).[56] He perpetuated his own ignorance, and along with those who acted similarly, contributed to the collective ignorance of the public.

Advances in brain scanning capabilities using magnetic resonance imaging (MRI) provide additional insights into paradigm formation within the brain. Harris, Kaplan, et al investigated the acceptance of religious and nonreligious propositions between equally sized groups of devoted Christians and atheists. The statements presented to study subjects—some true, others false—stimulated significant activity in the prefrontal cortex of the study participants. "A comparison of both stimulus categories suggests that religious thinking is more associated with brain regions that govern emotion, self-representation, and cognitive conflict, while thinking about ordinary facts is more reliant upon memory retrieval networks."[57] While these results applied to responses to events associated with religious and ideological paradigms, the same mechanism should likewise apply to Self paradigms. Thus, the filtering mechanisms described in Table 1

---

[56] Joe's Self paradigm may differ in other areas, such as sports or home repair work. In these areas, his fears may be subdued and his self-image better, which is why the term, situational, applies. Situational paradigms are largely associated with the Self paradigm and to a lesser degree with the Group paradigm. We should not expect the other dominant paradigms to have strong situational elements under normal circumstances except during stressful events, such as natural and man-made disasters.

[57] Harris, (in Abstract), 1.

that contribute to the neural framework of a person's Self paradigm similarly catalyze the neural structures responsible for an individual's emotions, self-representation, and cognitive conflicts.

In summary, from infant to adult, Self paradigm formation involves neural and biochemical processes under a plethora of stimuli. Development of the Self paradigm relies on both emotional and cognitive processes, which, through language and other symbolic representations, consolidate the individual's self-image.

Group Paradigms

A Group paradigm is a perspective strongly held by members of a social unit, an assembly of people typically bound together by physical, biological, and communal characteristics or interests. Geography and climate are two prominent physical factors that can influence group action and thoughts. Forest dwellers see the world differently than seafarers, urbanites differently than farmers, and so on. One's local surroundings certainly can affect self and group perspectives. Sociologists have found significant variances in worldviews when comparing, for example, those confined to inner-city ghetto life to those living in affluent suburban enclaves.

Biological factors play a significant role in shaping one's perspectives as well. Race, gender, hair color, and other biological variants influence the formation of MCs. We tend to identify with others of like color and physical traits. Experience can overwrite MCs, however. Racial perspectives stem primarily from parents, culture, history, myths, and other forms of verbal and non-verbal communications. Direct interaction among groups and individuals is the most accurate way to learn to distinguish the physical differences among the races and shift inaccurately developed paradigms (biases).

Infants innately develop attachments to the race(s) of their nurturing parents or providers, who may not have the same skin color and other physical characteristics that they do (refer to the studies on the attachment principle of infants exposed to nurturing caregivers). Other biologically related but less common paradigm bonds may occur. For example, consider the tendency for like-minded thoughts and behaviors among those with similar biological disabilities (e.g., blindness or deafness). The worldviews that develop from biologically similar experiences occur because of the unique ways these individuals and groups experience the world.

One's viewpoints also differ as a result of one's communal background. Ethnic, social, and cultural surroundings contribute to an individual's Group paradigm. A Slav raised in his native culture will likely have a vastly different worldview than a Chinese person raised in hers. Also, societal norms develop and drift over time, influencing how people think about and act toward their parents or the elderly, or their views on sexual preference, or a host of other socio-cultural matters. When evaluating the dominance of a Group paradigm, we must separate the ethnically, culturally, and socially driven influences upon perspectives from those influenced by religion. Often, we'll find the boundaries blurred, and the Group paradigm will overlap with the Religious or Ideological paradigms. For the purposes of this book, religious and ideological influences do not contribute to Group paradigms. They are separated out as individual paradigms because of their historical origins and impact on human interaction.

We should note, however, that when different dominant paradigms strongly align, they strengthen the common elements of the composite paradigm. In such cases, the mental filtering process reinforces similar content among the paradigms—meaning we see the world through more strongly biased composite paradigms. For example, the perspectives of the role of women in some societies often stem from both religious and ethnic/cultural influences. They reinforce each other. Thus, the composite paradigm in these groups will contain strongly biased attitudes and policies about women, their treatment, and the opportunities afforded them by society. History contains numerous examples of one or more dominant paradigms reinforcing a Group paradigm with powerful effects on the minds of group members. These include the racist fascists of World War II (Group and Ideological paradigms) and the Islamic extremists (Group, Ideological, Religious, and Power paradigms) of the present era.

Note that we should not confuse ideology with "group or one think." Ideological paradigms stem from a variety of factors not directly related to one or more groups. Ideological refers not only to what people think and believe about the way humans should live their lives but also how they react to specific stimuli. Accordingly, the following qualify as Ideological paradigms and not Group paradigms even though they involve groups: proponents of animal rights policies, sports and game clubs such as golf[58] and chess, and many other group or club-oriented activities based on shared ideologies or interests. A future section addresses the specific aspects of the Ideological paradigm.

Next we delve more deeply into certain aspects of the Group paradigm, three of the strongest influences identified in Table 1.

Key Group Paradigm Elements: Cultural-Racial-Ethnic

Cultural-Racial-Ethnic (CRE) paradigms have had and still have a powerful influence on the lives and thoughts of social groups. Members of a culture broadly experience non-ideological "one think," a unified perspective on most aspects of life, to include food, customs, and dress. In the modern era, the vast international communications network available through cell phones, the internet, radio, television, and wireless technologies has served as a catalyst to diminish the polarizing influence of many ethnic and cultural paradigms. Yet strong racial, cultural, and ethnic paradigms persist. For some groups, there is considerable overlap between the cultural-ethnic components of their paradigms and their religions, such as those who are both of Jewish descent and of the Judaic faith.

Many cultural paradigms resulted from the influences of geography and climate, giving rise to the perspectives of the seafaring, nomadic, and mountain/pastoral cultures of past eras. From Polynesia to the tundra, human groups developed paradigms in sync with their surroundings, including the local flora and fauna. Geographic latitude and climate are interconnected factors that affected seasonal growing and hunting patterns, such as the length of the day and animal migration. Over time, geographic and climatic influences embed themselves in a group's culture, becoming one of the many sub-elements of the Group paradigm. In past eras, geography, climate, and environment also affected the development of religious paradigms to include theisms rooted in volcanic activity, weather phenomena, animals, plants, and bodies of water.

---

[58] We must take care with certain club activities. A club that meets on the golf course to play rounds is different than belonging to a country club that may exclude individuals of an economic class due to fee structure or impose other limitations, thus qualifying as a Group paradigm.

CRE paradigms generally produce a set of socio-cultural norms within the society, anything from how women and men wear their hair to the living arrangements among extended families and even to artistic expression. Here again, the influence of geography, climate, and environment cannot be understated. The various art forms and construction projects of past societies depended upon the raw materials (plants, work animals, soil, minerals, and waters) available locally to manufacture the building materials, dyes, and tools to pursue the groups' artistic and engineering endeavors. These creations further solidified societal norms.

Over the past several centuries, globalization and technological advances have progressively broadened Group perspectives, eroding traditional cultural-ethnic worldviews. As a result, some cultural normalization has occurred among nations. The American Melting Pot effect has reached well beyond U.S. borders. One striking example is how people spend their time—watching television, surfing the web, and engaging in social media, all the while subjected to an onslaught of advertisements enticing the individual to buy. The advertising blitz stems from corporate and small business sources. Accordingly, most modern societies have shifted toward the paradigms of consumerism and materialism, subsets of the prevailing Economic paradigm (capitalism) discussed below. One could even take the cynical view that many societies exploit their ethnicities and cultures as a way of promoting consumerism among the local population and tourists. While the Westernization of economies and technological innovation have definitely weakened traditions that otherwise would have sustained cultural, ethnic, and religious paradigms, Group paradigm shifts are still stubbornly slow.

The discussion in the preceding paragraphs is yet another reminder of the interrelationships of dominant paradigms, wherein a multitude of competing and reinforcing mental filters direct the flow of thoughts within the human mind. The process results in thoughts and actions aligned to the individual's composite paradigm.

Even with the erosion of certain Group paradigms in the modern era, many of the most caustic CRE paradigms thrive, advancing gross ignorance. In particular, many composite paradigms include a strong racist component stemming from the Group paradigms of societies at large or factions within these societies. Over the civilized segment of our history, the racial component of the Group paradigm has been responsible for some of the most despicable and inhumane behavior by individuals and groups. The atrocities enacted by one group upon another, including those perpetrated by white Western Europeans and their colonial minions upon black-, brown-, yellow-, and red-skinned peoples, has been well documented. So too has the distorted CRE components of Nazism, which created a Master Race perspective under the Group paradigm. These actions stem from a paradigm of distrust of those who are different, a xenophobic response—not only racially, but also religiously, culturally, and ethnically.

CRE biases are the product of mental filters, a reflection of the inherent defense mechanisms for self and group survival. In nature, the hunted are generally wary of the prey; one species instinctively feels threatened by one or more other species.[59] Antelope scatter if a cheetah approaches. Similarly, humans treat non-group members with suspicion. For example, images of human faces of other races and cultures (such as reflected by dress, headgear, facial hair, skin color) can trigger the emotional centers of the human brain (amygdala), resulting in positive or negative responses. Experimental design can help determine whether a response stems from inherent (unlearned) origins or from exposure to prejudicial environments (learned). Clearly, children can readily adopt their parents' paradigms, particularly if the paradigms are reinforced through social and group interactions outside the family unit.

In summary, the Group paradigm derives from a combination of paradigmatic influences—most notably, cultural, racial, ethnic, geographical, and climatic. For example, seafaring cultures have entwined maritime themes within their food and leisure traditions. High latitude societies differ markedly from their equatorial counterparts in dress, food, and shelter. In addition, the proximity of different races, cultures, and ethnicities has often led to negative

---

[59] On the Galapagos Islands and other remote locales, some species have developed an indifference to humans, sensing no threat. If there had been significant interaction with *Homo sapiens* in the past, the species' defense mechanisms may have developed sufficiently through natural selection, making their descendants wary of humans.

intergroup interactions and paradigmatic clashes—often a blemish on human history.

Before examining the remaining dominant paradigms, we should review specific attributes of the ways other dominant paradigms can alter the Group paradigm. The Scientific paradigm broadly influences culture through technological innovations, profoundly influencing our collective actions and thoughts. [60] As mentioned previously, the cell phone, internet, energy production, and a plethora of other advances are shaping and shifting the cultural paradigms of the modern era—and thus, the nature of the dominant Group paradigm. One need only visualize a world totally without electricity (as it once was) and assess how our current cultures and paradigms would shift.

Ideological paradigms, such as isolationism, globalism, colonialism, and altruism, all have the ability to shift Group paradigms. Also, let's not forget the historical significance of Religious paradigms and their influence in shifting Group paradigms through the ages. Both Christian and Islamic paradigms had a powerful influence over nation-forming and regional politics. Also, well before the rise of Islam, the Roman Empire adopted Christianity. The Empire subsequently collapsed giving rise to diverse principalities—yet Christianity survived. Accordingly, the Group paradigms in these territories aligned strongly with the then-existing dominant Religious paradigm (Christianity).

Ideological Paradigms

Ideological paradigms stem from ideas and beliefs (opinions and values) that are not attributable to the other six major paradigms. They include both mental and physical activities, especially when the activities become an integral part of a person's life. The athlete, poker player, meditation practitioner, chess player, and the plethora of other individuals occupied by vocational and avocational pursuits have each adopted certain identities, at least for a segment of their lives. These pursuits stem from paradigms that influence their thoughts and behaviors. Eventually, occupations and pastimes become Ideological paradigms, which may reinforce or conflict with other Ideological

[60] Shermer, 30. Also, further discussion appears in Chapter 7.

paradigms held by an individual. Consider how workaholics act and what occupies their thoughts. They value, believe, or subscribe to certain work-related ethical principles—sometimes because of the recognition and rewards associated with their work and sometimes because the work strongly aligns with their composite paradigm, or both.

Ideological paradigms are tricky because they're easy to mislabel. For example, at first glance, we may assume a person with a socialist perspective subscribes to the economic sub-paradigm of socialism.[61] We may also assume a person who considers abortion immoral as an adherent of a religious paradigm. However, these positions may also result from ideological perspectives alone. A person with a socialist perspective may simply accept egalitarianism as a fundamental principle by which humans should live. Her socialist leanings are strictly ideological and not economic. She aligns with socialist perspectives because of the (economic) principle of wealth-sharing. She'd accept any economic system that supports egalitarian principles. Likewise, with no inherent scientific and/or religious rationale, a person who supports pro-life laws (e.g., no death penalty) may extend the umbrella of protected human rights to a fetus. As a human rights advocate, the person would seem to mirror a viewpoint of a religious right-to-life advocate. However, the person may hold this perspective on purely ideological grounds. In particular, if the person advocating fetal rights were an atheist or agnostic, his views would strictly stem from an ideological perspective.

Similarly, feminism is an Ideological paradigm and not a gender-based Group paradigm. Men can be feminist advocates. Feminism extends well beyond the biological role of women to bear and nurse children and beyond an accounting of the physiological differences between men and women. In fact, feminism stems from a broader humanistic ideology of the worth of individual humans, regardless of their gender.

In the preceding examples, it may seem difficult to separate the ideological paradigms from the religious, group, and economic perspectives. Thus, we should always examine the circumstances that allow Ideological paradigms to stand apart from the other dominant

---

[61] Note that socialism also encompasses a Power paradigm that dictates the means for the redistribution of wealth. The Power paradigm includes sociopolitical and military elements as well as systems for maintaining law and order.

paradigms. For example, there are ideological perspectives that favor the urban over the rural, isolationism over interventionist policies, organic farming over agribusiness, genetically modified organisms over natural selection, feminism over chauvinism, and a multitude of other opposing views. Rarely are ideologies black and white. As such, individuals and groups tend to align ideologically into a spectrum of conservative, liberal, and moderate camps. The divergences create political conflict. The seemingly perpetual ideological battlegrounds within the U.S. Congress over much of its history provide clear evidence of paradigm conflicts, many founded on ideological principles. However, we should never assume that political viewpoints are purely ideological. They rarely, if ever, are. Politics reflect the prevailing composite paradigms, largely encompassing the combined dominant perspectives of Economic, Group, Ideological, and Power paradigms. Thus, in an open society, we should always expect political friction.

While some positive outcomes occur from the associated social discourse stimulated by paradigm disagreements, social cohesion will remain elusive unless both citizens and their representatives undergo unifying paradigm shifts. Democracies can fail when paradigms are stagnant and entrenched. Eventually, obstructionism takes hold, resulting in high levels of ignorance within these societies. As we shall find, ignorance can beget greater ignorance, making it more difficult for people to shift their paradigms. Supporting evidence for this sociological phenomenon appears in studies on ignorance reviewed in Chapter 5.

As indicated in Table 1, people who subscribe to one or more non-religious and/or non-economic isms are thinking and acting under the influence of Ideological paradigms. The list of ideological isms is exhaustive, only a few of which were identified in this section and in Table 1. Note that mysticism is an Ideological paradigm rooted in the notion that metaphysical effects influence our lives, such as the positioning of planets or the zodiac sign under which a person is born.

Philosophies are usually rooted in Ideological paradigms. Like all paradigms, philosophies arise from the progressive development of neural networks in individuals over time. Sometimes, philosophies contagiously spread to groups (e.g. fascism). The philosophy of existentialism became an Ideological paradigm for many in the latter half of the 19th and first half of the 20th century. Existentialists maintain that individuals are responsible for their own actions. A person's true nature stems from his conscious self, not some social or family role he is fulfilling. How did such a philosophy heralding existence over essence come to be? To answer this question, we can usually examine the circumstances under which the ideology matures. For example, Jean-Paul Sartre and Simone de Beauvoir, well-known for disseminating existential perspectives, lived through the tumultuous rise of fascism and Nazism in Europe and the Nazi occupation of France. Their experiences (and knowledge gained from other philosophers) obviously stimulated a worldview aligned to existential principles, eventually coalescing as a neural network. Their dominant Ideological paradigm became existentialism. The brutality and rigidity of Nazi occupation forces obviously tainted their perspectives of human behavior.

Religious Paradigms

Religious paradigms are seemingly straightforward. People may believe that a divine influence governs human affairs (the faithful); others may have doubts (agnostics), and still others may find the notion implausible (atheists).[62] Although time and experience help people to personalize the religion of their youth and to mature their religious and spiritual perspectives, institutionalized religious paradigms still strongly influence societal laws, art, culture, and daily life. One need only examine the Judaic, Islamic, Hindu, and Christian societies of past and present to find divergent perspectives on divine influence, morality, gender roles, social hierarchies, and more. The societies where these religions dominate still vary significantly from each other.

As indicated in Table 1, religious sects and cults can influence the characteristics of one's Religious paradigm. Often, sects and cults enable (slight) shifts in Religious paradigms. These shifts don't necessarily lead to more enlightened religious perspectives; they could lead to stricter applications of religious traditions. As a result, most institutionalized religions are not unified. Sects persist (e.g., Sunni and Shi'a Muslims and the numerous Protestant denominations). Accordingly, "sect paradigms" have shaped or continue to shape the overarching Religious paradigms.

[62] For the purposes of this book, atheism is a Religious paradigm since it represents a perspective on divinity.

The faithful of any religion may take offense at labeling their religion a paradigm since it would seemingly consign their beliefs to mental and emotional models. To the faithful, religion represents an absolute truth independent of their existence. Paradigms, however, represent evolving tenets, which are products of the human brain. Still, as difficult as it may be for some to accept, Religious paradigm shifts have occurred under cultural, ethnic, economic, and societal pressures. Thus, existing religious norms largely differ from those of past eras, negating the notion that fundamental religious tenets originate from absolute truths.

Accordingly, some religions exist as incomplete or changing models of divinity. We simply are unable to know everything about a religion and the designs of its divinity/divinities. Still, the core content of institutionalized religious paradigms rarely shifts. The Bible remains the foundation of Christian sects as does the Koran for Islam. The core content of Ideological, Scientific, and Economic paradigms, however, has shifted significantly throughout history. Take, for example, the Scientific paradigm where the "center" of the universe transitioned from the Earth, then the Sun, and now the Big Bang. While cosmologists would be the first to confess that the existing cosmological perspective contains many unknowns—even errors—about our universe, the religious faithful cannot do so without weakening the pillars of their beliefs. They might admit that religious paradigms contain the unknown and the unknowable since only divine direction dictates what humans can know; however, any recognition that errors exist in their understanding of their God and His directives would undermine their beliefs. Sacred texts contain information about God from God Himself, and often specify His expectations for humans. To refute these would be blasphemy except where one could make reasonable metaphorical interpretations of the source wording.

Despite the high number of unknowns and the unknowable components of the many religions, humans haven't hesitated to claim a deep understanding of religious doctrines and conditions. Take, for instance, the afterlife. Many religions provide a description of paradise (and its antithesis) in the afterlife, but who living today can affirmatively state that they understand the nature of heaven? The essence of heaven is strictly a matter of faith. One common description of a heavenly paradise has us dwelling with our Divinity and reuniting with loved ones. Even when portrayed in spiritual terms, the depictions of heaven are both unrealistic and unexacting. Many questions arise.

How will differences in ages among family members and loved ones be resolved when reunited in heaven, such as a child who dies at age two from disease or accident and her parents who live to be octogenarians? What will each person remember of his or her life on Earth? Such questions typically lead to pushback by believers. To resist challenges to their belief structure, many of the faithful turn a blind eye to difficult queries as these and even to the evolving nature of their religions. By doing so, they fail to investigate the rich history and latest perspectives of the Religious paradigms they have accepted as the absolute truth.

Given the existing diversity of outlooks on religious matters, how did the existing multiplicity of perspectives develop? The answer is simple: Not any differently than any other dominant paradigm. The script goes as described in the next paragraph.

As we mature from infancy to early childhood and develop language skills, our neural networks acquire definitive structure. Our local environment—our homes, our schools and neighborhoods, our regions, and our nation-state—mold these networks. The foundations of our paradigms gradually harden as if a curing cement. One person's perspective may align with one denomination of a religion, and a second person may align with another denomination. Lineage is the primary influence. Parents and family largely dictate the religious (and denominational) paradigms to which their children are exposed. As children mature, the specifics of their Religious paradigms begin to coalesce. Their religious neural networks may weaken, shift, or strengthen over time. For example, an individual who studies religious doctrine in a formal setting will acquire a deeper understanding of the foundational precepts of his religion than someone who acquires a cursory notion of those same precepts, say, through listening to sermons. The two individuals' Religious paradigms will likely diverge.

One reason I had for writing this book is imbedded in the previous paragraph. My motive applies to all paradigms and not just dominant ones. We must accept the idea that our composite paradigm is largely a matter of chance. We align to certain perspectives, religious or otherwise, due to our genetics and our environment. The most common thing about our existence is that our DNA has species-wide characteristics we share. While our mental constructs of the world may be similar in one or more respects, they likely vary significantly in many other respects. We may have species-driven perspectives, but we also have individualized perspectives that depend not only on our genetic composition, but also on our environment. Thus, if we randomly redistributed the Earth's population about the six habitable continents, the approximate odds of encountering a Muslim would be one in seven, a Christian two in seven, a Hindu one in seven, an east Asian religious group member (e.g., Buddhist or Shinto) two in seven, and agnostics, atheists, or indeterminate secularists one in seven. Armed with this knowledge, we can come to terms with two important notions. First, it is illogical to assign fault to a person for having a specific religious outlook. Second, if paradigmatic impasses exist between and among individuals and groups, we must adopt a rational basis for dealing with our differences. This latter notion is an *extremely* complex matter, which we shall address in future chapters.

Typical of any dominant paradigm, another dominant paradigm may influence the content and intensity of a person or group's Religious paradigm. For example, under the influence of over two centuries of capitalism and about two millennia of monarchical rule, the Economic and Power paradigms have altered religious perspectives related to wealth. Being wealthy is now "okay" compared to earlier New Testament treatment of the accumulation of riches. The Bible describes barriers for the wealthy to enter the kingdom of heaven—a concept the rich televangelists rarely want to dwell upon.[63] Religions have also struggled with scientific advances such as artificial or medical means for birth control and drugs to assist in suicide for suffering, terminally ill patients.

The Crusades provide a prime example of how Religious paradigms can run awry and elicit unseemly behavior from the faithful. Christians wanted to free the Holy Lands from Muslim control. With Papal blessing, they set off on many Crusades during the twelfth and thirteenth centuries, both to the Holy Lands and even to other areas within Europe to rein in wayward Christians. To motivate the Crusaders, Popes offered plenary indulgences, a form of forgiveness in advance for sinful acts, such as murder and pillaging. The indulgences were effectively fast tracks to heaven. While indulgences have obscure biblical foundations, they moved to the forefront of the Christian Religious paradigm, particularly for those Crusaders who wanted to ensure a place in heaven in the afterlife. There were other types of

---

[63] See, e.g., The Holy Bible, Matthew 19: 23-24; Mark 4: 19: Luke 1: 53; 1 Timothy 6: 9: and James 1: 11 and 5: 1.

indulgences offered that had nothing to do with crusading, such as participation in ceremonial religious events on specific dates.

The concept of indulgences further illustrates the power of paradigms in influencing human thought and behavior. They motivated Crusaders to participate in a cause and a calling. Herein rests the primary danger associated with most Religious paradigms. Whether based on a longstanding institution or a modern-day cult, there remains a fundamentally profound pitfall in most religious perspectives: The divine seemingly always communicate with certain human agents to pass on directives to us. This specific paradigmatic component has and continues to be a source of corruption and abuse by those institutionally ordained to fulfill a position within the religious hierarchy or one self-ordained to assume control of a cult. Those faithful, who so willingly, and without question, accept the human agents called upon by their divinity, are also likely to accept centralized authority of the few, an inherent tenet of many Power paradigms. As we've seen in numerous examples, the interplay of dominant paradigms can create powerful mental constructs that give our thoughts and actions a deterministic quality. We will return to this concept when we discuss free will later in this book.

Are Religious Paradigms Humanity's Achilles Heel?

There's an obvious significant problem if one tries to come to terms with the varying religious paradigms: they're sufficiently diverse such that a one-divinity-fits-all supreme being cannot rationally exist among all religions.[64] One or more of the religions are wrong, in part or in totality. The faithful of each religion "know" they are right—a sure source for disagreement within and among societies. As a result, humanity has accumulated colossal casualties due to religious conflicts and prejudices over the past three millennia. The prospects for the future appear equally dismal. In the present, the world's two major religions, Christianity and Islam, promote ways of life which are at odds in many aspects of social and personal conduct. With Christians outnumbering Muslims worldwide, the Western viewpoint has prevailed in the modern era, but Westernization is meeting significant

[64] Islam, Christianity, and Judaism share the common singular divinity except for the Christian Trinity. Islam and Judaism do not accept Jesus as the Son of God—a major stumbling point for religious consolidation.

resistance, particularly in Islamic societies. What will happen late in the 21st century when the projected population of Muslims will be comparable to or exceed that of Christians, considering present birth rates between the two groups?[65] Will societies gradually adopt more Islamic religious, cultural, and social perspectives as the demographics shift?

While the two major religions draw the greatest attention in the news, secularism and Hinduism each have a billion or more followers, and there are numerous other religions or quasi-religions (e.g., Buddhism) with sizable followings in the hundreds of millions. Thus, religious paradigms abound in the present. Humanity is not gregariously shifting its religious perspectives toward a singular Religious paradigm any time soon. Not only does friction exist within and among the many religious paradigms, many religions clash with ideological paradigms, such as those involving the role of women in marriage and in society and alcohol usage. Without some shift within the many Religious paradigms toward a universal religious perspective, conflicts will undoubtedly flare up well into the future—a certain Achilles Heel in achieving world harmony. Later, we will devise an approach for moderately shifting religious paradigms to minimize the potential for religiously based conflict.

Are Good and Evil Products of Paradigms?

Good and evil are human MCs, concepts that have developed over time through cultural, ideological, and religious perspectives. There is no counterpart in the rest of the animal kingdom. In nature, when a band of chimpanzees attacks and kills members of another band over territorial squabbles, we would not judge these acts to be either good or evil. The chimps are just being chimps. The same is not true when humans do the same.

When a band of humans (e.g., tribe, ethnic group, or nation) acts aggressively, we try to determine a rationale for the actions. We at least want to understand if the action was justified—that one group was right and the other wrong. Right indicates good intentions; wrong evil ones. Our paradigms assist in our assessment of good and evil. When Nazi Germany attacked Poland in 1939 without just cause, triggering World War II, most people would assess the act as wrong

[65] Green, Emma. *The Atlantic* online.

and evil. To a Nazi who believed in Hitler's eastward expansion objectives in order to fulfill the then-perceived national survival policy of acquiring Lebensraum (living room), the attack might seem justified—i.e., a good thing. It depends on the observer's perspective or paradigm.

Human history contains way-too-numerous examples of one group subjugating another. Empire builders and imperialists were most extravagant in their conquests. For example, during the Age of Discovery, European colony builders pillaged the New World and Africa for its resources, introducing disease and forcing slavery upon their colonial subjects. These acts would qualify as evil to most rational persons yet for those who perpetrated these acts, they would disagree. They had a "calling" to colonize. They might have claimed that they were impelled by a religious cause (convert heathens to Christianity) or were fulfilling an ideological quest of expansionism or were simply searching for resources to improve the national economy and welfare of their fellow citizens or, worse of all, were elevating the peoples of these regions to the ranks of the civilized. Colonists undoubtedly viewed themselves as good people with good intentions. Whatever their reasoning, they were acting in accordance with the blended dominant paradigms of their era, their groups, and themselves.

After the United States rebelled from the colonial rule of imperial Britain, it followed its own expansionist goals, a westward movement spurred by the largely overt policy called Manifest Destiny. Native Americans suffered horrific atrocities, their lands taken and food sources depleted (e.g., buffalo). Is there a way to distinguish between what the Poles endured during World War II and what North American Native Americans endured in the eighteenth and nineteenth centuries?[66] Both groups suffered as a result of racist and expansionist paradigms.

Can we look to Religious paradigms to help resolve whether we can clarify what constitutes the good and what the evil? Not a chance. Religious paradigms have considerable flaws in their ability to distinguish between good and evil. Sure, there are commandments and decrees ostensibly emanating from divine sources, but humans have largely corrupted these by the application of non-religious, dominant paradigms. We discussed some of the corruptions and licenses taken during the Crusades. Killing is good if the person being killed is a non-

---

[66] This question is left to the reader to ponder.

believer, infidel, or just a hapless sinner who doesn't fit the mold of your Religious paradigm. Killing is evil when someone from your Religious paradigm dies at the hand of those from another Religious paradigm. Effectively, the Crusades exemplified theocratic tribalism.

Yuval Harari's take on this topic is instructive. In discussing the human quest for the meaning of life and the universe, he concludes that humanity effectively defaulted to a superhuman source—the divine.[67] Thus, the only reasonable explanation for why things are what they are is that a Supreme Being made them that way to provide us with meaning and purpose. Harari then concludes:

> This view made God the supreme source not only of meaning but also of authority. Meaning and authority always go hand in hand. Whoever determines the meaning of our action – whether they are good or evil, right or wrong, beautiful or ugly – also gains the authority to tell us what to think and how to behave.[68]

As we've indicated throughout this book, our paradigms are the real source of our thoughts and behaviors. Thus, you can slice and dice good and evil as many ways as you like, but they should lead you to only one conclusion: good and evil are paradigm dependent. As such, good and evil are not real. They are but subjective descriptors of events, ideas, policies, thoughts, and actions determined by viewing the world through paradigmatic lenses. One person's good is another's evil. The best humanity can hope for is to adopt a standard perspective in determining what constitutes the good and the evil and then live to a moral code. Religion has given us a great start in establishing basic elements of morality. Human rights organizations have done exactly the same from a more expansive secular perspective—to normalize the perception of good and evil so that people will act to a code of conduct in a way that treats other humans with dignity and respect. Unfortunately, such transitions require paradigmatic shifts, which, as we have indicated, are often difficult to attain.

---

[67] Harari, *Homo Deus*, 260.

[68] Ibid.

Economic Paradigms

The Economic paradigm is simply a MC defining how resources should be shared, exchanged, and/or appraised, ranging from the necessities of life to items of inconsequential value. Separate subsystems of valuations may govern the value of non-necessities (discretionary items), particularly in times of dearth and hardship. Similarly, the value of a lakefront home differs from the same house on a busy city street. The house is the actual necessity; in most instances, the location of the home is not generally a necessity. Culture plays a significant role in the valuation of goods and services. Africans value tribal art works differently than Europeans do Renaissance art pieces.

For an Economic paradigm to dominate within any group, it must be fundamentally simplistic and inherently stable. Many economic models satisfy these two criteria so usually other factors come into play for an economic system to thrive. When the political power structure supports an economic system, the Economic paradigm becomes further entrenched within a group (e.g., a nation or a political party within a nation) through an associated and enabling Power paradigm. As such, the Economic and Power paradigms are the two most prominent (and dominant) today. Thus, for example, socialistic principles may seem attractive to a large segment of the more populous middle classes, but political forces within the corporate establishment could easily minimize any attempt to effect change in the national and local economic agenda.

In the modern era, individual and group survival largely depends on economic well-being, a function of a society's ability to maintain socioeconomic order. The nation-state paradigm arose out of numerous attempts to guarantee group cohesion and economic success. Early in human history, royalty of all manner, dictators (self-appointed royalty), religious leaders (shamans, Popes, and prophets), and Alpha males (tribal leaders) helped to dictate the Economic paradigm within their spheres of influence. Groups without dominant leaders could also achieve the same, such as city-states in Ancient Greece and Rome's time as a republic. The longevity of these societies, in part, depended on the success of their economic systems. Of note, except for some hunter-gatherer societies, resources were rarely equally distributed.

As civilized societies rose and fell, the prevailing Economic paradigms did as well. Bartering systems fluctuated in how to deal with necessities and luxuries, from food and shelter to royal treasuries. Over the past four millennia, requirements for earning a livelihood also evolved, undergoing transitions from slavery to feudalistic farm labor to wages and salaried work. The concept of property and its supporting legal structures also matured.

Around the time of the Renaissance, mercantilism took root, which eventually spawned entrepreneurial capitalism. Capitalist "kingpins" displaced royals in their impact on society as parliamentary forms of governments relegated most royals to figureheads. Capitalism created a new elite based on wealth only and not on the royals' all-too-arbitrary genetic lineage. In the present, political power often derives from wealth, indicative of the aforementioned significant alignment between the Economic and Power paradigms. However, the Power paradigm stems from many other factors and not economics alone.

Table 1 provides the core influences upon the Economic paradigm over human history. Intrinsic to any Economic paradigm is unmitigated trust in the system—a belief that the paradigm is true. In a limited sense, one could argue that faith in a currency under an Economic paradigm parallels faith in a Divine Being in the Religious paradigm. A person develops a "valuation neural network" in a similar manner as a religions one. This phenomenon applies whether members of a society use a unit of currency at accepted exchange rates with other currencies or barter in specific possessions and goods. Valuation paradigms stem from cultural and social influences. The system only works if those engaging in financial transactions can justify the value of the currency used or the equivalence of non-currency items involved in a transaction (e.g., three hens are equivalent to a bushel of corn). They must accept the paradigm which arbitrarily assigns value to currencies, objects, and labor services.

The monetary value paradigm, a subset of the Economic paradigm, is arguably the most dominant sub-paradigm of the modern economy. We all acknowledge that a dollar, euro, yen, or other currency has an intrinsic value. This specific paradigm provides us the means to interact in a structured manner so that we can support each other's needs.[69] For this reason alone, I have set aside the Economic

[69] The current monetary value paradigm has evolved over the course of more than two millennia. However, its present format (paper currency and debit/credit tallies) in no way represents the only possible monetary value perspective. The monetary value paradigm will also include the valuation of labor services—at least until robots perform most services.

paradigm as a dominant paradigm of its own. Some may prefer to group the various economic viewpoints (capitalism, socialism, monetary valuation) as a subset of the Ideological paradigm, but by separating the Economic paradigm out as a dominant paradigm, it is easier to follow the historical transitions of the many economic perspectives from small tribes to great empires.

An economist might consider my treatment of the Economic paradigm overly trivialized. I recognize the complexities of modern-day capitalism and socialism, but have no intent to drag the reader through paradigmatic mires, discussing supply, demand, and market indices. Numerous economic sub-paradigms also can distract us. For example, corporations typically adopt one of two multinational paradigms to interact with foreign entities to promote their products or services—a global approach or one tailored to specific foreign markets.[70] The pros and cons of such considerations are unnecessarily detailed and would only complicate our discussion.

Economics: A Win-Lose or Lose-Lose Paradigm

The modern free enterprise system has certainly elevated the standard of living of a large fraction of the human population. From a purely ideological perspective, capitalism has appeal because it promotes innovation—the idea that we can create and/or improve a product or service (a supply), which consumers find useful and/or desirous (demand). But other paradigms—those of individuals (Self), alliances (Group), and authority (Power) have usurped this simplistic notion of capitalism to create an integrated Economic paradigm, which more often than not fails to serve the greater good.

Just because capitalism has grown in dominance does not mean it is the best Economic paradigm for humanity. Yes, the standard of living today is high for a significant fraction of humans, but is capitalism the only paradigm that could accomplish this feat? Capitalism has also created a grotesque difference in wealth—a win-lose system. The winners lavishly live in luxury; the losers plaintively plod through privation. In this and future chapters, we will examine the Economic paradigm in greater historical detail and evaluate the consequences of the excesses of today's capitalistic fervor.

---

[70] Aliber, 10-14.

Power Paradigms

The Power paradigm represents neurological patterns of thoughts and behaviors to control others through physical or psychological means and to control circumstances within one's immediate environment. In hunter-gatherer and other early societies, Alpha males and shamans affected the thoughts and behaviors of the group. The Alphas in a group employed physical and sometimes psychological intimidation. Shamans also used psychological tactics to advance religious, cultural, and ideological perspectives. The truth was irrelevant. As discussed previously, early societies depended on myths and stories to add meaning and purpose to their lives. The potent usually determined the narrative.

The Self, Group, and Ideological paradigms most often complement the Power paradigm. If the Power paradigm aligns with one's ego and self-perception, the individual is more likely to adopt and/or adapt to the perspectives of those in power. If people find, or in some cases, learn from others that the prevailing Power paradigm enhances their personal freedoms or control over their own circumstances and/or over others, they will come to favor the attributes of the paradigm. We experience this phenomenon in politics incessantly. If a political party wants to limit the extent of gun control laws or the ability of a woman to obtain an abortion, individuals and groups with similar agendas will support the party. Though these people may not strongly align to all the party's perspectives, one or more of their other dominant paradigms align(s) with their Power paradigms to fortify their composite paradigms. For example, those ideologically (or religiously) invested in preventing abortions have a desire to control the outcome for all women so they align with the Power paradigm that will help achieve that end.

Since the survival of hunter-gatherers and ancients meant coping with the imposed hardships of life, we should expect alliances and compromise between and among varying group perspectives in order to improve survivability. Alignments between Religious and Power paradigms have occurred as far back as our hunter-gatherer societies. Alpha males and shamans undoubtedly found their union of paradigms mutually beneficial. As civilizations expanded in size, royalty and other group leaders relied on soldiers, priests, and taskmasters to keep the minds and bodies of the group aligned to the group leaders' goals. As societies grew even larger and more complex, self-appointed or chosen leaders would ensure the prevailing Power paradigm leveraged CRE and Religious paradigms to bind groups together. A marriage of dominant paradigms could instill fears among the populace in order to keep them in check. Perhaps some would perceive threats from omnipotent beings while others would dread being ostracized by fellow group members. Fast forward a millennium or so to find definitive changes in societal power structures. The ruling classes recognized that power sharing and power brokering through a written system of regulations and laws would improve the stability and survival of the group and its position within the group. Through constitutions and similar charters, the nation-state gradually attained legitimacy. The resulting legal structures helped to enforce compliance with societal rules—a much improved system over past societies. Still, the existing Power paradigms have not eliminated the power brokers within present-day societies.

Refer to Table 1, which contains the fundamental influences that facilitated the development of the various Power paradigms over the course of history. Recall that paradigms never form in a vacuum so we should expect significant overlap among the influences which shape other dominant paradigms. For example, the nation-state paradigm enabled a paradigm shift to the capitalist economic paradigm in which corporations became ever more powerful. Paradigm overlap represents an oft-repeated theme in our discussions: One dominant paradigm often facilitates specific aspects of another dominant paradigm. The current Power paradigms have enabled a specific set of Group, Economic, Religious, and Ideological paradigms to take hold in different parts of the world. Wealthy and bureaucratic elites promote these specific composite paradigms to dictate the course of most nation-states. A nation like Saudi Arabia is a prime example. There, royal elites dictate social outcomes, leading to a narrow set of religious and group paradigms.

In the West, even though they enable each other, the nation-state (Power) and capitalist (Economic) paradigms clash at times, mostly because the corporate charter system supersedes the goals and welfare of the nation-state. Stated alternatively, the shareholders are the primary beneficiaries of the corporations, not the public. Thus, with few exceptions, profits trump any social, ideological, religious, and environmental “inconveniences” in motivating a corporation’s actions and decisions. Corporate enterprises that carry self-interest to the extreme may eventually feel backlash due to public outcry and diminishing political support, but few nations have the clout to inflict excessive damage upon a multinational global conglomerate. Since the wealth and assets of a large number of these corporations (banks included) exceed the gross domestic product of most nations, the ability of nations to effect change or to inspire even a small paradigm shift is minimal.

Table 1 also includes organizational or bureaucratic factors which may affect the formation of Power paradigms. Organizational structures within hunter-gatherer and nomadic cultures were trivial in comparison to today's bureaucratically complex societies. In the modern era, a person must navigate a plethora of singular and integrated bureaucratic hurdles to thrive. These rules help to sustain social order. However, the laws, regulations, and codes in today's nation-states generally erode individual powers (and freedoms). Obvious trade-offs exist. The best-case paradigmatic scenario would be those where organizational paradigms minimize social disorder while optimizing individual freedoms. Totalitarian states represent the worst-case scenario since they suppress individual power and freedom. Yet totalitarian paradigms continue to flourish in many societies, such as China, North Korea, and increasingly, Russia.

Catastrophe Alert: Power and Self Paradigms United

You'll need to read this section a couple of times to appreciate its content and context. I doubt you'll like what you read.

In the modern era, Power paradigms have menacing qualities, most of which are quite subtle. We'll return to a familiar issue: global warming. This time, however, we're going to examine the relationship between the Power paradigm and our behaviors and their many connections to a warming planet. Let's start with the automobile industry.

Cars have improved the mobility of humanity with great benefits to society, but along the way, car manufacturers, automobile enthusiasts, and their advertising agents have sold the public on the idea that fast, big, and/or sporty cars give the owner a form of mythological power. For a long time, pricey cars have been status symbols of success, wealth, and status—factors in leveraging power over others. Sporty cars add sexual overtones. Car envy may substitute for penis envy for some men—meaning there is also a component of ego associated with car ownership in many cases, stemming from the Self paradigm.

Cars have become more than a form of transportation. They also fuel modern societies' economic engines. Their integration within modern social structures has almost (but not quite) made them a necessity. We must then ask whether the aforementioned extravagances associated with the automotive industry are warranted.

The public and industry's fascination with specialty and high-performance cars has accelerated the rate at which carbon dioxide and other greenhouse gases have entered the atmosphere. Exemplifying the excesses promoted by capitalistic free expression, the practices of the automobile industry and its associated markets are simply gluttony on an unnecessarily grandiose scale. To understand the phenomenon, we'd have to examine the life cycle of a car from raw materials to junkyard, including lifetime maintenance and peripheral waste streams. We are not going to do that here due to the complexity of the analysis. We'll look at narrower aspects of the automobile's role in contributing to global warming.

To start, bigger cars are less fuel efficient due to their added weight and greater wind resistance at every speed. People tend to drive sporty cars faster, and faster means more wind resistance proportional to the third power or cube of the speed. More gasoline is consumed and a greater volume of toxic and greenhouse gases enter the atmosphere. Electric or hybrid vehicle owners who drive faster than conditions warrant are similarly guilty of wasteful practices.[71] Even if a car isn't big or flashy, a significant fraction of drivers exhibit extravagance in their driving habits, including unnecessarily high speeds. They heavy-footedly accelerate past other drivers rather than employing a more-efficient gradual acceleration. Internal combustion engines operate less efficiently under rapid acceleration conditions, discharging a greater volume of pollutants per engine revolution. I see this almost daily when I drive—someone zooms past me after stopping at a red light in an adjacent lane. The driver then moves ahead of me in my lane only to jam on his or her brakes before stopping at the next

[71] Electric vehicle owners who drive inefficiently may believe they're not contributing significantly to greenhouse gas emissions but they could be, particularly if they're charging they're batteries on an electric grid supplied by coal or other fossil fuel power plants. An exception would be if they charged they're cars from solar cells or some other alternative energy source.

light. The net result is a one car-length gain in position. That driver clearly showed me what power is all about.

Most of these behaviors stem directly from the Power paradigm, whether the driving public acquired these tendencies from parents, friends, advertising, movies, or innate personal qualities. Also, many people choose to drive their cars when public transportation is available and convenient because they want to be in control. And power is all about control. Motor vehicles give a person the ability to direct their lives—managing their speed, location, and destinations. Earlier humans relied on their legs and eventually animals to accomplish the same. And until the modern industrial era, humans only had control of domesticated animals (a few "horsepower"). Today, even with the smallest of vehicles, they'll easily have fifty horsepower at their disposal, adding a quantum leap in the physical power under one's control. The raw power of these vehicles can endanger others if used inattentively and recklessly. Our forebears had little such power.

The Self paradigm often factors into behaviors associated with the inefficient use of automobiles. For example, so as not to inconvenience themselves, many people sit in line at a fast food establishment with their engines idling. Parking and leaving their vehicles to stand in line in the store is too much of an imposition. Equally wasteful are those who sit in their cars in the heat of the day with their engines and air conditioners running, listening to the radio while they wait for someone rather than sitting on a nearby bench in the shade. If these people really cared about global warming, they'd shift their paradigms and modify their behaviors.

I know what you're thinking: the examples have a trivial impact on energy usage and global warming. Yes, I have chosen these intentionally. While I have selected some of the least prominent examples of negative behavior related to automobile ownership and global warming, I am speaking to mindset. Mindset equates to paradigms. The neural networks that dictate our actions for the trivial also control our behaviors for the egregious.

With respect to global warming, it's important to understand how the trivial can grow into the colossal. Take, for example, standby power. Before the advent of Wi-Fi, cell phones, security systems, and other gadgets for the home, devices were usually turned off or consuming no or minimal power. The types and numbers of devices that have standby states or are left on (e.g., Wi-Fi routers) have mushroomed. When not in use, they are either being charged or consuming small amounts of energy in standby mode rather than being turned off. However, collectively, they sum to massive amounts of energy being consumed for idle purposes. One shouldn't be surprised to learn that about 10% of the electrical energy consumed in the United States is due to devices and systems in standby mode.[72]

The Scientific Paradigm

In this section, we will describe the Scientific paradigm to complete the set of seven historically dominant paradigms affecting human thought and behavior. The word "science" stems from the Latin word for knowledge, but not any knowledge. The term refers to the understanding that comes with disciplined approaches to collecting data and performing analysis of phenomena. These processes will lead to results that either are observable and repeatable or fail to verify stated hypotheses.[73] The online Oxford dictionary defines science as "The intellectual and practical activity encompassing the systematic study of the structure and behavior of the physical and natural world through observation and experiment." Accordingly, science strives to determine testable truths and facts about ourselves and our surroundings. From these truths, we can extrapolate testable theories.

For *accepted* theories to enter the scientific worldview, the concepts from which the theories have arisen must have mathematical and/or observational rigor. For example, Albert Einstein's special and general theories of relativity have broad applicability to observed phenomena for very small, high-speed particles and for massive objects (planets, stars, and galaxies), respectively. Directly observing the effects of relativity theories on humans may never be possible. We will likely never be able to apply the forces and supply the energy necessary to accelerate humans and their vehicles to velocities where

---

[72] Bertoldi et al, Lawrence Berkeley National Laboratory report (online).

[73] Not all scientific endeavors are disciplined. Nutrition is one area of study where rigorous experimental design and discipline are difficult to achieve due to the many variables involved, not to mention the collusion and competing interests involved in determining the effects of foods on human populations. Advertising agencies and NGOs (e.g., lobbying groups) also play a significant role in promoting the food industry's paradigms about its products, scientific or not. The history of sugar and the research in evaluating the nutritional impact of this food is telling. See, for example, *The Case Against Sugar* by Gary Taubes.

relativistic effects become biologically relevant. For similar reasons, we should not expect humans to spend any part of their lives in intense gravitational fields. Quantum physics is another theory equally difficult to apply to the world of everyday objects, but it provides incredible insights to the workings of the atomic and subatomic realm from which we have derived many technological innovations.

Like all other dominant paradigms, the Scientific paradigm can have numerous constituent views. Some of these views reflect the subjectivity of various scientific camps that favor certain theories over others (e.g., a quantum statistical view of nature versus a general relativistic perspective). There may be psychological, sociological, epistemological, and ontological factors that drive the various views.[74] However, the Scientific paradigm eventually will lead to unified perspectives as the scientific method uncovers new truths. Such is not the case for the other dominant paradigms. We should not expect to see a melding of Christianity, Islam, Hinduism, and Judaism, among others, to produce a unified religion. Nor should we expect to wake up one day to an economic system that combines the elements of communism, socialism, and capitalism. Science has the greatest probability of a "grand unification," although it could take quite a while. The existing "scientific paradigms influence what experiments are done, how they're performed, and how the results are interpreted."[75] Thus, a Scientific paradigm could remain static, a victim of its own success. Thomas Kuhn devoted an entire book, *The Structure of Scientific Revolutions*, to this topic, analyzing the means by which the Scientific paradigm matures or stagnates. Over the past two millennia, the scientific worldview has made incredible transitions—from Aristotelian, to Newtonian, to relativistic, and to quantum. The accompanying paradigmatic shifts have given us a more accurate means of understanding Nature's past, present, and future. The details will always remain murky, however. We can piece together Nature's puzzles, but a complete picture will never be in sharp focus.

Even distinguished scientists can become entrapped within certain paradigms. Earlier in his life, one of the greatest minds of the twentieth century, Albert Einstein, could not break free of his view that the universe is inherently unchanging. He added a term to his

---

[74] Shermer, 39-40.

[75] Becker, 182.

basic equation for general relativity to be consistent with his perspective that the universe is static. He later regretted his blunder (although today the term has become relevant).

Of special note, the Scientific paradigm can fall prey to other paradigms, dominant or otherwise. Ideological and Group paradigms have tainted the Scientific paradigm, leading individuals and groups to call for the sterilization of people in the name of science. The idea was to limit the ability of those with certain birth defects to reproduce, to stop their "inferior" genes from spreading. Such ideas went beyond science and gained much publicity in the United States and Europe in the first half of the twentieth century—a sad chapter in human affairs that contributed to the genocidal inclinations of numerous groups, most notably the Nazis.

Accordingly, when evaluating whether a system of belief adheres to the Scientific paradigm, one must exercise extreme caution. If the scientific method was loosely or improperly applied to develop a worldview, the paradigm may be pseudo-science—most likely, an Ideological, Group, or Religious paradigm. For example, creationism does not utilize the scientific method since it (intentionally) ignores data that is readily available, verifiable, and systematically developed. As stated early in this book, the same methodologies employed to develop the theories and principles used to design and manufacture the cell phone, refrigerator, and automobile were similarly utilized to develop a theory of evolution. To accept the processes in one instance and reject them in another is truly supreme willful ignorance.

The reverse notion also applies. "Science will always be a political threat to some institutions, simply by virtue of its attempts to respect no authority other than data and logic."[76] Thus, the Scientific paradigm often finds itself at odds with the Group, Power, Religious, and Ideological paradigms. For example, if groups don't like the implications of new scientific endeavors, they may simply choose to ignore them and/or minimize their visibility. As we noted in numerous examples in this book, the scientific perspective doesn't always supersede other dominant paradigms even though the substance of the scientific view is verifiable and those of the other dominant paradigms are rarely so. Why is this so?

First, the Scientific paradigm stems from the human brain's ability to process sensory data in abstract terms (e.g., through language

[76] Becker, 280-281.

and symbols) and create a rigorous approach for observing the surroundings. The same is not true of the other dominant paradigms. They rely *only* on the brain's innate ability to derive connections between events and their causes.[77] The brain makes these connections to help the individual and group survive. Facts and truths may or may not be relevant. The same neural connections that help us to identify poisonous plants also contribute to the development of false perspectives. When early humans experienced phenomenon for which they had no reasonable explanation, such as the source of lightning, their brains tried to make connections. That's what brains do. The connections weren't and still aren't always accurate. In an effort to explain the world, people once assumed that a mystical or divine force must be responsible for lightning. To a hunter-gatherer or early ancient with limited information about the world, an unbridled imagination could derive highly specious explanations. These explanations eventually become a network within the nervous system, giving birth to a paradigm. The same is true today of many other phenomena, whether a person is versed in science or not.

The paradigms of prejudice form the same way. Unless we have evidence to the contrary, our brains instinctively tell us that people who are different than we are *may* pose unknown threats. Our genetic wiring is in protection mode. Our guard is up, much as a gazelle gazes suspiciously at potential predators in the grasslands. In the human realm, fear of these unknowns creates and/or magnifies racial, cultural, religious, and/or ethnic biases—a potential source of extreme, prejudicial ignorance. Fear-driven biases and paranoia often originate with parents, peers, and authority figures. Over time, experience can strengthen, weaken, or erase the biases and their related paradigms.

The human propensity to explore the unknown, and to subsequently infer relationships from those explorations, has led to a progressive objectivism in the Scientific paradigm. Those who truly embrace the tenets of scientific methodologies find ways to erase their biases, at least within the scientific realm. By doing so, they contribute

---

[77] Shermer, 56. The word *only* in this sentence does not mean that the other dominant paradigms cannot employ disciplined methods and advanced symbolism, such as the use of calculus in economics, but that they can thrive without the analytical processes. The Scientific paradigm would become immaterial without the advancement of mathematics, technology, and disciplined methodologies.

positively to the collective human potential. However, the other six dominant paradigms often thwart our efforts to establish a scientific reality we can readily accept.

On the one hand, our brains respond to our survival instincts and attempt to fabricate the most accurate MCs of reality.[78] This cognitive talent far exceeds that of any other Earthly living entity. It drives humankind's affinity for tool making and symbolic abstraction. The combination of science, tool making, and symbolic capabilities—what we call technology—has become so sophisticated over the past 10,000 years that some humans claim that we are evolving to a higher state (but we emphatically are not).[79]

On the other hand, establishment of Scientific paradigms requires significant effort and diligence, the latter a quality very few humans possess. As a result, competing paradigms set obstacles in our path toward enlightenment, limiting the degree to which science becomes part of our lives. If we had advanced toward enlightenment as a species, we would not have devoted a large fraction of the tools we've created to killing fellow humans. Instead, one or more of the other six dominant paradigms compel us to convert tools to weapons with ever greater killing efficiency. Consider the differences between a primitive stone arrowhead and a thermonuclear weapon—truly mindboggling. That's how far we have "advanced."

To summarize, in this section, we have learned that only the Scientific paradigm, in its purest form, is capable of establishing consistently logical and verifiable perspectives within the mental constructs through which we experience the world. Let's explore in greater detail the significance of the Scientific paradigm with respect to the other six dominant paradigms.

Scientific versus the Other Six Dominant Paradigms

The reader is probably wondering, "Why can't the Scientific paradigm "overpower" the other six dominant paradigms?" Is it simply a matter of exercising greater diligence in life as alluded to in the

---

[78] Not all MCs, as discussed earlier in this book, are survival-oriented.

[79] Our technological achievements mesmerize us and convince us that our minds have somehow evolved to a higher state, but we are no more intellectually capable than our pre-ancient forebears were.

previous section? History holds the answer: The Scientific paradigm was chronologically the last of the seven dominant paradigms to influence human thought and behavior in any significant way. In early societies, technological progress provided tools of warfare to both the aggressors and the defenders, *independently* of rigid scientific methods. Bows, arrows, and spears developed under trial-and-error tool-making practices. These unscientifically derived products helped to solidify authority within and among societies.[80] Power paradigms evolved from these primitive advances in technology. Alpha males once only used their personal physical prowess to intimidate others. Over time, they were able to sustain their dominance by outfitting armies with armor, arrows, and bladed weapons to control their own and other societies. Facilitated by the prevailing Power paradigms, several other dominant paradigms took hold of the neural networks of group members. In simplistic terms, these paradigms translate to "We are individually better than each of you (Self), "Our Group is superior to yours," "Our Religion is true; yours is false," "Our Ideologies supersede yours," and "Our Economic way of life is better than yours."

Consider, for example, that religious paradigms were already well-established in ancient and first-millennium-Common-Era societies. Through decree and force, Christianity and Islam became the Religious paradigms of Eurasia and Northern Africa. Back then, the highly immature Scientific paradigm had little influence in the development of Religious paradigms. Arguments questioning religious doctrines were considered heresies.

Later, due to significant shifts in the Scientific paradigm, objectivism gained a foothold, but that didn't stop other dominant paradigms from exploiting the tenets of scientific methodologies. As capitalism gradually emerged as the dominant Economic paradigm, it survived largely because of science, destined for stagnation without prolonged technological advances. Science and technology rescued capitalism by improving the efficiency of production, the extraction of resources, and the distribution and advertisement of products and services. Bolstered by a wave of technological innovation, individual capitalists accumulated great wealth. Wealth translates to power. To sustain their power early in the Industrial Revolution, capitalists

[80] The early tools that came about through trial and error leveraged the human mind's ability to draw connections and find uses for the resources in their immediate environment.

supported royalty and lobbied state leaders when it was to their advantage. They also leveraged the ideologies of imperialism and colonialism to further fuel the steamroller of capitalistic expansion. This interplay among the dominant paradigms led to the present, prevailing composite worldview.

Despite its strength of veracity in the modern era, the Scientific paradigm still lags behind the Power and Economic paradigms in its ability to influence human thought and behavior. We've seen direct evidence of this phenomenon during the worldwide COVID-19 pandemic.

The Scientific Paradigm and Truth

Of the seven major models influencing our behaviors and thoughts, the Scientific paradigm has a quality none of the others possesses: the ability to establish verifiable truths.[81] The truth may exist in facts, trends, principles, and physical theories and laws. Truths also exist in human relationships and events, but they are harder to determine because experiments rarely have exacting controls and because the blended effects of the other dominant paradigms often dissuade our senses. The other six dominant paradigms cloud our ability to accept our own ignorance.

The Scientific paradigm stands out in another critical quality: it admits to ignorance. If data doesn't provide a means to evaluate a hypothesis, then either the hypothesis is faulty or the data is inconclusive. Stated alternately, one may expose a greater ignorance about an area of inquiry in the pursuit to uncover a truth. However, there's a subtler effect going on as science advances. As Firestein puts it:

> Curiously, as our collective knowledge grows, our ignorance does not seem to shrink. Rather, we know an even smaller amount of the total, and our individual ignorance, as a ratio of the knowledge base, grows.[82]

---

[81] The ideological paradigm, under certain conditions, can establish truths if we apply a system of logic to derive these truths. In this book, however, we treat logic as part of the sciences due to its mathematical rigidity, a foundation of the Scientific paradigm.

[82] Firestein, 13.

We noted this concept previously when discussing the noösphere. Thus, within the sciences, knowledge may increase and truths become uncovered, but an individual's ability to acquire this knowledge and process these truths diminishes. Science will always be a Catch-22 when it comes to ignorance, but at least there's an acceptance and an awareness of the conundrum. Compare, for example, the Scientific and Religious paradigms. The former concedes ignorance where the latter generates absolutism among the faithful. An example will illustrate the disparity between these two dominant paradigms.

One of the hallmarks of the Scientific paradigm is its ability to uncover the truth about the nature of things. Imagine a sphere with one hemisphere colored blue and the other yellow. A person sitting directly facing the blue hemisphere would say the sphere is blue. Another person, directly opposite the blue observer, would claim it is yellow. Other observers would claim different proportions of blue and yellow depending upon their perspectives (observational locations). So what is the true nature of the sphere? If people can't or won't communicate their perspectives, they will incorrectly characterize the sphere. There is a universal truth about the sphere for the normal range of human sensory acuity (e.g., no observer is colorblind), but that truth may remain elusive without a cooperative and scientific approach to analyzing the true nature of the sphere. The truth is that it is half blue and half yellow.

Next, imagine trying to develop a common perspective about the nature of God, His or Her doctrines, and religious practices among a group composed of those from the Hindu, Judaic, Christian, Islamic, and Buddhist faiths, not to mention the various sects within these beliefs and a host of lesser-known but extensively accepted religious perspectives. The Scientific paradigm facilitates the characterization of the sphere by the observers. The Religious paradigm, differing in each participant, would likely lead to chaos and disagreement.

The preceding example exemplifies the quandary of finding legitimate and exacting characterizations for human socialization and interaction. The Self, Group, Religious, Economic, Power, and Ideological paradigms are highly subjective. The worldview of an Irish, Catholic, rural fieldworker typically differs significantly from that of an Arab, Muslim, urban shopkeeper. The disparity amplifies if one factors in the Power paradigms under which they separately exist. At present, only one dominant paradigm provides a pathway to universal truths,[83] the Scientific paradigm. No legitimate scientists from any of the various cultures, races, ethnicities, and religions will ever argue over the ballistic trajectory of a near-Earth projectile given its initial parameters. The Scientific paradigm allows them to determine and agree upon the results.

Thus, the human condition today is one where conflict persists within and among societies because six of the dominant paradigms generate largely divergent views of life—views with limited room for negotiation. The Scientific paradigm, however, is founded in methodologies which rely on evidentiary reasoning, therefore providing an avenue to a united humanity. We also cannot neglect the role of the other six dominant paradigms in misdirecting the potential benefits of the advances that have occurred under the Scientific paradigm. Under the influence of these other six paradigms, science and technology pose a threat to our own existence and to the Earth's biosphere. Accordingly, the path to enlightenment requires a significant reduction in ignorance by diminishing the influence of religious, economic, power, ideological, self, and group perspectives in shaping human thought and behavior.

Are There Yet-to-Mature Dominant Paradigms?

Is it possible that in the future one or more minor paradigms will gradually supplant one or more of the six dominant paradigms with better outcomes for the welfare of our species? In a later section, we will evaluate a set of possible dominant paradigms which can brighten the prospects. We briefly introduce the idea now to gain further appreciation of the role of dominant paradigms in human history. Imagine, for example, a Holistic paradigm, which, in

---

[83] For this book, universal truths are not absolute truths. They are truths based on scientifically structured processes (or their equivalent) that we use to characterize reality, meaning they are verifiable through rigid experimentation. They are universal within the realm in which they apply. For example, within our local reality, (1) gravity has certain effects on matter and (2) specific cells unite to reproduce a given species. We have determined exacting universal truths related to these phenomena. We have not done the same for religious, socioeconomic, and ideological matters.

conjunction with the Scientific paradigm, can help shift our existing way of life toward truth and cooperation. Holism refers to the notion that the parts of the whole are strongly interconnected with each other.[84] Thus, under such a paradigm, we could acknowledge that human livelihood relies heavily on the local and global ecology and then respond accordingly. Holism also means that our MCs must encompass the greater reality interconnecting all parts of Nature.[85] To the greatest extent possible, holistic MCs of the world would be comprehensive and unbiased compilations of our experiences and ideas. Holistic perspectives will greatly reduce ignorance by shifting our current composite paradigms away from the influences that elevate "I" and "We" above all others, including fellow species. The Self, Group, Power, Ideological, Religious, and Economic paradigms represent a historically harmful hexad of perspectives responsible for the needless deaths of hundreds of millions of people over the short expanse of human existence. I must reiterate, however, that given the historical sway of this dominant hexad, the present state of human development was largely unavoidable. Later, when we explore holistic principles, we will examine the marriage of a currently weak Holistic paradigm with the Scientific paradigm. From there, we will assess whether a shift in human fate is plausible.

Scientific and Religious Paradigms: A Review

I have tried to present the idea of a Religious paradigm in an honest and straightforward manner consistent with the reality that religiously and spiritually nurtured neural networks determine what a person's religious and spiritual worldviews are. Obviously, the

---

[84] The reason for a needed shift to the Holistic paradigm will become clear. Other dominant paradigms were considered to help minimize ignorance, such as a Humanistic/Humanitarian paradigm and a universalist paradigm. The former can lead to anthropocentric ideologies and the latter easily mistaken for a religious philosophy.

[85] The theory maintains that parts of a whole are in intimate interconnection, such that they cannot exist independently of the whole, or cannot be understood without reference to the whole. The whole can thereby become greater than the sum of its parts. Holism is often applied to mental states, language, and ecology. With language, for example, sentences can convey meanings beyond that of the individual words summed together.

religiously devout readers will find this and other evidentiary analysis an assault on their beliefs. They would claim to know the truth about their God(s). However, any believers, if honest, would have to admit that God and His realm are a mystery. By their nature, mysteries contain unrevealed truths. The content and origins of scriptures provide limited insight only into religious mysteries, making it impossible for anyone to say he or she truly knows the truth about God. There are varied interpretations of God's word even after scholarly theological review. Let's return to the expectation of a heavenly afterlife, which serves as a prime motivator for many to sustain allegiance to the religion of their parents. No person alive today can describe the true nature of heaven and a "life" of everlasting bliss. For example, past writings only add to the Christian God's mystery—such as biblical references to a Throne existing in heaven. Does a throne imply a real of metaphorical social hierarchy in heaven? Is heaven egalitarian or do the early prophets occupy a different tier of existence?

Admitting that the truth about God remains a mystery does not deny the existence of God but only points to the need for more exacting research into the nature of God using scientific methodologies, such as through archaeological findings and improved translations of ancient writings. Science itself contains many mysteries. Among the most prominent is the troubling weirdness within quantum physics where the constituent particles of Nature act as if mathematical probabilities represent their real properties and *not* an abstract model of their behavior—a very puzzling situation. Quantum physics has an advantage over religious inquiry, however, since the results derived from quantum theory match observations—repeatedly. Religious research has yet to develop a consistent view of the divine given the numerous religions and their associated denominations. I have met and know of many scientists who affirm the existence of God. They trust both scientific and religious tenets. Their Religious and Scientific paradigms have common characteristics, indicating an integration of their neural networks governing these paradigms.

The Blended or Composite Paradigm

Summed together, the dominant paradigms create an overall worldview within an individual, an integrated neural network of reinforcing and competing mental constructs. The aggregate or resultant paradigm is what truly drives our general thoughts and actions, but situational factors can cause one paradigm to prevail over the others and force thoughts and behaviors to deviate from the composite norm. We reviewed this idea when discussing the Self paradigm since mental and physical health problems, traumatic events, fear, love, sleeplessness, medications, drug usage, and unusual social settings can alter or negate the effects of one or more of the dominant paradigms. In some cases, traumatic events may reinforce and/or dramatically shift a person's existing composite paradigm. For example, a drone attack against terrorists may trigger extremist views in innocent bystanders or other non-radical survivors.

At present, we can only speculate on the actual mechanisms that cause a multiplicity of dominant paradigms to condense into a composite or blended paradigm to influence thought and behavior. Yet, we do know the human brain is very proficient at making connections and finding common threads (associations). Thus, for example, consider Christians who accept at face value the commandment, "Thou shall not kill," and who also develop pacifist ideologies. Whether the religious perspective preceded the ideological may be difficult to ascertain in all cases. Regardless, pacifism is part of their Ideological paradigm, which in turn is reinforced by their Religious paradigm (and vice-versa). The resulting composite paradigm might easily motivate some of these individuals to become conscientious objectors, refusing to serve in the armed or police forces.

We will investigate the composite paradigm in greater depth in Chapter 4.

Ignorance Primer

In Chapter 5, we will look in detail at research into the various situational types of ignorance. In this section, we provide an overview of what we mean by the term ignorance and formalize the link between paradigms and ignorance. Up to this point, we've only partially described the role paradigms play in creating ignorance. We need to bring additional clarity to the paradigm-ignorance relationship.

Since paradigms largely steer our thoughts and actions and since we exhibit our ignorance through our thoughts, words, and behaviors, the framework of our paradigms determines our level of ignorance. That framework stems from our individual composite paradigms. Our decisions may be flawed, uninformed, or reprehensibly inappropriate. We are all ignorant to some degree, but some of us more so than others. If our paradigms keep us from accepting, acknowledging, or understanding evidence and verifiably accurate information, we are clearly ignorant. If our paradigms impel us to accept, positively acknowledge, or blindly believe falsehoods, unproven claims, and exaggerations, we are clearly ignorant.

We could qualitatively assign a level of ignorance associated with our thoughts, actions, and decisions. If we always "get it wrong," that is, fail to accept any verifiable truths, we could classify ourselves highly ignorant. If we accept certain verifiable information and reject other verifiable information, we may classify ourselves moderately or mildly ignorant. If we just don't know certain things but are willing to honestly consider the consequences associated with not knowing these things, we are slightly ignorant. Malice of forethought is a factor in assessing one's level of ignorance. Someone who knows he's acting ignorantly (e.g., intentionally ignores data) and/or does so with malicious intent is highly ignorant. Some of the ignorance research discussed in Chapter 5 will address this last phenomenon.

In the field of medicine, paradigms typically dictate treatments. Some have potentially dangerous outcomes for patients. Doctors may not be sufficiently aggressive in initial diagnoses, failing to uncover a medical condition. Doctors who fail to remain current in their fields may use procedures and medications with much lower probability of successful treatment than newer methods. We would classify these doctors as moderately ignorant. To assist medical professionals in understanding ignorance "traps" in their practices, M. Witte, Crown, Bernas, and C. Witte adapted an ignorance map to evaluate the curriculum at medical schools and to determine what would help future practitioners to remain up-to-date in general medicine and/or their specialties. We shall use this model in this book, but before providing details, we should understand why medical professionals would find ignorance mapping beneficial. The answer lies in the paradigms that govern medical practices.

How medical practitioners treat an individual or members of a group is largely dependent upon their perspectives about the patient and his or her symptoms. Treatment also relies on the practitioners' knowledge of latest methods. Numerous bizarre treatments and processes have elevated to the level of best practices throughout medical history. These have included bloodletting, the use of leeches, unsanitary surgeries leading to deadly bacterial infections, and lobotomies. Medicine has matured significantly but treatment paradigms still persist—many not in the best interest of patients or not qualifying as properly vetted science and research. We should also not neglect "counterculture" medical paradigms held by patient populations, such as those who shun vaccinations and other immunological methods as dangerous or unproven and those who adopt unproven natural remedies as scientifically proven cures. The medical community must deal with the pushback associated with these largely baseless backlash paradigms.

Ignorance about medical matters usually stems from the mix of existing medical practices. Some doctors may recommend surgeries for a given diagnosis; others, medications; and still others, physical therapy. These treatment options reflect medical paradigms. In this regard, medical ignorance parallels general ignorance, which similarly arises from a blend of and/or conflict among paradigms, typically among the seven dominant paradigms. Thus, the methods for understanding and assessing ignorance in the medical arena, known as ignorance mappings, will apply equally well to the ignorance occurring in everyday life. Thus, we will borrow from the medical field to apply ignorance mappings to construct ignorance tables for selected historical periods. The tables will facilitate our assessment of ignorance levels and their paradigmatic origins.

We start with Table A below. The first column (left to right) identifies the major sources of ignorance as established for the medical field. The second column provides a description of key mapping attributes for each major source of ignorance. I have added the descriptors in brackets to provide a more expansive understanding of unfamiliar terminology, such as "known unknowns." The italicized text is the description used in the medical mapping analysis. The third column provides my assessment of the highest and lowest ignorance levels for each ignorance source, where the range varies from very low ignorance to very high. The ignorance assessments shown are tailored to the seven dominant paradigms and not paradigms specific to medical fields.

Before proceeding, we should note that what is truly known and agreed to by all concerned is not a part of the ignorance assessment. Using a modern media term, we might say there are no "alternative facts" to assign to the known. These "known knowns" contribute zero to a person's ignorance and are therefore disregarded. The fact that there are more known knowns today than in the past is irrelevant when determining ignorance level in a given era. As we shall see, our paradigms determine our ignorance level not necessarily what we know.

The classification of ignorance levels for each ignorance source in the table reflects only the very high and very low states of ignorance. Actual ignorance may fall in between as determined by the influence of our paradigms on processing the knowledge in the noösphere and by what we think we know—whether or not our paradigms are founded in misconceptions, misjudgments, beliefs, incomplete knowledge, taboos, prohibitions, dissent, defiance, or a host of other factors that keep a person from acquiring or applying knowledge. Although unknowns are inescapable, our paradigms are the reasons why uncertainties, knowledge gaps, and poor assumptions inform our thoughts and behaviors and why errors, taboos, and denials are so prevalent among all humanity. A few examples will help to clarify the cause-effect relationships between existing dominant paradigms and ignorance.

A known unknown is typical within the Scientific paradigm. Science aims to develop testable hypotheses. If a hypothesis is not verifiable by rigorous means, it is an unknown, or at best, a speculation—nevertheless an unknown. By its very processes, science acknowledges what is unknown. Most Scientific paradigms include numerous known unknowns (e.g., cosmological dark matter and microbiological mechanisms for fetal development). However, since they are acknowledged, the ignorance level associated with these unknowns is low or very low. Uncertainty is minimal, assumptions are fact-based, and efforts are underway to identify the unknowns to bring them into the realm of knowns.

Power paradigms are markedly different. They aim to control others and the surroundings. Control also means an attempt to shift the other dominant paradigms to align with the Power paradigm. Thus, those in power try to control the narrative to shape the composite paradigm of others. Power paradigms are largely opinions and beliefs—MCs prone to errors—with little use for factual knowledge. They create blind spots, preventing people from accessing or accepting what they know, thereby increasing their unknown knowns or uncertainties. Power paradigms accordingly promote high ignorance. Totalitarian systems are one such example where governments try to control the narrative with little regard for true representations of reality.

The Self paradigm can manifest itself as egoism, as introspection, or as a state in-between. Introspection provides a means to find one's place in the world but rarely provides a pathway to reduce unknowns. Introspection may reduce errors, denials, and taboos, however, if the individual can clarify what is known. Since survival is generally the first priority of any Self paradigm, a person will try to determine what needs to be known to improve one's chances of survival. This would tend to make a person slightly ignorant only. However, highly egoistic individuals place self-interest first, which often impels them to make errors and deny factual knowledge. Thus, a Self paradigm governed by ego will result in high or very high ignorance.

Note that survival rarely depends upon knowing and acknowledging what is true. While our hunter-gatherer forebears lacked considerable knowledge of their place in the universe, they did acquire sufficient functional knowledge to survive and thrive. Hunter-gatherers also understood that survival depended upon group cohesion and cooperation.[86] Self paradigms in these societies were largely suppressed and supplanted by Group paradigms unless or until Power paradigms imposed by Alpha leaders took root.

Group and Religious paradigms have tribal or parochial roots, meaning errors, denials, and taboos are prevalent. Groups and religious factions inherently promote their agendas, customs, or ideologies, resulting in high or very high ignorance. They can develop a sense of superiority and exclusivity, reject the perspectives of others, or feel threatened by opposing views (e.g., political party platforms). Thus, when Group and/or Religious paradigms dominate our neural networks, highly ignorant decisions and policies are common.

[86] Herman, class notes.

Since agricultural civilization matured into sizable societies, Economic paradigms and their associated economic systems have been largely founded on self-serving assumptions about the way life *should be* lived and society *should* operate—at least in practice. The systems writ large favored the few over the many, excluding many in the group from the benefits reaped. Such assumptions are prone to errors. Even more significant is the impact of unknown knowns. Due to unjustifiable assumptions and failures to address socioeconomic uncertainties and risks, what should become known remains unknown, increasing ignorance. For example, by failing to acknowledge, assess, and integrate other economic perspectives into an Economic paradigm, an economic system can do a great disservice to the society it supposedly serves. The draconian and misguided application of communistic perspectives in the former Soviet Union was one such example. And we see it today in the United States where deregulation, special-interest tax codes, and expediency limit wealth-sharing and threaten fragile ecosystems.

Table B below applies the foundational concepts of the ignorance type model presented in Table A to a modern source of ignorance: the acknowledgement of climate change. To assist readers in their review of Table B, we have specified five factors related to the origins of human-induced climate change and its consequences. The factors represent a collection of knowns or unknowns related to climate change. Individuals and groups will have a range of knowledge of these climate change factors, and similarly, a spectrum of perspectives (composite paradigms). Note that any attempt on the part of the general populous to clarify unknowns related to human-induced climate change results in a low level of ignorance, even if these people lack specific knowledge of the factors contributing to climate change. As for denials, taboos, and errors, these can be obviated by genuine efforts to seek pertinent knowledge related to climate change.

We will return to ignorance mapping tables in the next chapter as we explore the historical effects of paradigms from ancient times to the present.

Table A: Sources of Ignorance

Ignorance Source	Description of Factors	Ignorance Extremes
Known Unknowns	*What you know you don't know* (Identifiable Risks, Fact-based Assumptions, Known Uncertainties, or Incomplete Knowledge)	Very Low Ignorance: Aware of and attentive to factors that would improve assumptions, uncertainties, and knowledge and reduce risk. Very High Ignorance: Unmindful of or oblivious to factors that would improve assumptions, uncertainties, and knowledge and reduce risk.
Unknown Unknowns	*What you don't know you don't know* (Unidentified Risk, Unjustifiable Assumptions, Irresolvable Uncertainty, Lack of Knowledge)	Very Low Ignorance: Vigilant in examining factors influencing one's environment. Very High Ignorance: Indifferent and careless in examining factors influencing one's environment.
Errors	*What you think you know but don't* (Superficial Knowledge, Poor Assumptions, Flawed Certainties or Claims)	Very Low Ignorance: Cautious examination of factors influencing one's environment. Very High Ignorance: Inattention to the factors influencing one's environment.
Unknown Knowns	*What you don't know you know* (Incomplete or Untapped Knowledge, Ineffective Identification of Risks)	Very Low Ignorance: Diligent in examining factors influencing one's environment. Very High Ignorance: Negligent in examining factors influencing one's environment.
Taboos (Avoid Knowledge)	*What's dangerous, pollute, or forbidden to know* (Unexplored or Neglected Knowledge, Corrupted or Prohibited Knowledge)	Very Low Ignorance: Fearless in pursuing and exposing the truth. Very High Ignorance: Apprehensive in pursuing and exposing the truth.
Denials	*What's too painful to know, so you don't* (Knowledge Avoidance, Rejections of Assumptions, Defiance of Risks)	Very Low Ignorance: Pursues knowledge and truth despite their consequences. Very High Ignorance: Eschews and refutes new knowledge and truth because of their consequences.

Table B: Ignorance Determination, Climate Change Example

Knowns and Unknowns: 5 Major Factors in Understanding Climate Change	(1) Mechanisms of climate change (2) Impacts of climate change (3) Relevant climate data and trends (4) Methods to minimize climate change and reduce impacts (5) Extraneous factors (e.g., politics of diminishing resources and increased taxes)

Ignorance Source	**Ignorance Determination (Extremes)**
Known Unknowns	*What you know you don't know* Very Low Ignorance: Attentive to all 5 factors. Very High Ignorance: Oblivious to all 5 factors.
Unknown Unknowns	*What you don't know you don't know* Very Low Ignorance: Is aware there are factors that cause climate change and is open to examining their impacts. Very High Ignorance: Does not consider there are specific factors affecting climate change and is unaware of their impacts.
Errors	*What you think you know but don't* Very Low Ignorance: Exercises caution in examining the factors associated with climate change and their impacts. Very High Ignorance: Capriciously dismisses all 5 factors associated with climate change and their impacts.
Unknown Knowns	*What you don't know you know* Very Low Ignorance: Diligently seeks out information about the factors related to climate change Very High Ignorance: Disinterested in learning about any factors related to climate change.
Taboos (Avoid Knowledge)	*What's dangerous, polluting, or forbidden to know* Very Low Ignorance: Overcomes fears and impediments to learn about the factors responsible for or related to climate change. Very High Ignorance: Uses personal, religious, and/or group (e.g., political) justifications to avoid learning about factors responsible for or related to climate change.
Denials	*What's too painful to know, so you don't* Very Low Ignorance: Pursues an understanding of climate change despite the real and potential consequences of climate change to the individual and humanity. Very High Ignorance: Irrationally dismisses climate change as a hoax, conspiracy, or falsehood to avoid considering the real and potential consequences of climate change to the individual and humanity.

Chapter 4: Paradigms and Ignorance through the Ages

"It is certain, in any case, that ignorance, allied with power, is the most ferocious enemy justice can have."
- James Baldwin [87]

The focus of this chapter is to improve our understanding of the historical effects of the seven dominant paradigms over the past three millennia. To this end, we turn to Figures 2 through 7 to qualitatively examine the dominant paradigms from six specific historical eras. Tables 2 through 7 accompany each corresponding figure to help identify common attributes of each dominant paradigm during the timeframe in question. Additionally, we will include an ignorance assessment table pertinent to each historical period (Tables D through I).

Previously, we've shown how the collective attributes of dominant paradigms determine a person and/or group's composite paradigms. Thus, by projecting what composite paradigms were prevalent in past eras, we can qualitatively determine their effect on history and the level of ignorance in each era. The selection of eras

[87] *No Name in the Street*, 149.

was not arbitrary; my aim is to illustrate the progression of paradigms over the past several thousand years. In a given era, we will focus on the confluence of dominant paradigms and then assess the extent of ignorance in broad terms. As a reminder, there are many ways to dissect paradigms and assess ignorance. I believe the format I've selected for this book best facilitates an understanding of the significant impact paradigms have had and continue to have on our lives and human destiny.

Each figure displays a paradigm funnel similar to the baseline representation of dominant paradigms in Figure 1. Again, the funnels represent paradigmatic mental filters. As the brain calls on memories and receives sensory stimuli, the filters allow specific ideas and behavioral responses to prevail. These thoughts and actions stem from a mix or blend of the various dominant paradigms, or what we have labeled a composite paradigm. The color (or shaded)[88] sections at the top of the filter represent the relative filtering strength of each dominant paradigm. The larger the wedge or "pie piece," the greater will be a dominant paradigm's influence on a person's thoughts and actions. Thus, a devoutly Christian capitalist sees the world through mental filters whose composite paradigm is largely influenced by his specific Religious and Economic paradigms. As the figures shall illustrate, throughout history, the prevailing composite paradigm undergoes shifts from era to era, but usually only gradually. We expect the wedge sizes at the top of the funnel to change somewhat from historical era to historical era. The smaller increments of time we examine, the smaller the paradigmatic shifts, in general. However, the magnitude and scope of the filtering and blending of specific paradigms could undergo significant shifts in perspective over the course of several consecutive eras. Such significant shifts have occurred for the Scientific paradigm, particularly since the seventeenth century when the mathematically rigorous depiction of physical phenomena began in earnest.

The figures also contain an era-adjusted ignorance level based on three primary criteria: the maturity of knowledge people had of

---

[88] E-book diagrams are in color; printed book diagrams are in black, white, gray, and various shades.

their surroundings (knowns), the capability of the people to acquire knowledge in a disciplined manner (the ability to accurately clarify known unknowns), and the level of turmoil in their societies at the time in question (distinctive conflicts *and* the effects of errors, taboos, and denials). For example, it is difficult for people to reduce their ignorance through intellectual or scientific endeavors if they are frequently fighting off invaders. Similarly, societies burdened by taboos, myths, and supernatural beliefs will struggle to compete with their more enlightened neighbors due to their ignorance.

Note that the assessment of ignorance level differs somewhat from the previous chapter, which examined ignorance level strictly on the basis of global attributes, such as the scope of the prevailing unknown knowns. Here, we factor unique aspects of each era into the assessment of ignorance level. For example, if warfare dominated a specific historical era, many obstacles would arise that would diminish the ability of peoples to broaden their knowledge. The group or national effort would focus on winning the war—survival.

We shall, therefore, now introduce a ranking or scoring system (numerical scale) to ascertain the level of ignorance during a given era. We shall apply Table A to perform ignorance assessments with the criteria illustrated in Table C.

Table C provides a way to characterize the total effect of the sources of ignorance based on the paradigms existing in a specific era in history. The last row of Table C is not reproduced in future ignorance assessment tables; this row provides numerical ranges for assigning ignorance levels. The table establishes an ignorance level for the era based on the weighting of dominant paradigms during the era. For example, if mythological creatures dominated the paradigms of an era, we'd expect that taboos, denials, and errors should be a source of very high ignorance, resulting in a score of 5 in each of these ignorance sub-categories. If the myths existed but were not significant in the era, the ignorance score could be lower, say a 2 or 3. Similarly, if scientific or ideological foundations of paradigms were highly immature, we'd expect a very high level of ignorance due to a dearth of knowns and a mischaracterization of the unknowns. Since the content, scope, and dominance of paradigms vary with time, their impact will vary from era to era.

Let us now examine the circumstances portrayed in Table C by referring back to Figure 1 and Table 1 for the highly irregular case where all the dominant paradigms are equally weighted. Previously, we qualitatively assessed the overall ignorance as "Very High" by averaging the contributions of all sources of ignorance—a direct reflection of the composite paradigm of the hypothetically balanced or equally-weighted composite paradigm. Now, however, we will develop quantitative determinations of ignorance levels from the funnel figures for each era.

With the situation in Table C consisting of seven equally weighted dominant paradigms, we surmise that six of the seven will tend to mute the impact of the Scientific paradigm. Thus, unknown unknowns, unknown knowns, taboos, denials, and errors will have ignorance level values in the four-to-five range. We justify these assigned levels based on the many examples provided in this and preceding chapters, including the Cuban Missile Crisis, Saipan, and global warming. Effectively, perspectives will vary widely since neural networks will exist in unstable states—flip-flopping among the dominant paradigms depending on the situation (refer to discussion of situational paradigms in Chapter 3). However, we can assign a moderate ignorance level (3) to known unknowns since a single dominant paradigm is, on balance, unable to limit the impact of any other dominant paradigm. A person having equally weighted dominant paradigms would often fail to identify and distinguish among numerous known unknowns—for example, being unaware of identifiable risks and dismissing fact-based assumptions. Thus, we should expect the assigned levels in Table C to lead, on average, to a high or very high level of ignorance for situations where dominant paradigms have equal or near equal neural network weighting (i.e., the average score of 4.5 is borderline high to very high ignorance).

Accordingly, we will use this system of analysis in the following pages to examine the dominant and composite paradigms in selected historical eras, followed by an assessment of the ignorance level during the same time period. Before proceeding, the reader should review Table C and its accompanying discussion.

Table C: Ignorance Determination for Hypothetical Era
Note: For Equally Weighted Dominant Paradigms as in Figure 1
This Table Complements Figure 1 and Table 1

Ignorance Source	Era Score	Explanation
Known Unknowns	3	The comparative strength of the Scientific paradigm keeps uncertainty and knowledge gaps at relatively moderate levels.
Unknown Unknowns	5	Dominant paradigm balance prevents knowledge from advancing.
Errors	5	The social narrative lacks regard for the truth since the other dominant paradigms compete strongly with the Scientific paradigm.
Unknown Knowns	4	The other dominant paradigms often contradict the Scientific paradigm, limiting the advance of knowledge.
Taboos (Avoid Knowledge)	5	Balance among the dominant paradigms promotes an atmosphere that evades the true and the relevant.
Denials	5	Six dominant paradigms serve group and individual self-interests and contradict the true and relevant.
Total Score	**27**	The composite paradigm (1) limits what is and can be known, (2) applies the scientific and unscientific to explain unknowns, and (3) instills prohibitions impeding advancement of knowledge.
Average for Era	**4.50**	**"Balanced" Era Assessment = High to Very High Ignorance**

Era Score and Average Score Ratings	Very Low Ignorance = 1; Range = 1.0 to1.5 Low Ignorance = 2; Range > 1.5 to 2.5 Moderate Ignorance = 3; Range > 2.5 to 3.5 High Ignorance = 4; Range > 3.5 to 4.5 Very High Ignorance = 5: Range > 4.5 to 5.0

Ancient Era

Figure 2: Ancient Era Composite Paradigm

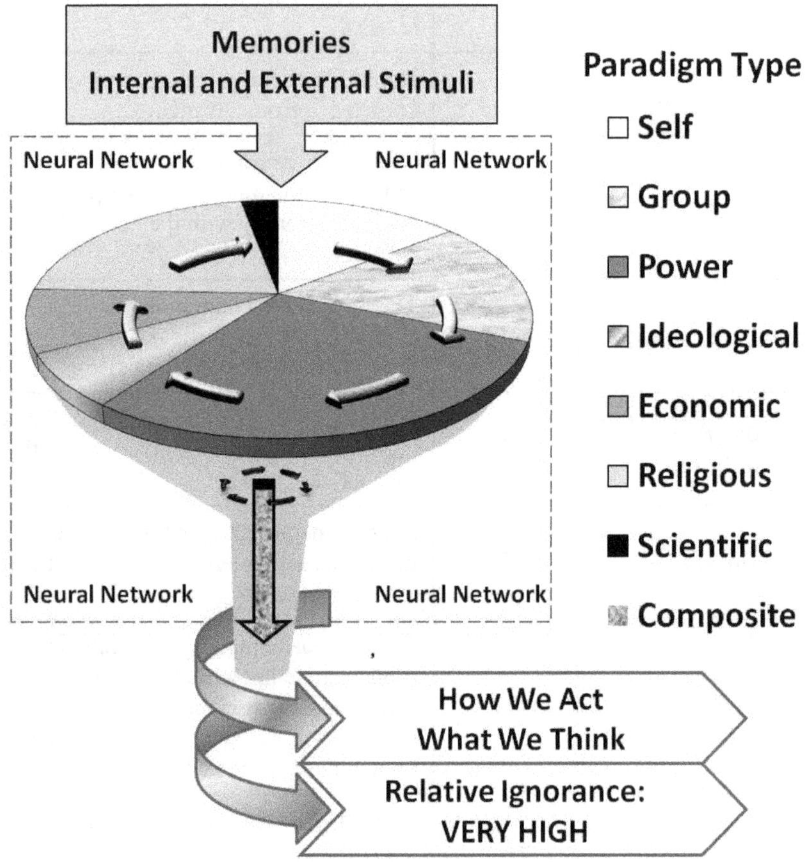

Table 2: Ancient Era Dominant Paradigm Neural Filters

Dominant Paradigm	**Major Filters Affecting Thoughts and Actions**
Self	Neural/Bodily Needs, Fear of Unknowns/Attack or Plunder, Disease, Survival Instinct, Ego, Introspection
Group	Societal Preservation, Tribalism
Power	Rule by Royalty, Democratic elitism, Emperor-gods; Militarism
Ideological	Sexism, Slavery, Militarism
Economic	Bartering, Monetary Exchange, Property Rights
Religious	Mono- and Polytheisms, Shamanism, Sacerdotalism
Scientific	Crude Observations, Metaphysics, Simple Tool-Making Technology

Table D: Ancient Era Ignorance Determination

Complements Figure 2 and Table 2

Ignorance Source	Era Score	Explanation
Known Unknowns	**5**	The Power paradigms controlled the narrative stifling the ability to clarify the unknown.
Unknown Unknowns	**4**	Religious and Group paradigms dictated knowledge of the routines of life and the mysterious.
Errors	**5**	A lack of rigor in scientific endeavors and the acceptance of myths could not overcome the misconceptions held.
Unknown Knowns	**5**	An immature Scientific paradigm inadequately stimulated the search for new knowledge, leaving Power and Religious paradigms the motivation for technological innovation.
Taboos (Knowledge Avoidance)	**5**	Self, Group, Religious, and Power paradigms subdued the acquisition of knowledge.
Denials	**5**	Group and Religious paradigms thwarted the establishment of a factual foundation for describing nature and human interaction.
Total Score	**29**	The composite paradigm limited what is and can be known, relied on the supernatural to explain the unknowns, and established prohibitions to impede the advancement of knowledge.
Average Ignorance Level	**4.83**	**Era Assessment = Very High Ignorance**

Figure 2, Table 2, and Table D Overview

In the Ancient Era, the Power, Group, Ideological, and Religious paradigms dominated (Figure 2 funnel wedges). On the continents of Europe, Asia, and Africa, the empires of Egypt, Persia, China, and Rome serve as examples. In these and other seats of power, royalty or strongmen served as self-appointed agents of the gods.[89] The royals endorsed some or all divinities, or in some cases, marketed themselves as gods. Priests fulfilled the sacerdotal nature of the religions, a carryover of the tribal shaman.

In most cases, the royals attained their status from a past or recently ascended Alpha-male or other group notable, who emerged as a leader and subsequently bestowed his legacy upon his heirs. As a result, the concept of royalty acquired an enduring status as a Power paradigm.

Geographic-cultural-ethnic paradigms and ideological perspectives also contributed significantly to human thought and behavior during the ancient era. Warfare and slavery became survival ideologies. Ancient belief systems essentially evolved with a singular purpose in mind: To survive among others with different worldly perspectives. The Power paradigm effectively became a way of life: Conquer or be conquered. The ideologies of warfare and slavery promoted acts of subjugation by force. Those in power leveraged these ideologies and integrated them into the Power paradigm. "To the victors belong the spoils"[90] was never so apt, including the option to enslave the vanquished. Group ideologies during the ancient era were often situational, a response to intersecting and conflicting perspectives. Warfare largely evolved from an instinctive risk-benefit survival strategy. A bird will swoop in and steal food from another bird or animal if the bird (instinctively) assesses that the benefits outweigh the risks. An ancient society that believed it had a high

---

[89] Other seats of power include the Greek city-states and Rome under republican government. Eventually, these were supplanted by kings and Caesars.

[90] The quote is from New York Senator William L. Marcy, a staunch defender of the political spoils system of his time. He made the statement in defending an appointee of U.S. President Andrew Jackson. Spoils refer to valuables or benefits taken from the loser in any form of competition. See https://www.britannica.com/biography/William-L-Marcy, (online) Encyclopaedia Britannica.

probability of victory on the battlefield would wage war on its neighbor(s). The rewards could be significant. Militarism developed from the inherent aggression found in the ideology of warfare. Groups attempted to resolve their conflicts through diplomatic means if they believed the risks were too high or a stalemate was the likely outcome.

Militarism has its roots in the neural constructs of both the Ideological and Power paradigms. Both perspectives developed naturally out of the need for individual and group survival. Survival depended both on force and cunning. Military cunning refers to the ideology of warfare as an organized undertaking. Thus, militarism became both an art and philosophy utilizing structured armed forces that served the offensive and defensive needs of a group—a tribe, nation, or confederation of states. When a group adopts militarism, it accepts the necessity of violence to preserve the society through formal defensive or offensive measures. From ancient times to the modern era, militarism has remained a key aspect of the Power paradigm.

At its core, militarism stems from the evolution of neural networks—a behavioral set of connections that protect the species, and more specifically, social units. Similarly, ants, bees, chimps, and other social species respond aggressively when outsiders threaten the collective. As a Power paradigm, militarism achieves an end—to exert influence over others to shape outcomes for a group. As such, militarism is in all of us (to varying degrees), meaning we tend to readily accept the authoritative systems that may materialize to improve our own security. Unfortunately, groups often had to endure weak, self-serving, or tyrannical leaders who also directed the military or mercenary forces to maintain control over their societies.

One obvious development during the ancient era was the plethora of Religious paradigms spread across a multitude of societies. The exact nature of each is well beyond the scope of this book, but each paradigm contributed one or more of the following belief structures within society: (1) divinities help explain why things happen the way they do; (2) divinities provide purpose to life; (3) divinities provide a pathway to an otherworldly existence; (4) divinities dictate authority relationships and hierarchical systems; (5) divinities establish both individual and group identities; and (6) divinities define the sacred, the moral, and societal norms. Not every Religious paradigm embodies these six belief structures. The Greek gods were often as fallible and petty as humans, certainly lacking a moral code.[91]

Archaeological studies and the many writings scattered among ruins and/or passed down to posterity provide historians a rich foundation for characterizing the ancient era. Historians have filled volumes with evidence and evidence-based supposition on what transpired within and among ancient societies. Because of the scope involved, we will not burden ourselves with the details. The reader is encouraged to access any of the multitudes of textbooks and articles on world history and/or on the specific periods of history evaluated in this book. They will confirm that power, religion, and ideology (often myth-based) played a significant role in determining the course of history in the ancient era.[92]

In evaluating the collections of paradigms throughout our history, one must first consider the preeminence of survival. To endure, societies developed Power, Religious, and Ideological paradigms to motivate individual and groups to action. Those who ascended to positions of authority communicated ideological and religious doctrines as enticing stories. They convinced the greater ancient populations that life followed certain courses. Deviating from these prescribed pathways would lead to negative consequences in this life and the afterlife. Adhering to dominant paradigms would lead to positive outcomes.

The motion picture and theatrical industries have attempted to portray the times and paradigms under which the ancients lived. Such efforts are laudable but rarely portray reality. We today cannot truly comprehend the varied subtleties of ancient perspectives because our present-day paradigms cloud our ability to see the world as it once was. We cannot divorce ourselves from the paradigms that occupy and steer

---

[91] Cavendish, 120-135.

[92] Note that ideologies may be buried within a paradigm or masked by other paradigms. For example, slavery may appear to be a dark extension of the Self, Group, and/or Power paradigms. At first, victors made slaves of the vanquished, driven in part or on whole by a paradigmatic hatred of the conquered. However, slavery subsequently matured into a societal theory and institution, not driven by hatred but to attain personal and group comfort and wealth. Slavery is simply a constituent part of and an early precursor to more imperious ideologies, such as racism, colonialism, fascism, and Nazism.

our thoughts and actions from moment to moment today. Yes, the seven dominant paradigms still exist but not as they once did.

We've addressed most of the dominant factors from the ancient era that contributed to the formation of the neural filters specified in Table 2. While the Economic paradigm was not as significant as other dominant paradigms, property rights emerged as a strong neural filter during this period. As populations increased, arable lands took on increasing value as food sources. Proximity to water was obviously prized as were the crops and animal husbandry the water supported.

In addition, construction projects became a priority. Structures provided shelter and security. Societies could wall themselves in cities, allowing commerce to blossom, but they also had to ensure they could protect their domesticated animals and crops. Doing so within the confines of an urban environment proved problematic, given the need for sanitation to prevent disease. These challenges stimulated technological and scientific advancements to agricultural and city life. As crude as these efforts were, the ancients made great use of simple machines such as the lever, wedge, and wheel. These devices enabled them to make great strides in altering their environments, from irrigation projects to the construction of massive monuments. Without knowing much science, real and perceived necessity proved the Mother of Invention. The ancient composite paradigm spurred technological innovation not due to the Scientific paradigm, but largely the Power and Religious paradigms.

In Table D, I rate overall ignorance "Very High" during ancient times for several reasons. While there were numerous scientific developments in this era, they failed to mature. Thus, the ancients' ability to uncover unknown knowns rarely materialized, which had a significant effect on the everyday lives of their societies. Mythology, lore, and a smorgasbord of religions played a significant role in developing socially detrimental errors, denials, and taboos. Both the acts of those in power and the inherent tribalism of groups fostered a lack of awareness among the general populace. The masses had minimal understanding and certainty of knowns. They also failed to grasp the significance of any unknowns. They believed in a narrow depiction of existence and an even narrower portrayal of the possibilities life afforded them. The masses could only claim certainty about their plight: Life was a persistent challenge.

The Dark Ages

Figure 3: Dark Ages Composite Paradigm

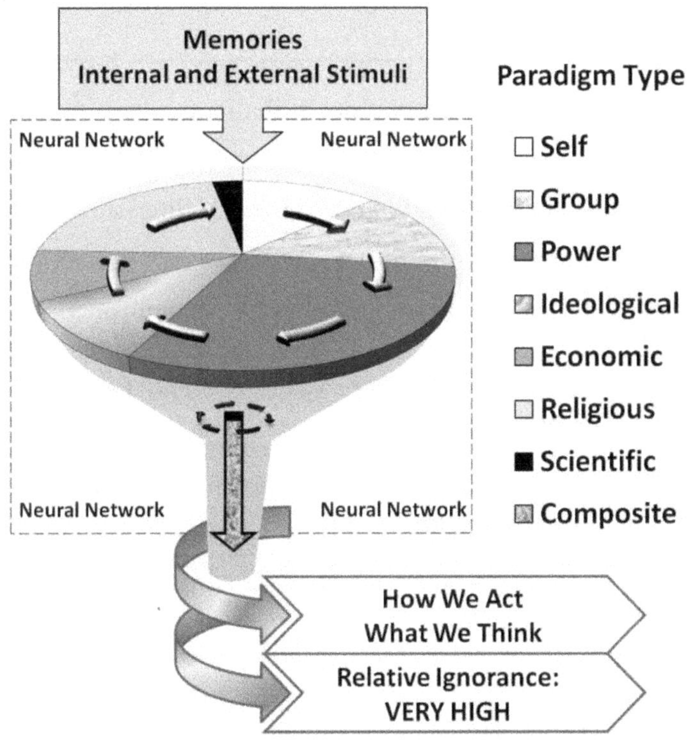

Table 3: Dark Ages Dominant Paradigm Neural Filters

Dominant Paradigm	Major Filters Affecting Thoughts and Actions
Self	Neural/Bodily Needs, Fear of Unknowns/Attack or Plunder, Disease, Survival Instinct, Ego, Introspection
Group	Societal Preservation, Tribalism
Power	Rule by Royalty and Alphas; Militarism
Ideological	Sexism, Militarism, Slavery, Metaphysics
Economic	Bartering, Monetary Systems, Feudalism, Property Rights/Laws
Religious	Mono- and Polytheisms, Institutional Theologies, Sacerdotalism
Scientific	Crude Observations, Minor Tool-Making Advances

Table E: Dark Ages Ignorance Determination

Complements Figure 3 and Table 3

Ignorance Type	Era Score	Explanation
Known Unknowns	**5**	Power, Religious, and Group paradigms controlled the narrative.
Unknown Unknowns	**4**	Religious and Group paradigms prevented uncovering the uncertainties and risks associated with everyday life.
Errors	**5**	A lack of rigor in scientific endeavors and the acceptance of myths could not overcome the misconceptions held.
Unknown Knowns	**5**	The Scientific paradigm stagnated then regressed, providing little stimulus to the search for new knowledge.
Taboos (Knowledge Avoidance)	**5**	Power and Religious paradigms stifled the acquisition of knowledge.
Denials	**5**	Group and Religious paradigms thwarted the establishment of a factual foundation to describe nature and human interaction.
Total Score	**29**	Similar to ancient times, the composite paradigm limited what is and can be known, relied on the supernatural to explain the unknowns, and established prohibitions that impeded the advancement of knowledge.
Average Ignorance Level	**4.83**	**Era Assessment = Very High Ignorance**

Figure 3, Table 3, and Table E Overview

In the Dark Ages, the Power and Religious paradigms continued to dominate, particularly Power. The institutionalization of religion thwarted the advances of competing religions but failed to counter the inherent violence and lawlessness of the period. Islam emerged and spread in the southern and eastern Mediterranean. Christianity progressed under the might of Rome, thanks to Emperor Constantine. When Rome finally dissolved in Western Europe, the resulting separate states sustained Christian tradition. Power remained with royalty [93] and other leaders who exploited institutionalized religions as a way of keeping the populace in check. Cultural-ethnic paradigms and ideological paradigms also sustained their prominence. Nomadic groups led by Alpha males tried to expand their power base, eventually leading to the militaristic adventures of the Vikings and Mongols, operating beyond the traditional timeframe of the Dark Ages. Warfare and slavery remained ideological imperatives to improve the chances of survival. Physical comfort required the ability to leverage the labors of others through servitude or slavery. Physical security required prepared fighting forces.

Ian Mortimer has concisely summed up this period of history:

> The human race in 1001 was not just illiterate, superstitious, ignorant of the outside world and devoid of spiritual supervision; it faced continual hardships and dangers. Hunger and deprivation were widespread. Society was violent, and to protect yourself you had to meet force with force.[94]

The Power and Religious paradigms together provided a means to an end. As for other dominant paradigms, they advanced little. Group paradigms were varied and many, but small states managed to

[93] If one traces royalty back to its origin, one will always find an Alpha Male or other notable personality who had managed to hold sway over others. Royalty is both story and history.

[94] Mortimer, 11.

band together at times to engage common enemies, despite their paradigmatic differences. The Scientific paradigm stagnated, then regressed, and did not mature significantly beyond ancient times; the struggle to survive outweighed the luxury of intellectual exploration. Additionally, the advent of feudalism late in the Dark Ages did little to spur the persistent economic inertia brought on by societies perpetually distracted by basic survival needs. The Economic paradigm changed little from ancient times in its composite-paradigm weighting.

In Table E, I have assigned an ignorance level of five to all but one contributing element of overall ignorance, the Unknown Unknowns. However, even this element of ignorance doesn't vary significantly from ancient times. The fractured nature of regional societies and the incessant struggles among hordes, tribes, fiefdoms, kingdoms, and conquerors made it difficult to expand the human knowledge base. Much knowledge was lost because of the social upheavals accompanying warfare. Power, Group, and Religious paradigms took hold of neural networks leaving humanity highly ignorant.

In the preceding discussion, readers should have found an answer to the question, "What made the Dark Ages dark?" While insecurity, lawlessness, and hardships abounded then, they were not the root cause. Paradigms were—ones that created the thoughts and behaviors catalyzing the aforementioned outcomes (see Table 4 below). The general mindset existing during the Dark Ages followed from paradigms leading to despair and desperation. When humans experience hopelessness and extreme stress, their thoughts and behaviors may undergo severe corruptions. Other mechanisms may also be at work. Power (control) and ideology may be the cause or ego and tribalism or any numerous combinations of dominant paradigms. They all can lead to periods of despondency, both local and global in scope. For example, the Mongols were a destructive force well beyond their regional bounds. The same applies to the Axis powers during the Second World War. Most dark periods have their origins in the dominance of Power paradigms.

The Renaissance

Figure 4: Renaissance Composite Paradigm

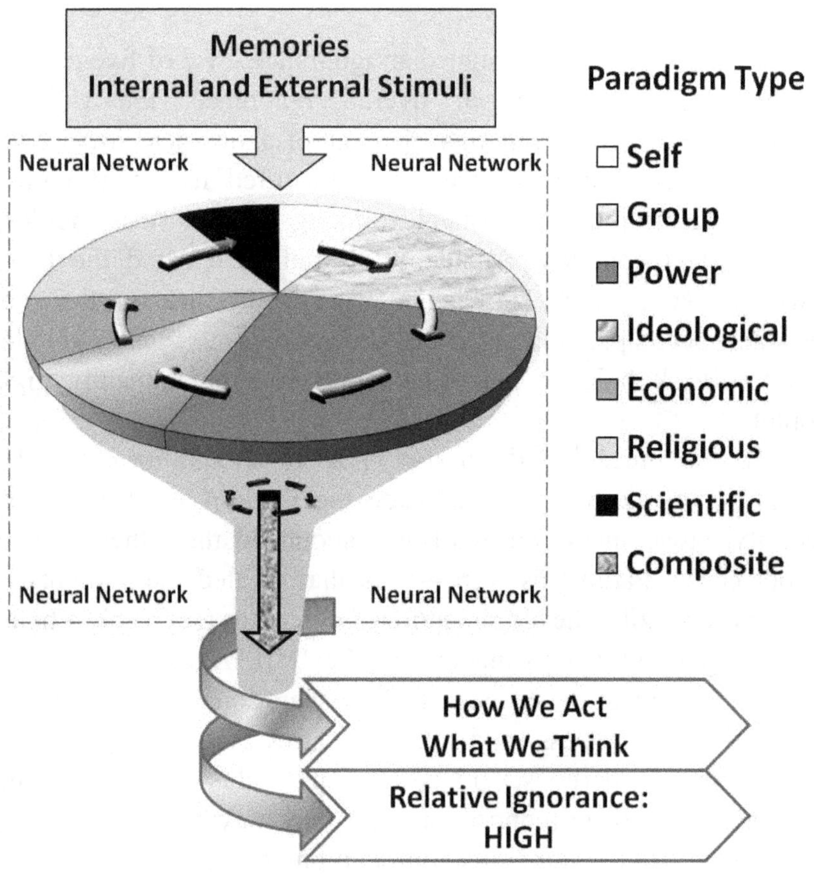

Table 4: Renaissance Dominant Paradigm Neural Filters

Dominant Paradigm	Major Filters Affecting Thoughts and Actions
Self	Neural/Bodily Needs, Fear of Personal Safety and Disease, Ego, Survival Instinct, Introspection
Group	Tribalism, Racism, Elitism
Power	Royalty, Fiefdoms, Militarism, Church-States, Armies
Ideological	Militarism, Imperialism, Colonialism, Slavery, Constitutionalism
Economic	State Monetary Systems, Feudalism, Mercantilism, Banking, Property Rights/Laws
Religious	Consolidated, Multi-State Religions: Catholicism, Islam, Protestantism, Hinduism
Scientific	Mathematics, Physics, Technology-Aided Observations, Scientific Method, Rationalism

Table F: Renaissance Ignorance Determination
Complements Figure 4 and Table 4

Ignorance Type	Era Score	Explanation
Known Unknowns	4	With science taking hold, the Power and Religious paradigms begin to lose some control over the narrative.
Unknown Unknowns	4	The Scientific paradigm began to demystify some unknowns, but Group and Religious paradigms remain dominant.
Errors	4	Though scientific endeavors offer alternative perspectives, they still cannot dispel the misconceptions held due to myths.
Unknown Knowns	5	The Scientific paradigm did little to enlighten the populace. Imperial and colonial attitudes (Ideological paradigms) decimated New World peoples, siphoning their resources.
Taboos (Knowledge Avoidance)	3	The printing press eroded the Power and Religious paradigms' impediments to the acquisition of knowledge.
Denials	4	The printing press eroded Group, Ideological, and Religious paradigms' impediments to establishing a factual foundation that describes nature and human interaction.
Total Score	**24**	The composite paradigm limits what is and can be known, but begins to explore unknowns with greater fervor, while prohibitions that impede the advancement of knowledge decline.
Average Ignorance Level	**4.00**	**Era Assessment = High Ignorance**

Figure 4, Table 4, and Table F Overview

The Renaissance represented an awakening of human thought and behavior that changed the relative balance among the dominant paradigms. The Scientific paradigm gradually began to sway human thought and behavior with the development of scientific methods. Emboldened by the widespread rise of technologies, societies shifted their Ideological and Economic paradigms, fostering imperialism and colonialism and nurturing formalized currency exchange systems. Despite these shifts, Power and Religious paradigms largely determined outcomes—from the New World to the Old and from the Middle East to the Far East. Institutionalized religions and royalty obstructed changes to paradigms stimulated by emerging scientific perspectives. Despite the rigidity of religious institutions, Protestantism managed to gain a foothold and rapidly expanded. Inventions such as the printing press provided the means to expand communications even though literacy was uncommon. Royalty sustained power largely by aligning with established religions. The royals professed their allegiance to God whether a Christian (Anglican, Protestant, or Catholic), Muslim, or Hindu.

The Age of Discovery fostered a competitive fervor among European nations regarding the Ideological paradigm of colonialism. In addition to colonialism, aggressive imperialistic objectives matured. Visions of empire integrated with the Power paradigms of major European powers. The impact on the New World was devastating. Natives of Africa and North, Central, and South America suffered the consequences, enduring slaughter, slavery, disease, and brutal indignations. Their worlds were shattered. Their composite paradigms evaporated rapidly with European conquests—one of the greatest examples of physical, mental, and emotional “shock and awe” in human history, particularly for the Inca, Maya, Aztec, and a host of African tribes.

Though power and religion dictated the overall course of history, science and technology were gradually disrupting long-held views. The Earth was no longer the center of the universe (despite resistance from the Vatican), and the forces of nature were not whimsically directed by God or gods but followed discoverable natural laws. Such revelations freed some minds from the darkness of their caves.

Integrated economic systems began to coalesce under the influence of mercantilism, the predecessor to capitalism. Though many nations were at war, mercantile trade fueled the rising interactions among societies. Colonialism made global trade very profitable, particularly in the New World and the Pacific where Western Europeans effectively stole the riches of most of their colonies. Wealth was for the taking for the enterprising and bold.

As societies grew in population and in their global reach, governing became increasing challenging. Royalty was ill-equipped to handle the magnitude and scope of domestic and international matters. Constitutionalism emerged as a way to compensate for the incompetence and limitations of royalty. In some cases, constitutional forms of bureaucratic governance partnered with royalty to manage national affairs. An ideological shift reoccurred after remaining dormant since ancient times—that the people should have a say in their own governance. The republicanism of Rome and the democratic inclinations of Greece had re-emerged.

In summary, during the Renaissance, the Power, Group, Ideological, and Religious paradigms controlled the perspectives governing everyday life, keeping ignorance high. People aligned strongly with the perspectives of their group (e.g., nation-state), their religion, or their authority figure(s) (e.g., royal, political party, etc.). With colonialism and imperialism intensifying in Europe, the Economic paradigm expanded to include a globalization initiative, albeit one founded on pillaging the resources of colonies.

With respect to ignorance (Table F), the discovery of unknown unknowns and the purposeful cataloguing of known unknowns remained difficult, but some headway occurred due to the strengthening insertion of the Scientific paradigm into everyday life (e.g. pre-industrial technology). Science was improving certainty about the world, demystifying many previously held misconceptions about Nature and uncovering methods to explore the unknown. The Scientific paradigm began to erode the effects of errors, denials, and taboos in fostering ignorance. Exploration, the identification of physical laws, and the rising utilization of sophisticated tools all reduced the ignorance associated with unknown knowns.

The Industrial Revolution

Figure 5: Industrial Revolution Composite Paradigm

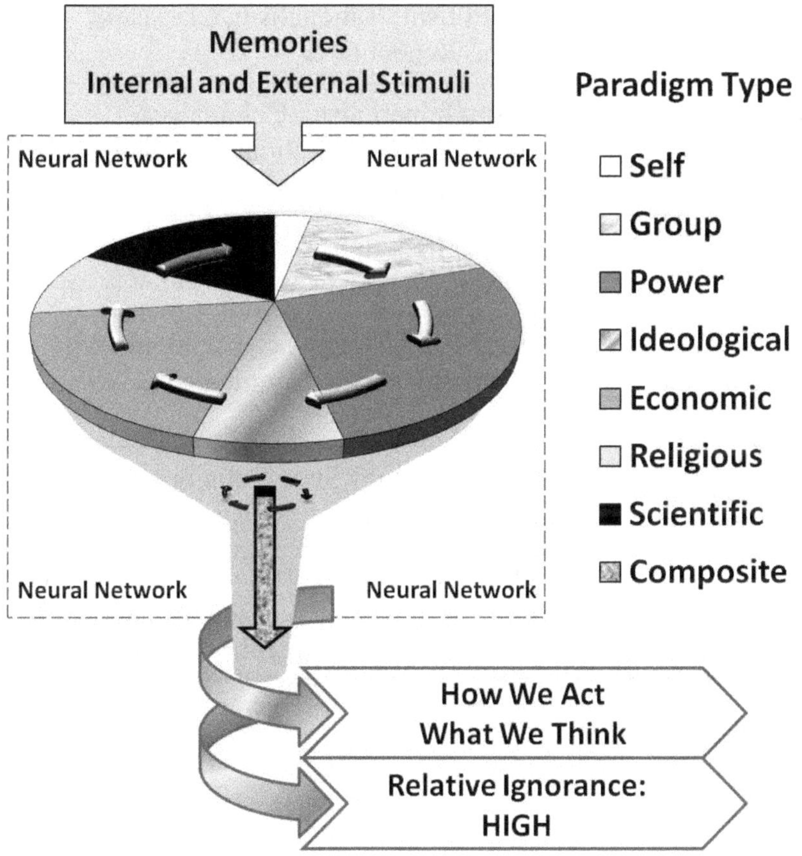

Table 5: Industrial Revolution Dominant Paradigm Neural Filters

Dominant Paradigm	Major Filters Affecting Thoughts and Actions
Self	Neural/Bodily Needs, Fear of Disease, Ego, Survival Instinct, Introspection, Behaviorism
Group	Racism, Elitism, Nationalism, Classism, Ethnicism, Xenophobia
Power	Militarism, Imperialism, Colonialism, Republicanism, Constitutionalism, State and Local Police, Nationalism
Ideological	Militarism, Imperialism, Colonialism, Materialism, Nationalism
Economic	Banking, Monetary Exchange Systems, Capitalism, Socialism, Communism, Incorporation
Religious	Consolidated, Multi-State Religions: Catholicism, Islam, Protestantism, Hinduism
Scientific	Reductionism, Mathematics, Physics, Chemistry, Scientific "-ologies" (e.g., Biology), Scientific Method, Electro-Mechanical Machinery

Table G: Industrial Revolution Ignorance Determination

Complements Figure 5 and Table 5

Ignorance Type	Era Score	Explanation
Known Unknowns	4	With science taking hold, Power and Religious paradigms lose some control over the narrative but Economic and Group paradigms offset these gains.
Unknown Unknowns	4	The Scientific paradigm began to demystify some unknowns, but Group, Economic, and Religious paradigms remain dominant.
Errors	4	Though scientific endeavors offer alternative perspectives, they still cannot dispel the misconceptions propagated under Group, Economic, and Ideological paradigms.
Unknown Knowns	3	The Scientific paradigm reduced uncertainty about the world by providing the means to expose and clarify unknown knowns.
Taboos (Knowledge Avoidance)	5	Power and Group paradigms minimized the acquisition of knowledge, eventually leading to xenophobic perspectives.
Denials	5	Group, Ideological, Economic, and Power paradigms thwarted the establishment of a factual foundation to describe nature and human interaction.
Total Score	**25**	The composite paradigm limits what is and can be known, but begins to explore unknowns with greater fervor, even while prohibitions that impede the advancement of knowledge grow.
Average Ignorance Level	**4.17**	**Era Assessment = High Ignorance**

Figure 5, Table 5, and Table G Overview

The Industrial Revolution awakened humanity to new and varied options for living one's life.[95] The balance among the dominant paradigms shifted, stimulating new perspectives of reality. The Scientific paradigm gradually began to sway human thought and behavior. Under a rapid-fire growth of technologies, societies deepened their ideological outlook and shifted their economic perspectives. Colonialism, imperialism, and capitalism all found enabling support within the power structure of nation-states. The Self paradigm was largely supplanted by the Group, which leveraged the Power, Economic, and Ideological paradigms in an effort to compete with neighboring groups (nation-states). This largely Eurocentric phenomenon disrupted the continental peace, eventually leading to World War I. Nationalism and militarism united under nation-state authority, legitimizing these isms under the Power paradigms by incorporation into constitutions and parliamentary process. Some cracks in the foundation of institutionalized religions began to appear.

Noteworthy during the Industrial Revolution was the rising dominance and eventual decline of "Super" Self and Group paradigms, such as fascism and Nazism and the personalities behind them. Enabled by Ideological and Economic paradigms, such as racial supremacy and communism, individuals and groups took control of societies to force their paradigms on others. Royalty had often taken such steps, but the rise of Lenin, Stalin, Mussolini, and Hitler, and lesser-known ideologues, demonstrated the strength of the subtle stains imprinted on the neural networks of these individuals and their followers. Their reach was profound. Technology, such as radio, film, and photography, provided direct pathways into the minds of millions, overwriting paradigms contrary to the propaganda being spewed or catalyzing new, darker ones. The power of repetition cannot be understated in the formation of paradigms. Consider Adolph Hitler's own words:

---

[95] For the purposes of this book, the Industrial Revolution spans the period from 1760 to 1944, approximately a century more than usual, to include World War I and World War II and the substantial industrialization of 20th-century warfare.

> The receptive powers of the masses are very restricted, and their understanding is feeble. On the other hand, they quickly forget. Such being the case, all effective propaganda must be confined to a few bare essentials and those must be expressed as far as possible in stereotyped formulas. These slogans should be persistently repeated until the very last individual has come to grasp the idea that has been put forward.[96]

Hitler certainly had no training in neurophysiology, but he did understand the nature of Pavlovian responses. Ring a bell enough times when you feed a dog, and the dog will come to salivate with the sound of a bell only. Repeatedly tell the German people that they are a Master Race or that the Jews are the cause of social strife, then the neural network's start to give credence to even the vilest ideologies and xenophobic notions. The mind remembers what the senses repeatedly perceive; the truth doesn't matter. These memories can alter mental filters and the paradigms they support. This phenomenon is the most troubling of all aspects of paradigm formation—that we and our paradigms can fall prey to mental meddling founded in falsehoods.

A more subtle and pervasive Group paradigm also emerged during this era by integrating with the prevailing Economic paradigm. Corporations and their Captains of Industry became to capitalism what royalty was to feudal society—the top of the wealth chain. As previously mentioned, corporations exist to serve their shareholders—the national, public, or social impacts of business operations are secondary. Profits trump social consequences of their efforts. The true cost of doing business, even with visible benefits to society, such as improved mobility, rarely falls upon the corporation. Corporations build cars for profit, but the burden of building and maintaining the roads the cars drive on is borne by the taxpayers. Air and water pollution are other examples of this phenomenon unless businesses are held to high standards.

The industrial era demonstrated how toxic our paradigms can become and how lethally our technology can be applied when those same paradigms dominate our thoughts and actions. We must remember, however, that the non-Scientific dominant paradigms are the root cause of these despicable acts. Scientific endeavors and tool-

[96] Hitler, 116.

making (technology) are responses to the needs created by our other paradigms. In effect, the Scientific paradigm is a product of the other six dominant paradigms that gradually transformed into its own dominant paradigm, eventually taking on the rigid qualities that helped discern the truth from unfounded information.

Throughout the Industrial Revolution little change occurred in the dominant paradigms except the Economic paradigm, which stimulated actions that remodeled many social structures, and the Scientific paradigm, which revealed and identified truths about our universe and ourselves. Thus, the same greed and self-serving objectives of individuals and groups in ancient times governed the neural networks of the power brokers of the Industrial Revolution. By reviewing the accompanying figure and tables in this section, one can make a simple intellectual leap to grasp the paradigmatic significance of the (expanded) Industrial Revolution. Here are just a few of the most noteworthy events spurred by its dominant paradigms:

(1) The U.S. Civil War and Reconstruction
(2) Worldwide anti-Semitism
(3) Globalization within the structures of imperialism and colonialism
(4) Two World Wars and numerous lesser wars (e.g., Napoleonic wars)
(5) Ideological fanaticism: Nazism, fascism, Master Race, Social Darwinism, Bolshevism, capitalism, communism, et al
(6) Slavery and its aftermath, racism, xenophobia, eugenics
(7) Air, water, and soil pollution, child labor

These occurrences were the direct result of the dominant paradigms in play in the 19th and first half of the 20th century. As identified in Table G, ignorance was high. The reader might judge ignorance "very high" based on the list of significant events presented, but truths about the world were beginning to help people escape their paradigmatic caves (e.g., women's suffrage). The social order was in transition via an intense and seemingly perpetual War of Paradigms, within and among nations. Relatively fewer people accepted the status quo. Neural networks were shifting.

The Atomic Age

Figure 6: Atomic Age Composite Paradigm

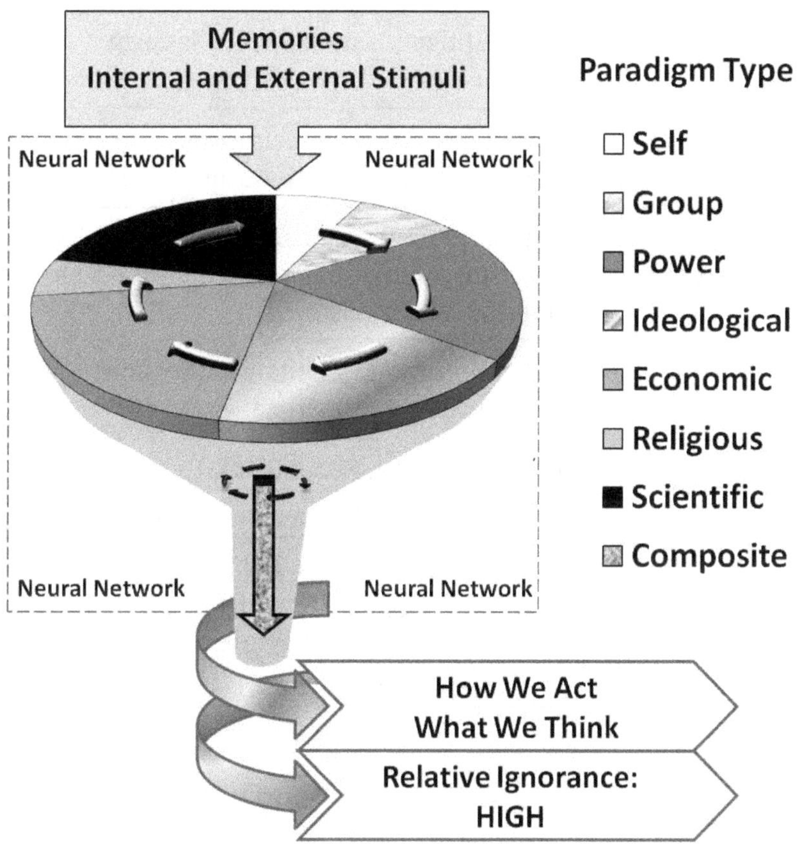

Table 6: Atomic Age Dominant Paradigm Neural Filters

Dominant Paradigm	Major Filters Affecting Thoughts and Actions
Self	Neural/Bodily Needs, Fear of Disease, Ego, Survival Instinct, Introspection, Behaviorism
Group	Racism, Elitism, Nationalism, Classism, Ethnicism
Power	Militarism, Military-Industrialism, Totalitarianism, Mutually Assured Destruction
Ideological	Militarism, Republicanism, Constitutionalism, Humanism, Internationalism, Anthropocentrism, Globalism, Materialism
Economic	Banking, Corporate Capitalism, Socialism, Communism, Consumerism
Religious	Monotheism (All), Secularism, Evangelism (mostly in the U.S.)
Scientific	Reductionism, Quantum-Relativistic Physics and Chemistry, "-ologies" (e.g., Biology), Scientism, Electronics, Integrated Circuitry, High-Energy Physics, Cosmology

Table H: Atomic Age Ignorance Determination

Complements Figure 6 and Table 6

Ignorance Type	Era Score	Explanation
Known Unknowns	**4**	Cold War Power and Economic paradigms controlled the narrative for most of the world's population.
Unknown Unknowns	**4**	The shift in the Scientific paradigm toward quantum perspectives confined the scope of what could be known, limiting deterministic outcomes.
Errors	**5**	The Cold War created a disparity of views and misinformation on a global scale, germinating errors through opinionating.
Unknown Knowns	**4**	Although preeminent in reshaping modern society through technology, the Scientific paradigm lost some public trust due to the destructive effects of nuclear weapons and power plant accidents.
Taboos (Knowledge Avoidance)	**3**	An era of protests regarding civil rights, war, and poverty was marked by a search for truths by large segments of the world's population.
Denials	**5**	Competition between the two major Economic paradigms (communism and capitalism) thwarted the establishment of a consistent perspective of the human condition.
Total Score	**25**	Cold War politics and all-powerful scientifically developed weapons and technology impeded the advancement of knowledge.
Average Ignorance Level	**4.17**	**Era Assessment = High Ignorance**

Figure 6, Table 6, and Table H Overview

Humanism made strides after World War II, a brief but poorly reinforced paradigm shift in human behavior toward each other, but the Cold War and Asian wars (Korea, Vietnam) quickly negated any such tendency. Industrialism proceeded at an accelerating pace, fueled by anthropocentric visions of a world that would yield to human desire. Entropy caught up with human greed as ecological degradation followed on the heels of rampant consumerism and materialism. Capitalism reinforced its grip in the international arena, leveraging new labor and material resources in foreign markets. Economic globalization was relentless. Religious paradigms declined in dominance early in the era only to see a resurgence of fundamentalism in Islam later in the era. At the same time, in the United States, political expediency allowed Christianity to reemerge as a force in influencing public policy, narrowing the separation between church and state. Evangelists gained a handhold and still maintain a grip.

In the United States, technological progress fueled the dominance of the Scientific, Economic, Power, and Ideological paradigms, ultimately shifting societies toward urbanism and revitalizing classism. Given the American global influence, these perspectives infiltrated other nations, particularly consumerism and materialism. Financial elites largely dictated socioeconomic outcomes thereby influencing the resulting composite paradigms of the Atomic Age.

The Atomic Age promised to restructure the world's energy infrastructure to meet the rising demands of overindulging human populations. This effort fizzled with the end of the Cold War and the reactive responses to nuclear power plant accidents, most notably Three Mile Island, Chernobyl, and Fukushima. Fossil fuels, the primary contributor to human-induced climate change, became and remain the energy source of choice. While the Atomic Age began to fade, the Information Age (or Computer Age) was on the rise, bolstered by the establishment of the internet which could link information and computer systems together. The human thirst for energy and information seemed unquenchable.

The Present Era

Figure 7: Present Era Composite Paradigm

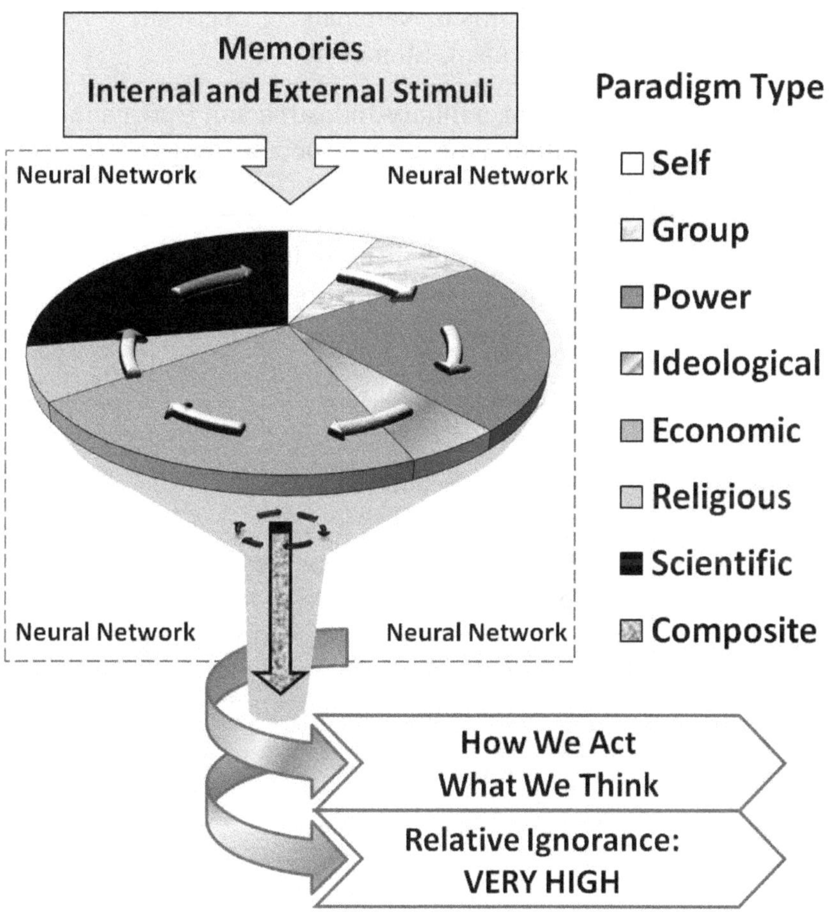

Table 7: Present Era Dominant Paradigm Neural Filters

Dominant Paradigm	Major Filters Affecting Thoughts and Actions
Self	Neural/Bodily Needs, Fear of Disease, Ego, Survival Instinct, Introspection, Narcissism
Group	Racism, Elitism, Nationalism, Classism, Republicanism, Ethnicism
Power	Militarism, Military-Industrialism, Bureaucracy, Constitutionalism, Technocracy, Mega-Corporate Imperialism
Ideological	Militarism, Globalism, Individualism, Materialism, Economic Imperialism
Economic	Banking, Globalized Corporate Capitalism, Socialism, Consumerism
Religious	Monotheism, Secularism
Scientific	Scientific Method, Unification Theories, Computer Technology, Cosmology, Big Data, Integrated Circuits, Nanotechnology, Genetic Engineering

Table I: Present Era Ignorance Determination

Complements Figure 7 and Table 7

Ignorance Type	Era Score	Explanation
Known Unknowns	4	The Scientific paradigm has begun to control the narrative, but pushback from power brokers and a chaotic noösphere prevent meaningful exploration of known unknowns.
Unknown Unknowns	4	The Power and Economic paradigms prevent establishment of Big Picture principles within the public sphere, limiting the options for dealing with increasingly complex problems.
Errors	5	The Power and Economic paradigms continue to thwart the ability of science to expose and correct errors.
Unknown Knowns	5	The Power and Economic paradigms thwart the public's education of Big Picture principles, providing little stimulus to the search for new knowledge in the public arena.
Taboos (Knowledge Avoidance)	4	Power, Ideological, Religious, and Group paradigms and growing tribalism distract people from and stifle the acquisition of knowledge.
Denials	5	Power and Religious paradigms intentionally discredit the factual foundations of knowledge and promote unverifiable "alternative facts."
Total Score	**27**	The composite paradigm lacks the discipline to deal with the increasing challenges of knowns and fails to establish and/or apply Big Picture principles to address uncertainties. Decisions and workable solutions are impeded.
Average Ignorance Level	**4.50**	**Era Assessment = Very High Ignorance**

Figure 7, Table 7, and Table I Overview

The Scientific, Power, and Economic Paradigms have combined synergistically in the current era to dictate thought and action. By pouring resources into the military-industrial complex, the U.S. has ensured that these dominant paradigms sustain technocratic capitalistic imperialism.

In many respects, science and government have become the tools of the superrich and globalism a muted form of economic imperialism. MCI is driving humanity to an unsustainable techno-capitalist vision controlled by special interest groups. Consumerism and materialism rank supreme among the public's economic ideological perspectives. Meanwhile, religious and cultural norms are teetering against the onslaught of evidence that minimizes the validity of their founding theological and cultural tenets, leading, in many cases, to extremism. Ignorance is expanding under the influence of competing paradigms and an overload of digitized information. In the U.S., a widening disparity between the Haves and Have-nots has created stress and frustration within the public sector, a distraction that prevents the Have-nots from reducing their ignorance. While the public's quality of life has actually improved materially over time—meaning the poverty baseline has shifted upward, people feel less certain about the future. Their insecurity limits their ability to shift their paradigms, effectively becoming victims of survival mode paradigms. The Power and Economic paradigms largely dictate outcomes for the Have-nots.

As for the Power paradigm, militarism remains the dominant perspective, largely because of American military infrastructure. In the present nation-state era, the Power paradigm relies on the armed forces, which fall under the authority of presidents and premiers, and police forces, which operate within local communities. Notably, after over a century of isolationist policies, the 20th century opened with the United States adopting militarism as a way of influencing outcomes in the international arena. After a short respite following World War I, militarism expanded greatly in the 1940s, mostly in response to the threats generated during and after the World War II. The U.S. has extended the umbrella of its militarism to other nations, influencing the perspectives held by its allies. With the U.S. military-industrial complex heavily supported by U.S. internal spending, it can also offer weapons and weapon systems to allies, such as members of the North

Atlantic Treaty Organization (NATO) alliance and other friendly nation-states. This dependency is not always ideologically in the best interests of the affected nations, but is usually economically favorable. The paradigm of continuous improvement in offensive and defensive capabilities fuels a perpetual arms race even while relative peace has become the new norm, with a few exceptions such as Syria. The perpetual armament paradigm complements MCI, providing yet another pathway for national and multinational conglomerates to fill their coffers.

The militarism paradigm definitely has a firm grip on the American political mindset, egged on by corporate interests. As a result, a Military-Industrial Complex has burgeoned that consumes a significant portion of the annual federal budget, vastly outspending any other nation. Federal spending steers a disproportionate amount of resources toward military systems. Paradigm conflicts occur because domestic spending falls short of the objectives promoted by other paradigms. "We are what we spend" may be an appropriate summation of present-era paradigm structure—with Power, Economic, and Scientific paradigms leading the way.

Paradigm-Ignorance Historical Summary

Early civilized life, such as in ancient Greece, freed some individuals from routine survival needs. Of these, many pondered different ways of living; some even contemplated a utopian and communal Good Life (discussed later in this chapter). However, the ancient Greeks could not overcome their paradigmatic immaturity and suffered the consequences of their own perspectives. The ancient Greeks had numerous detrimental dominant paradigms concerning slavery, religious matters, women, warfare, and foreigners. As a result, they could not break the chains that confined their societies to their two-dimensional shadow-caves. The ancient Greeks were only able to superficially penetrate the many aspects of social, economic, and political life that keep societies functioning for extended periods. Their successes stemmed from a focus on militaristic principles and from advances in knowledge and intellectual processes, particularly compared to neighboring societies. Both phenomena were relatively short-lived. Paradigms failed to evolve or shift within Greece, in part, due to the weak communications and cooperation among the dispersed Greek city-states. Ultimately, Greece and other ancient societies depended heavily upon warfare for their survival. The warfare paradigm has persisted since then. Only since the early 21st century has the warfare perspective begun to lose its grip in most societies—at least for now.

Paradigmatically, however, the course of history has not deviated. The seven dominant paradigms have persisted in every society since our hunter-gatherer origins, albeit some, such as the Scientific paradigm, barely registered initially. The elements making up each paradigm vary with historical period and reflect the values, behaviors, and systemic characteristics of each period. We provided Figures 2 through 7 and their associated tables to illustrate the broad implications of past and current perspectives. These representations do not apply to every geographical region for the selected periods of history, but they do approximate the historical realities of their eras. Nor is there a fine line delineating the end of one era and advent of the next. The overall paradigmatic structure of each period broadly identifies the influences upon the societies of their time, and consequently the impetus behind the then-existing way of life and underlying attitudes. The funnel wedges in the figures crudely represent the degree of influence each dominant paradigm contributed to the lives and thoughts of the people in each era.

We also estimated the degree of ignorance of each historical period. We found some common threads. For example, if the Power and Religious paradigms have a high degree of influence over "how we live" and "what we think," one should expect, at the very least, a high level of ignorance among the population. This may not be an obvious conclusion, but everyone should recognize that Power and Religious paradigms lack objective consistency. They can create biases or impose erroneous notions upon society, sustaining and even elevating the ignorance of group members. Consider how the Catholic Church refuted and condemned Galileo's work in astronomy during and long after his lifetime. Consider also the petty wars among the medieval states of Europe, some at the whim of royal decrees and others based on ethnic or religious differences. These actions represented severe ignorance. In accepting the paradigm that royals have a divine connection or represent superior bloodlines and intelligence, many societies of the past fell into a deep abyss of ignorance.

Can the Power paradigm have a positive effect on society and reduce ignorance? In theory, yes, but in practice, no, it does not. The world is still awaiting its first philosopher king or benevolent dictator to lift the shroud of ignorance from his or her subjects. Corruption and power seem inexorably linked, even within democratic societies or nation-states with constitutional governments and elected representatives. Power paradigms can thrive over the short-term—years to centuries—by controlling the inherent chaos of large social systems (e.g., the Roman Empire); however, long-term stability (centuries to millennia) results from coherently blended paradigms. One such example was the strong cohesion between certain power-religious paradigms in the Egyptian empire's pharaonic system that lasted over a millennium. This single data point of paradigmatic consistency is highly unusual in most human systems, however, and is cited as an exception and not a rule.

Although many of the perspectives within Christianity, Islam, Judaism, Buddhism, Confucianism, Hinduism, Shintoism, and other isms can bring order and a communal spirit to society, they do not foster a climate for reducing ignorance. Power mongers utilized institutionalized religions to create a spiritual model of life that subsequently stifled the quest for truth and enlightenment. Societies largely dominated by a Religious paradigm will eventually wither under corruption, oppression, or the suppression of individual freedoms. These circumstances have repeated themselves with such regularity throughout human history that they appear an inevitable consequence of any dominant Religious paradigm.

The periods of history encompassing the Crusades, the Inquisition, and the seemingly perpetual persecution of Jews provide sufficient evidence of the negative outcomes created by societies dominated by narrow Religious or Ideological paradigms. Throughout history, the slaughter of millions occurred in the name of divinities. Religious conflicts have continued into the twenty-first century, albeit on a contracted basis.

We should also not neglect phony religious convictions. Advocates of secularism usually experience significant pushback from political leadership, who hypocritically use religion to improve their electability. Imagine a present-day U.S. presidential candidate admitting he or she was an agnostic or atheist. He or she would not survive the primaries. Accordingly, paradigm shifts to less rigid religious perspectives are generally difficult to establish in most societies, which contributes to the relatively high level of religiously-based ignorance in the present era.

In addition to the Religious paradigm, the Power paradigm creates a political environment that often promotes a specific Economic paradigm. The current state of capitalism couldn't survive without the support of governments, even while governments seemingly impose restrictive regulations upon the industrial/business sectors. Unbridled capitalism is its own worst enemy. Adam Smith got it wrong when he alluded to an Invisible Hand guiding capitalists to make the right decisions about production, wages, investments, capital improvements, and so on—decisions that *should* ultimately lead to a common good. [97] Rather, Smith should have acknowledged a Clandestine Manipulator, acting behind the scenes, to steer wealth toward the few at the expense of the many. The rise of corporate "fundamentalism" early during the Industrial Revolution ensured the shareholder was more important than society at large. That mentality persists today. Consider how globalization effectively moved industrial production to nations of cheap labor and weak regulations, with little regard for employee welfare and the local environment. Capitalism tends to hide the true cost of doing business, which includes the global impact to the environment, the degradation of air and water quality, ecologically unsound infrastructure development to support business enterprises, the inherent cycles of unemployment, and a host of direct and subtle influences on our way of life, such as noise pollution, traffic congestion, and plastic-ravaged oceans. To date, no one can provide a cost-benefit analysis that adequately weighs the consequences of our current Economic paradigm against any other Economic paradigm, hybrid or otherwise, because we are too euphorically invested in our own consumerism and materialism. This makes us Moderns too prone to errors and too ready to deny alternative economic systems, a sure sign of significant ignorance.

Thus, the most noteworthy effect of the Self, Group, Power, Ideological, Religious, and Economic paradigms over the course of human history is the sustainment, and more often, the expansion of ignorance among the world's peoples. The ignorance studies reviewed in the next chapter will illustrate how ignorance thrives in our societies today.

---

[97] Smith, 349-350.

Implications for the Future

Of the billions of humans alive today, relatively few actively seek to lessen their ignorance by remaining open to even small shifts in their paradigm structure. A paradigm structure is the resultant, integrated neurological network responsible for a person's composite paradigm. Thus, paradigm structure refers to the set of dominant and weak paradigms that create an individual's belief system. Even though paradigm structures are different for each individual, thematic tendencies exist among the general population. The phenomenon is similar to what Plato described in *The Republic* about Socrates' Parable of the Cave. Let's revisit this parable yet again to reinforce some additional aspects relevant to our historical review of paradigms and ignorance.

Individuals confined to a cave are part of a cave society where the artificially-lit shadow world of events, persons, and objects take on an enigmatic reality. The occupants live in a cave-world paradigm of obscurity, unable to fathom the larger world outside. Their paradigm structure remains inflexible and closed to new ideas. For the fortunate of humanity living in comparative comfort, blissful ignorance similarly holds them acquiescently chained within their Socratic caves—unable, unwilling, or uninterested in accepting a larger reality. They prefer to dwell in their caves rather than escape their paradigms or consider other paradigms.

Accordingly, Moderns are far from achieving anything resembling a communal Good Life. The communal Good Life refers to circumstances when human thought and action convey respect for others and the environment—a state of stewardship for everyone and everything, including one's self. If people and societies do not respect each other, conflicts will occur and ultimately escalate. Within the United States, Red-state and Blue-state mentalities persist. In the Middle East and other parts of the world, religiously and ethnically based paradigms create discord and violence. Paradigms also differ widely among the Haves and Have-nots. In these respects, today's world remains unchanged from the recent past.

Similarly, disrespect for the environment—the subjugations of lands, waters, air, and other species—create tensions among peoples that will ultimately undermine what respect they have for each other. A Good Life is impossible to claim if one is breathing polluted air or drinking tainted water.

If we can shift our paradigms to create greater cooperation among individuals and societies, we can manage our ignorance. We can focus our attention on factual and relevant matters that will lead to better decision-making. Otherwise, the high level of ignorance will equate to poor and oftentimes irresponsible decisions and planning.

Respect for others and the environment implies that a social consciousness exists among group members. A social consciousness, then, is a prerequisite for the communal Good Life. In effect, social consciousness is part of a quest for meaning—a journey that examines and interprets the world through the fewest cultural filters. Alternately stated, a society can only attain the communal Good Life if the society's dominant Ideological paradigm values the truth and the continued quest for the truth. In Harari-speak, numerous communal imagined orders would exist, with the search for the truth preeminent among all.

If people and/or groups continue to believe that one race or religion is superior to another when the evidence is overwhelmingly contrary, their ignorance (and perhaps obstinacy) would deny humanity the opportunity to advance as a global community. Their actions would neither serve the greater good nor help achieve the communal Good Life. The current state of ignorance, a product of the existing dominant paradigms, is accordingly the major obstacle in this Truth Quest[98] and a roadblock to achieving the communal Good Life.

In the modern era, the concept of a holistic truth often seems foreign. Despite factual evidence and a highly refined and disciplined process to seek the truth—specifically, the scientific method—people remain largely ignorant of the physical workings of their immediate environments. More importantly, they fail to comprehend the meaning and significance of the physical relationships and principles of Nature that they rely on for their survival. The troubling aspect of this phenomenon is that in no other period in history have people had greater access to the truth than those living today. Access to information, both factual and fake, in post-industrial societies, is literally at one's fingertips. Instead, being a consumer within a global economic machine is job one, not reducing one's knowledge deficits or understanding the true and the relevant. Thus, a significant number of individuals doubt the systematic logic and the accumulation of knowledge associated with the Scientific paradigm. They can't make

---

[98] Herman, Class notes.

the connection that the technology at their disposal is undeniable evidence that the scientific method is valid—the same method used to develop the theory of evolution and the molecular science behind the Earth's thermodynamic changes. Ignorance reigns supreme among a large and unfortunately influential segment of the U.S. and world populations.

It is imperative, then, to explore the reasons for the preponderance of ignorance and determine viable ways to break the persistent grip ignorance has on humanity. In the next chapter, we will review research that examines political and social ignorance. Our review will assist in categorizing types of ignorance and facilitate an analysis of the causes behind ignorance.

As a prelude to the next chapter, let's examine a specific contemporary example that illustrates ignorance's impact on the human future. Stephan Schwartz has applied the term willful ignorance to people who have developed a rationale for ignoring the human impact of their actions.[99] Willful ignorance is perhaps less a type of ignorance and more an attempt to control human perspectives in order to achieve a desired result for group and/or personal gain. From Schwartz's perspective, by controlling information, the power elite can create critical knowledge deficits and cognitive deficiencies that contribute to the public's ignorance. These deficits and deficiencies will form a framework for analyzing ignorance in the next chapter.

Willful ignorance can have legal implications within the justice system. The reader can find numerous examples in the public health arena, such as the willful efforts of the tobacco industry to mislead the public on the dangers of cigarette smoke and of the chemical industry to take adequate protections to prevent air and water pollution. Willful ignorance should not be confused with culpable ignorance or considered a form of self-deception.[100] Lynch gives a medical example in which a doctor fails to review the latest treatment options and side effects associated with a procedure he performs on a patient.[101] As a result, the patient suffers a serious condition. The doctor is culpably ignorant, not willfully ignorant, in this case because his actions were not intentional, but he is, nevertheless, still legally accountable.

---

[99] Schwartz (2012), 268-269.

[100] Lynch, 505-523.

[101] Ibid, 506.

Lynch also goes on to use famed Nazi, Albert Speer, to explain why willful ignorance cannot be synonymous with self-deception.[102] Speer himself described how a top Nazi official warned him not to visit concentrations camps because what he would see there would probably upset him. Speer took the advice but obviously had a suspicion that something despicably egregious was happening at these facilities. Speer was not deceiving himself, either intentionally or unintentionally, but he was deliberately avoiding learning a truth—a meaningful truth within his sphere of influence. Since Speer should have had a suspicion of prisoner maltreatment, there is no way his actions can be classified a self-deception. For him to deceive himself, he would have had to claim that he had allowed himself to believe a falsehood that conditions at the camps were satisfactory—a highly unlikely scenario in this case. Additionally, Speer could not reasonably claim that the act of determining concentration camp procedures would have been exceptionally demanding on him. He was willfully ignorant by keeping himself uninformed of camp operations. (Note: "Demandingness" is one of Lynch's terms for situational tests to determine whether a person's state of ignorance is willful. One cannot expect an individual to expend an unreasonable, personally dangerous, or extremely demanding effort in pursuit of a truth. Ignorance would not be willful under such circumstances. Speer's situation was definitely not one of demandingness.)

The different forms of ignorance presented above are easily subject to teleological misinterpretations. One should not assume that a hidden, higher purpose is at work or that conspiracies to manipulate knowledge are prevalent. Such assumptions will derail any efforts to attain a communal Good Life. Paradigms control both the perpetrators and their victims. We shouldn't prematurely assume that someone or some group is willfully "out to get us" through their ignorance, feigned or not.

Still, many of the paradigms in which ignorance flourishes stem from belief systems that lack logical legitimacy. These include faith-based perspectives of the way the world came to be and is. Those who consider themselves on a Truth Quest should not feel discouraged by their encounters with those with a religious agenda. A divinely inspired paradigm may appear an impenetrable fortress, but statistically, the unreasonable and irrational zealots of religion are a

[102] Ibid, 505-506.

minor fraction of the world's population. The religious experience is not immune to using the evaluative processes of the Socratic and scientific methods. Even hunter-gatherer societies have evaluated their own and others' perspectives through formal processes. Native Americans, have employed concepts such as the Medicine Wheel to understand the paradigmatic nature of the human mind. [103] Religious paradigms can and do shift.

Many other paradigms of ignorance exist beyond those associated with faith. Other types of ignorance include political, racial, ethnic, social class, educational, and psychological. Political ignorance stems from paradigms based on narrow socioeconomic perspectives, which includes the role of societal authority. Ignorance founded in racial, ethnic, and social class beliefs often has an historical context stemming from a fusion of multicultural paradigms. Educational ignorance has two major contributing factors, the inability of an individual to acquire knowledge due to educational system deficiencies and the individual's failure to acquire knowledge when the opportunity exists to do so. Psychological ignorance includes, but is not limited to, a failure to explore beyond one's current knowledge base because of emotional circumstances. These emotional states cause the person to remain wary of changes from the status quo or to create a longing for a mythical past when life was purportedly better.

Whatever its origin, ignorance is nothing new. Our historical review has demonstrated how ignorance has persisted from era to era, typically at high or very high levels. Whether people lived as hunter-gatherers, pastoral herders, agricultural societies, or industrial nations, the bulk of humanity has failed to make use of its opportunities to lift its shroud of ignorance. In the present, the phenomenon persists despite a growing prosperity and advances in formal education. The present era has seen a dramatic rise in the number of people with specific knowledge and skills, in the dispersion of general knowledge, and in the scope and frequency of communications. Technological capitalism, which requires a skilled workforce, has helped to shape the education systems largely responsible for these knowledge gains. Yet, this expanding public knowledge largely consists of a mass-media set of information of known knowns, which have minimal impact on the level of ignorance. (Recall the earlier discussion that removes known

[103] Storm, "The Teaching of the Medicine Wheel," from the introduction to *Seven Arrows.*

knowns from the assessment of ignorance level.) Thus, the current Age of Ignorance perseveres due to the corruptive forces upon the noösphere and the inadequate identification of Big Picture knowledge.

Only by exploring the causes of ignorance can humanity enter a New Age of Enlightenment, develop the skill sets to engage in a collective Truth Quest, and prescribe the ethical principles that define the communal Good Life.

The next chapter explains many of the causes of our current Age of Ignorance.

Chapter 5: Ignorance Research

"Real knowledge is to know the extent of one's ignorance." - Confucius

Fortunately, academia has not ignored the topic of ignorance. Researchers have found numerous ways to assess the cultural, social, and political aspects of ignorance in the modern era. In the following sections, we sample pertinent studies on present-day ignorance and examine the role of paradigms in effecting the varied states of public ignorance. The results of the research provide direct evidence that ignorance is a widespread characteristic of modernity. The research has also been able to assign ignorance types to specific behaviors, providing a means to determine correlations between an explicit brand of ignorance and the associated enabling paradigms.

Trust in Government and Avoidance Behaviors

Two researchers, Shepherd and Kay, conducted five related studies in the areas of economics, the environment, and energy to test their hypothesis that "ignorance—as a function of the system justifying tendencies it may activate—may, ironically, breed more ignorance." [104] Their study is pertinent because of the way the

[104] Shepherd, 264.

researchers constructed their hypothesis and applied system justification theory to sociopolitical issues. In simple terms, the researchers attempted to demonstrate how individuals can rationalize an ignorant position.

Understandably, people have some level of ignorance about certain topics—climate change, foreign affairs, economic policies, and more. For the many intertwined and complex issues that exist in the modern era, most citizens rely on government to "figure it out." Citizens have generally come to accept that government either has or can acquire the resources to solve problems. Thus, the public finds it easiest to justify the systems that are in place to deal with the intricacies and challenges society faces (<u>interpretational or dependency ignorance</u>). Accordingly, citizen trust in governmental authority remains generally strong.[105] The reality is there are few options in addressing the significant issues of the day. However, by relying on the government, citizens can then rationalize their reasons for not learning relevant information about complex issues, thereby furthering their ignorance.[106] Their avoidance behavior—the failure to invest time in understanding pertinent issues—feeds their ignorance. Thus, in Shepherd and Kay's situational model, ignorance begets greater ignorance. Their findings are worth quoting:

> Across five studies in which diverse methodologies were used, we have provided evidence for a psychological chain of events that serves to increase system support and status quo maintenance in two related ways: first, through increased government trust and support for extant government procedures and, second, through the avoidance of information that would challenge this trust and might otherwise educate the individual and lead to action as opposed to inaction. Evidence for this model was found in the context of both novel and familiar issues, including

---

[105] Though people are wary of government and will protest against authority on a number of issues, they inherently recognize that significant problems require a significant effort to resolve. Problems won't fix themselves. The complexities of the modern era demand, at the very least, a limited government or authority system.

[106] Ibid, 264.

energy technology, the management and depletion of oil reserves, and the 2008 economic recession.[107]

Shepherd and Kay's results provide a conceptual foundation for one cause of our current Age of Ignorance: To sustain existing cultural and authoritarian paradigms, the power elite find ways to manipulate a socio-psychological causality-dependency chain to increase the public's ignorance. In simple terminology, the dependency boils down to "We (in power) will tell you (the public) what you need to know." Sadly, the more complex issues become, the less likely the public will delve into the details with sufficient scrutiny. The public's ignorance only elevates. To some degree, the media and the internet facilitate the growth of ignorance, oversimplifying facts and events through video clips and sound bites. Both the Self and Power paradigms are the greatest drivers of this type of ignorance. If there's no imminent danger or personal discomfort associated with a policy or area of concern, the self will defer to authority and focus on more pleasurable endeavors. Also, under the prevailing Power paradigms in the U.S. and other nation-states, most of us have been acculturated into accepting the notion that authority, in the form of parents, institutions, and government, has the wherewithal to tackle problems.

Research bottom line: People tend to defer to government or authority when confronted by complex matters—a state of dependency for interpreting and assessing multifaceted information. By putting their trust in authority and avoiding their own independent appraisals, they sustain or increase their ignorance. In effect, they avoid acquiring new knowledge as if the effort were taboo. (Recall that the taboo is a source of ignorance.) The public will be especially vulnerable if the knowledge required to reduce its ignorance is nuanced or susceptible to distortions.

Can anything be done to minimize the influences driving the growth of ignorance among the public? Yes, but to do so would require targeting the public's fears about its own inadequacies, which are buried within Self paradigms. It would also require exposing organizational weaknesses in existing authority structures, thereby diminishing the influence of the prevalent Power paradigms. Hostility would likely arise between the public and those in power, creating a

---

[107] Ibid, 275.

climate of mistrust. One way to overcome such obstacles is for competent authority to provide a helpful, sufficiently detailed Big Picture overview of an issue. Trust in authority should subsequently strengthen. The Big Pictures should be presented as "teaching moments" in story format, such as carefully measured explanations for the causes of climate change or of the means to combat a pandemic or of the impact of economic policies and more. In the United States, a president known for his or her integrity would be the ideal deliverer of such a Big Picture message.

Unfortunately, as we'll see in the next section, the message between the government and the governed often contains incomplete and/or barely comprehensible information within a cluttered background of printed, audio, and video noise—the fake news, half-truths, falsified information, and other misrepresentations from a variety of seemingly competent sources. Many information panhandlers provide misleading data across a spectrum of media and social media platforms, including some from foreign sources. Ultimately, the public ends up accepting the sources with which they are most comfortable, not necessarily the most reliable.

Factual Ignorance and Belief Perseverance

Shepherd and Kay are not the only researchers to draw a conclusion about the relationship between autocratic structures and ignorance. In an effort to characterize research done on political misperceptions, Nyhan and Reifler reviewed numerous results from a spectrum of research related to political ignorance. Their analyses pertain directly to one of the contributing factors to the Age of Ignorance—misinformation. The researchers identify dissimilarities between the "uninformed" and the "misinformed."[108] Distinctions between the uninformed person and the misinformed individual are relevant from a causality perspective (determining the source of one's ignorance) but irrelevant when assessing outcomes. Whether people are uninformed or misinformed, the net effect is a collective increase in public ignorance. As discussed below, the results of Nyhan and Reifler's research align with the two foundational precepts in this book: (1) a blended composite of the seven major paradigms drives our ignorance and (2) ignorance remains high in the present because

[108] Nyhan, 304.

people fail to take advantage of their ready access to factual and well-vetted knowledge—including access to information that could clear their misperceptions. Though both the uninformed and the misinformed can take action to limit their ignorance, they rarely do.

Based on the work of other researchers, Nyhan and Reifler maintain that political preferences stem from the misinformation a person accepts as factual, which is why they also refer to collective misperceptions as factual ignorance. [109] They designed four experiments to determine whether corrective information contained in credible media reports could decrease the political misperceptions held by a misinformed public. Nyhan and Reifler wanted to build and improve on the work of Bullock, who found that the psychological condition known as the belief perseverance paradigm would generally cause research subjects to intensify their belief in information that is subsequently discredited. [110] Belief perseverance refers to the persistence of a belief system, even in the presence of contrary factual evidence. Thus, any attempt to shift a paradigm will encounter emotional resistance, even after competent authority has discredited the original information.

Significantly, unlike Bullock's experiments, Nyhan and Reifler added an additional step after providing participants corrected information. The researchers always informed their participants whether the revised information was, in fact, truthful. In their hypotheses, Nyhan and Reifler took the psychological position that "humans are goal-directed information processors who tend to evaluate information with a directional bias toward reinforcing their pre-existing views." [111] Their results validated the psychological effect.[112] A person's existing political ideology affects his response to corrective information. Subjects who held perspectives aligned to the content of the corrected (true) information generally accepted the revised information. Subjects with opposing perspectives to the content of the corrected (true) information more staunchly held to their misperceptions even after being told that the corrected information was factual.

---

[109] Ibid.

[110] Ibid, 306.

[111] Ibid, 307.

[112] Ibid, 323.

Research bottom line: In the face of factual information, people will likely not change their perspective, and tend to hold onto false perspectives even more resolutely. Since these people have been presented the facts (truthful information), their ignorance is no longer "blind." Their ignorance level has actually elevated.

In accordance with the paradigm-ignorance theory presented in this book, we would state that a person's composite paradigm dominates his thoughts and behaviors preventing both paradigm shifts and any desire to access and/or accept new, clarifying information.

Voter Ignorance

The way the public votes in U.S. elections seems puzzling at times. One way to assess voter acumen is to take measure of an individual's depth of knowledge of the political landscape. The results should indicate whether individuals would make informed decisions in casting votes and whether they would contribute in a meaningful way to the public discourse on the spectrum of socioeconomic issues. This is precisely what Carpini and Keeter did when they conducted a follow-up study on the U.S. public's political knowledge thirty-five to forty years after a series of initial studies were conducted in the 1940s and 1950s.

The earlier studies repeatedly found the public insufficiently informed on political matters, including basic civics.[113] Carpini and Keeter expected that the higher overall level of education attained by the current population should improve their general political knowledge compared to the population in the original study.[114] From the late 1940s to the late 1980s, there was a four-year grade jump in the public's (average) level of education. They also considered other societal change factors, such as the greater use of television and other mass communications technologies, which should also improve overall political knowledge.

In their 1989 study, the researchers constructed their survey to "measure a range of substantive political knowledge, including government institutions and procedures, contemporary issues, civil

[113] Carpini, 583.

[114] Ibid, 584.

rights and liberties, and current government policy."[115] Fourteen of the questions used in their random telephone survey duplicated the past studies, adhering to original question style and format. Statistical analysis of responses determined that overall knowledge level is stable but the 1989 participants were less knowledgeable about the politics of their time. From their findings, Carpini and Keeter concluded that the U.S. public education system holds much of the responsibility for the lack of improvement in political knowledge.[116] Their results also indicate that school systems are failing to motivate citizens to fulfill their civic duties since respondents were only able to average about fifty percent correct answers on a test of fundamental political and civic knowledge.[117]

Research Bottom line: Approximately half of the U.S. public is poorly prepared and/or lacks sufficient interest to deal with the plethora of political and socioeconomic complexities of the modern era. Such broad political ignorance degrades the institutions of democracy. The U.S. educational network bears some responsibility for the overall state of voter knowledge, at least up to the time that internet usage became so pervasive. In the twenty-first century, the situation is no better. Surveys conducted in 2006 found that "only 42 percent of Americans could even name the three branches of the federal government" and that "only 28 percent could name two or more of the five rights guaranteed by the First Amendment to the Constitution."[118] The 2016 U.S. presidential election provides more recent evidence of factual and voter ignorance and the effects of belief preservation and Self paradigms—not because of the outcome of the election but because of contradictory rationales during exit polls.[119] Below, we will see that rationality is not always rational.

---

[115] Ibid, 586.

[116] Ibid, 606-607.

[117] Ibid, 588-589.

[118] Somin, 258.

[119] See https://www.cnn.com/election/2016/results/exit-polls.

Ignorance and Liberties

Surveys are not the only confirmation that ignorance limits citizens' abilities to support democratic institutions. The concept is also rooted in political philosophy. Garnett conceptually dissected the effects of ignorance and physical incompetence on the philosophical foundations of liberty.[120] Physical incompetence refers to the lack of physical ability to act due to limited strength, coordination, or other physiological factors. Ignorance (for the purposes of the study) refers to the lack of mental ability to act due to knowledge deficiencies and/or limited cognitive abilities. Both affect an individual's capacity to exercise her personal and political freedoms. Garnett concludes that liberty is quantifiable and functionally dependent on both a person's level of ignorance and his physical competency. The less ignorant a person is, the greater his liberties. To illustrate, a person may be at liberty to vote for candidates or referenda under a political right or freedom; however, that liberty diminishes if a person cannot meaningfully cast his vote, such as lacking knowledge of the candidates or issues.

Research bottom line: The masses of uninformed voters worldwide illustrate that liberty is often a façade. The political paradigm of democracy relies on a voting populace that is knowledgeable and not capricious. Evidence points to the contrary, even in societies with formal education systems. Garnett's work reinforces the conclusion drawn from earlier assessments in this book that our current Age of Ignorance is a real phenomenon.

"Talk is Cheap" Ignorance and Rational Irrationality

No contemporary issue reveals the rampant state of ignorance in modernity than the debate over climate change.[121] Humphrey confronts the issue head-on in his examination of recent public surveys in the United States and United Kingdom regarding the actions

---

[120] Garnett, 428-446.

[121] Later in this book, we acknowledge that there is finally, in 2019, a majority of U.S. citizens who accept that human-induced climate change has contributed to recent global warming. However, this statement in no way reflects the public's level of understanding of the mechanisms responsible for worldwide temperature increases and the associated impact on the biosphere.

necessary to address the effects of climate change. In simple terms, he found that "talk is cheap," however, his own words are poignant:

> . . . we can instead understand simulative eco-politics as a manifestation of rational ignorance combined with rational irrationality. This can lead to political posturing, an over-moralized politics, 'cheap-talk' solutions and the manipulation of information costs on the part of interested lobbies. While 'simulative eco-politics' does not mark a radical new departure, it does mark out some high-profile environmental problems, such as climate change, as seriously intractable.[122]

In the surveys, people were strongly in favor of actions to reduce the effects of climate change, yet when the survey asked if they would support increases to their taxes or accept changes in their routine, few accepted these options. The "inconvenient truth" was that people opted not to inconvenience themselves. Humphrey called this trait rational ignorance or rational irrationality depending upon the cause of a person's reluctance to accept inconvenience. A rationally ignorant person is protective of his comforts. A rationally irrational individual acts out of blind spite, fancy, or whimsical illogic, ignoring the data and arguments against his position. Rational ignorance and/or rational irrationality stem from the Self paradigm, especially if inconvenience, personal comforts, or wealth are at stake. They may also stem from the influence of a Group paradigm where an individual blindly follows others in their misguided belief system(s).

With respect to climate change, Humphrey also refers to these types of rationalizations on the part of the public as simulative eco-politics, where politicians and/or the public promote ideas in the abstract either never intending to act on them or trivializing the effort required to implement them. The political platitudes such as "we need to find ways to "x"—where x is something like "reduce our use of fossil fuels"—are bantered about without purposive intent. Sloganeering and cliché proclamations only add to the public's collective ignorance because they give the impression that there are meaningful plans or policies in place or proposed, or that "we are doing all we can" to address the significant problems of our time.

[122] Humphrey, 156

Humphrey's premise of simulative eco-politics parallels Shepherd and Kay's thesis that the public will default to government oversight as the complexities of issues become increasingly evident.

Note first that rational ignorance implies intent. Humphrey viewed the rational irrationality and rational ignorance of study participants as a means to avoid inconvenience. Participants would make an irrational decision by "rationalizing" that the policies or actions that levy a personal cost or burden on them take precedence over policies or actions that cost or burden society on whole. People protect their own comforts first, then society's. Thus, for example, people would rather allow carbon dioxide levels in the atmosphere to rise than pay more for fossil fuels. Additionally, some participants in the study rationalized that some information was not pertinent, and chose to ignore it.

Humphrey's use of rational ignorance and rational irrationality are important and require a closer look. We must understand their mechanisms if we expect to break our patterns of ignorance and our blind adherence to our paradigms. Understanding the influence of rational ignorance and rational irrationality will help us to communicate meaningful and relevant (truthful) information and to develop schemes to promote low-ignorance, communal group-think.

Research bottom line: Rational ignorance and rational irrationality play a large role in sustaining and even elevating ignorance levels. Fear of loss of socioeconomic standing, of personal freedoms, and of personal conveniences and/or comforts (e.g., driving one's car versus taking public transportation) entrench people in their paradigms. The Self, and secondarily, the Group paradigms are the major contributors to these states of ignorance.

Rational Closed-Mindedness

Bayern doesn't take such a negative view as Humphrey in the application of rational ignorance, or even in the use of what he calls rational closed-mindedness. Bayern argues that rational ignorance largely serves as an information filter.[123] A rationally ignorant person is one who decides not to seek or examine new knowledge since there is little or no return on investment for doing so. People prioritize their time and focus on interests they value. According to Bayern, one can

[123] Bayern, 943-945.

acquire excessively extraneous knowledge, which can lead to confusion and faulty decision-making.[124] Information can overwhelm or distract people, such as occurs when too many details obscure the critical factors which are the basis of sound decisions. Similarly, according to Bayern, a rationally closed-minded person would dismiss certain information, concepts, and processes based on prior experience or knowledge.[125] For example, a rationally closed-minded person would choose not to read a suspected junk e-mail before pressing delete. Similarly, a rationally closed-minded atheist would have little patience in listening to a divinity-based sermon. While rational ignorance and closed-mindedness can serve the practical interests of the individual, their indiscreet application can have serious consequences by preventing people from taking the necessary steps to understand and/or question the information they receive. Such people would rarely consider the merit of ideas of opposing political parties. Thus, one group's rationality could be another group's irrationality. Under these circumstances, democratic processes will stumble and perhaps fail.

Research bottom line: Since rational closed-mindedness serves to filter information, it effectively acts as a composite paradigm that locks people into certain perspectives. Society rarely benefits from rigidly-held perspectives. We can expect ignorance levels to be high within these groups and within the larger organizational structure in which such groups and individuals exist.

Rational closed-mindedness is not a paradigm of its own, however. A person's composite paradigm contains the mental filters that cause him to think and act in a rationally closed-minded manner. Likely causes for this behavior stem from one or more dominant paradigms: Self (e.g., ego, comfort), Group (e.g., tribal), Power (e.g., control), Ideological (e.g., adherence to one or more isms), and/or Economic (e.g., financial self-interest).

Functional Knowledge

Ungar takes a more menacing view of knowledge in the modern era by describing a strengthening "undertow of ignorance"

---

[124] Ibid, 944.

[125] Ibid.

that characterizes the "knowledge society." [126] His historical perspective follows:

> Ignorance is anything but a new phenomenon, but it was largely unremarkable and tolerated as more or less inevitable until the relatively recent advent of the so-called information age.[127]

His focus is neither ignorance of highly esoteric scientific knowledge nor the narrow-mindedness of stereotyping. Rather, Ungar's interest is the deficit of functional knowledge that prevents people from making informed decisions. The deficits affect both individual lives and the greater society. As an example, Ungar cites the shortsightedness of American military planners and geopolitical analysts in the 2003 Iraq War. Although information was readily available about the ongoing disputes between Sunni and Shiite Muslims, which could undermine postwar reconstruction, the people in charge excluded the input of knowledgeable sources.[128] By doing so, they created a functional knowledge deficit (FKD), miscalculating the resources required to win the peace.

FKDs abound according to Ungar. They exist in the political, scientific, economic, healthcare, social, and mathematical disciplines, among others. His observations about mathematical skills are especially relevant to sustaining a well-functioning society. Ungar underscores the need in modern society to have the capacity to perform numerical comparisons and deal in probabilities, such as understanding risk.[129] Mathematical illiteracy can affect individuals' abilities to make rational financial choices, which taken together, can have significant socioeconomic impact (e.g., a society entrenched in debt). Thus, ignorance is partly a lack of functional knowledge and partly, the inability to process and interpret existing and new knowledge. In effect, FKDs create ignorance. Thus, FKDs represent cognitive deficiencies that can prevent people from emerging from

---

[126] Unger, 301.

[127] Ibid, 302.

[128] Ibid, 306.

[129] Ibid, 309.

their social, political, economic, religious, and cultural caves. They may "see the light" that could lead them to wisdom but lack the wherewithal to figure out how to reach it. An alternate way to state this: FKDs represent a deficit of the cognitive tools necessary to function properly in one's society. When the deficits exist, ignorance will prevail.

Ungar's analysis includes a discussion of Bauer's knowledge-information paradox or KIP.[130] KIP refers to the exponential increase of information in the modern era and the inability of the human mind to absorb the quantity of meaningful knowledge contained within that information. The phenomenon occurs both in specialized fields and in the generalized aggregate of knowledge necessary to navigate through the challenges of life. (Refer also to the discussion of the noösphere and Pascal's expanding sphere of knowledge in previous chapters.)

For example, doctors who have difficulty keeping up with medical advances will find themselves unable to prescribe the latest treatments for their patients. Citizens may find themselves similarly unable to comprehend the increasing complexity of taxes, insurance, banking and financing, and responsible consumerism. KIP theory aligns well with Shepherd and Kay's thesis that people will defer to governmental authority when political issues begin to overwhelm them. KIP also fits nicely with Humphrey's notion of cost-benefit ignorance. Similar to Humphrey, Ungar has found sufficient theoretical and empirical evidence that "for most persons the costs of attaining specialized knowledge or becoming broadly knowledgeable has become too great for the expected benefits."[131] Ungar, here, is simply expressing Bayern's rational ignorance in alternate terminology.

While the KIP effect—more precisely, the proliferation of knowledge—increases the number and scope of the FKDs that exist within modern society, Ungar identifies a more troubling and sinister effect: the cultural and institutional creation of ignorance, including misinformation.[132] Ungar has numerous examples, such as the tobacco industry's tactics to withhold information, sponsor its own research, and peddle uncertainty about the effects of smoking, or special interest groups' ploy to fund climate-change naysayer-experts, and school

[130] Ibid, 311.

[131] Ibid, 313.

[132] Ibid, 321.

systems' refusals to provide a comprehensive sex education program.[133] As Ungar implies, a cult of ignorance is beginning to plague society—one rooted in preventing the public from acquiring the truth by leveraging and manipulating paradigms favorable to their perspectives.

Research bottom line: FKDs limit how effectively individuals and groups can function in the information age. The scope and magnitude of the information stream in the modern era places an even greater burden on those ill-equipped educationally and emotionally to navigate the complexities of modern life. A reduction in FKDs across society would likewise reduce the overall ignorance level and facilitate paradigm shifts.

FKDs stem largely from dominant paradigms that put too little emphasis on educating the populous on both critical functional knowledge skills and overarching Big Picture themes pertinent to modernity. Through paradigms that stress relevant education, holistic ideologies, and an interconnectedness among society's members, we can make significant inroads into reducing FKDs and, therefore, ignorance. We shall address this in detail in Chapter 9.

The Quirkiness of Political Ignorance

An ignorant populace will severely impede the efficient and effective workings of a democratic society—unless, of course, people were somehow *truly* "rationally ignorant" and collectively acted in an educated and enlightened manner.[134] Accordingly, Gilens decided to evaluate whether the various attitudes Americans held on political issues would differ if the public were better informed. In an elaborate study with detailed statistical analyses, he first determined which study participants had a broader general knowledge of political issues. Then, he exposed all participants to policy-specific information covering the same issues. Based on participant responses, the policy-specific information had a greater influence on the judgments of those with the greater general political knowledge.[135] However, Gilens realized that

---

[133] Ibid.

[134] Gilens, 379.

[135] Ibid, 391-392.

most studies have found Americans ignorant of political matters.[136] Thus, providing policy-specific information to the public at large would only have a small impact in shifting the public's political perspectives.

Research bottom line: Having a strong general knowledge of a topic and subsequently enhancing that knowledge with specific information on that topic increases the possibility of paradigm shifts. The weaker a person's general knowledge, the less effective specific information becomes in stimulating a change in perspective. The study suggests that preexisting ignorance begets continued ignorance. In the political arena, this phenomenon is similar to Shepherd and Kay's government-dependency model. If the government presents complex issues to the public of which they know little, the public will defer policy formulation and action to the government rather than engage with the government or other citizens on the topic.[137]

This study also supports the notion that the greater and more diverse one's knowledge is, the more receptive one is to evaluating and perhaps accepting other perspectives and the less ignorant one is compared to those with a limited scope of knowledge. Big Picture thinking becomes more probable the more diverse one's knowledge is.

Willful Ignorance Revisited

At first glance, the creation of ignorance by groups, corporations, the government, and institutions has similarities to a concept introduced earlier—willful ignorance. However, ignorance generated for political or financial gain differs significantly from willful ignorance. According to Schwartz, willful ignorance arises from the act of denial, not from deception or intentional misinformation.[138] Schwartz uses the example of the religiously faithful who subscribe to creationist theory, denying the validity of data obtained from the scientific method. Many deniers are sincere in

---

[136] Ibid, 379.

[137] The dependency model does not apply to public issues in conflict with strong belief systems. Segments of the public will attempt to shape government policies on such issues as abortion, the death penalty, and same-sex marriage if the policies fracture their personal-religious-ideological paradigms.

[138] Schwartz (2010), 137.

their assertions. Ignorance peddlers are usually disingenuous, seeking an advantage. The deniers and peddlers may join forces for their mutual benefit, in which cases they can become a formidable political force, drowning society in ignorance.

Does a Natural "Veil of Ignorance" Exist?

We consider next an evolutionary biological contribution to human ignorance. Are we predisposed to ignore certain traits in others in order to improve our individual or group survival? Queller and Strassman, two evolutionary biologists, suggest there are heritable factors that work to this end, shrouding individuals in a veil of ignorance, concealing information that might otherwise lead to aggressive behaviors. For example, many males in a honeybee hive mate with a single queen. While genetic markers are available that would allow the various bee clans within the hive to distinguish from each other, the bees collectively acquire an odor that suppresses the information. This veil of ignorance prevents competitive behaviors and facilitates group cohesion.

The researchers note that the red fire ants don't possess this ability. As a result, worker ants can distinguish which genes are similar to theirs within the colony. The workers will kill all queens without their genetic marker.

Researchers have yet to uncover an equivalent, genetically-based veil of ignorance among humans that would benefit the species. In fact, history supports a contrary condition. We seem genetically disposed to recognize differences within the species, much like the red fire ant. In fact, we seem overly conscious of these differences. Human history has followed the pattern exhibited by red ants where we aggressively subdue those who are different. The Ideological paradigm of colonialism is a prime example. The prevalence of racism is another.

Analysis and Discussion

The preceding sections provided numerous examples of the ways modern researchers have characterized public ignorance. They applied concepts from psychology, philosophy, political science, and sociology in analyzing their results and in developing their ideas. The significance of the varied concepts and theories of ignorance presented thus far will become clearer by applying them to a singular issue: the recent controversies surrounding climate change.

Within the political realm, most people find complex and challenging issues overwhelming, so they block out their concerns and defer the problems to government authority, and by doing so, as Shepherd and Kay's studies found, increase their ignorance of specific issues. Deference to authority is indicative of a dominant presence of the Power paradigm. Climatologists, however, could also inflict this ignorance upon the public unintentionally by providing unnecessarily complex descriptions of the science behind climate change. The climatologists may be so entrenched in their science that they fail to communicate effectively to the public, such as failing to present Big Picture elements associated with climate change. The media could intentionally or unintentionally do the same by presenting, as credible sources, the profiteers and climate-change naysayers who add confusion and intricacy to the issues by putting their own spin upon the science and origins of climate change. These two simple scenarios illustrate how easily the misinformed can join the uninformed in a dizzying array of contradictory perspectives of the causes and repercussions of climate change.

Psychological effects also come into play when people are presented with new knowledge that differs from their longstanding beliefs, such as highlighted in Bullock's belief perseverance paradigm and Nyhan and Reifler's goal-directed information processing. Thus, when the public processes information on the anthropogenic causes of climate change, they may not be psychologically ready to accept the information. Negative learning events from their past may keep people from accepting scientific consensus, or perhaps they fear that government actions to address climate change will threaten their livelihood (e.g., coal industry unemployment). The Self and/or Group paradigms begin to dominate.

A fine line exists between goal-directed information processing and the self-interest Humphrey exposed in his studies. Humphrey found that the public, on whole, is unwilling to pay more or endure personal inconvenience to mitigate the human contributions to climate change. The origins of these types of head-in-the-sand ignorance are difficult to determine. One could even rationalize that ignorance based on self-interest stems from a genetic survival instinct (Self paradigm). Another could make a case that cultural influences have shaped behaviors, persuading people to accept a specific socioeconomic paradigm—which, in the modern era, is the current capitalist mindset whose roots extend back to the ideas of John Locke and Adam Smith (Economic paradigm).

A danger lurks in too-quickly accepting many of the plausible causes of ignorance, however. Defaulting to the cultural, physiological, and psychological motivations behind ignorance may entangle the analysis in oversimplified themes or distracting side issues. For example, if one applies Bayern's rational ignorance and rational closed-mindedness concepts to climate change, how does the researcher distinguish between rational ignorance and self-interested ignorance? The selective filtering of information may appear rational but in fact be selfish. Anyone could claim that they are acting rationally by disregarding the scientific principles behind the anthropogenic causes of climate change. They might argue that they recognize that they don't possess the cognitive abilities or have the time to invest to understand the science (perhaps a self-demandingness test). Are such excuses rational or motivated by self-interest? For now, the question is rhetorical, but it leads to a fundamental question not yet addressed in this book: Who decides what information is worth knowing? The answer lies in Ungar's concept of FKDs.

To understand the significance of the current Age of Ignorance, we must reiterate that ignorance does not describe the human condition of "not knowing everything." No one knows everything. Rather, much of the ignorance in the modern era stems from significant deficits in functional knowledge. Functional knowledge not only refers to knowledge of certain information (facts and concepts) but also the ability to process information logically and unemotionally. We shall refer to this latter ability as cognitive processing.

More precisely, deficits in functional knowledge could be either or both of the following: the lack of certain critical information and/or the inability to acquire the information even though it exists. The second deficit illustrates poor cognitive processing skills, such as allowing an emotion or a belief system to cloud one's perspective.[139] Another processing deficit may include the inappropriate application

[139] This in no way implies that people can "flick a switch" and discard their emotions and beliefs, only that they must understand how their emotions and paradigms are affecting their actions and behaviors. Plato might say that people must be able to determine when their emotions and beliefs are strengthening the chains that bind them to their darkened caves.

of the scientific method or of another logic-based approach to analyze a situation. As Ungar warns, some of the deficits may be by design, such as when governments or corporations keep facts from the public or place an emotional spin upon events.

Functional knowledge is superior to general knowledge because it enables the individual to make decisions and choices that contribute to his own and his society's well-being. Historical era, environment, and culture determine a large part of the functional knowledge an individual must acquire to avoid a deficit. For example, about fifty years ago, a San male in the southern African bush had to acquire functionally critical hunting skills to support himself and his clan. With the outside world infringing upon their lands, the San had to acquire new functional knowledge in order to thrive. [140] In pre-industrial history, a society's neighbors, geography, and climate helped to shape the knowledge that was functional. As technological innovation transformed societies from agricultural to industrial to globalized post-industrial (technocratic) economies, the effect has been to standardize functional knowledge across societies.

Technology has dramatically increased the types and breadth of functional knowledge one must acquire. This means a larger number of people in the modern era must have a minimum threshold of functional knowledge to make positive contributions to society. Use of the internet is one obvious example. Still, Moderns and their immediate families can survive with a narrow scope of functional (and general) knowledge. Socioeconomic systems and their associated services provide the general public in most nations the ability to earn a living and thrive despite their ignorance. Technology and science have supplied some of the leverage necessary to overcome many of the ills associated with the Age of Ignorance—"There's an App for that." However, with the effects of FKDs being moderated by software tools, we should evaluate whether we are mechanically marching toward a

---

[140] Although I wish the San could retain their lands and way of life, the San must face their new reality, adapt, and acquire new functional knowledge to survive and thrive. The experience of the San is only one of the many tragedies that have occurred throughout history—societies, ethnicities, cultures, and subcultures being overwhelmed either intentionally or unintentionally by outsiders. For example, had truth-oriented, functional knowledge-promoting societies existed during the European colonization era, the indigenous peoples of North and South America would not have suffered many of the miseries they endured under European imperialism and colonialism (except perhaps disease).

tipping point of global disparity and despair. A pandemic of ignorance could arise from software-based paradigms. More so than in any previous era, we must raise the level of our personal and collective functional knowledge to force paradigm shifts that allow us to deviate wisely from the paths our current set of dominant paradigms are paving. We must do so without relying on or being seduced by paradigms imbedded in software, such as advertising algorithms or suggestive ideologies encountered in our web browsing experience. We must greatly enhance two distinct components of our functional knowledge, the personal and the socially conscious.[141] Both are necessary to minimize ignorance.

A hypothetical climate change example using automotive engineers will illustrate the differences between functional and general knowledge and exemplify the social consciousness component of functional knowledge. A fictitious automotive engineer, Mr. Van Carson, earns a good salary and sees to his and his family's immediate needs. Carson's functional knowledge is highly specialized. His general knowledge is diverse; he knows much about sports, theater, fishing, and home-project carpentry. While Carson's functional knowledge contributes to society's transportation needs, he and his associates have failed to focus on engineering solutions that would reduce the automobile's contributions to global warming. Though highly skilled, they have a FKD in an area that would improve outcomes for society. Carson and his fellow engineers continue to design inefficient, gas guzzling, greenhouse-gas-emitting "muscle" cars, trucks, and SUVs for the public. Gadgets, power, and luxuries are more important in the present than an overheated Earth in the future. Carson and his team lack the functional knowledge to embrace the Big Picture, living their lives in their automotive-engineer cave. Obviously, Carson has bosses who have bosses so the cave is crowded. This hypothetical lack of functional knowledge is a real-world systemic problem similar to Ungar's description of the shortsightedness of

[141] A Marxian economist might view the division of functional knowledge as an inevitable social-evolutionary development associated with the persistent division of labor under capitalism.

American military planners in the 2003 Iraq War.[142] This sample FKD phenomenon is widespread and encompasses every facet of life. In the present example, without the government setting fuel efficiency standards, Carson, his bosses, and his fellow engineers would have little incentive to create more fuel-efficient vehicles.[143]

The prevalence of the FKD problem in the modern era is unrelated to Bauer's KIP. The explosion of information drowning the human senses in the present is not responsible for the wholesale FKDs that have created the Age of Ignorance. A person can avoid FKDs through exposure to holistic educational opportunities that help him acquire interactive life skills, diversified knowledge, and cognitive processing acumen. A weakness in any of these three critical areas can signify a sizable FKD. Thus, an individual with expansive general and highly specialized knowledge could easily have FKDs, such as automotive engineer Carson. The reverse is also true; a person without a FKD could lack general knowledge. Functional knowledge usually includes occupational knowledge and skills—from janitor to field worker to the production line to CEO. However, as seen in the automotive engineering example, functional knowledge must also include the incorporation of Big Picture themes and the ability to cognitively process elements of the Big Picture. Social consciousness evolves from Big Picture knowledge and cognitive processing skills.

Big Picture knowledge consists of raw information, concepts, and attitudes that support the acquisition and assessment of verifiable content about our world. Cognitive processing represents the methods that enable the individual to uncover the interrelationships among disparate elements of Big Picture knowledge. Cognitive processing skills allow the individual to apply scientific and Socratic methods to

---

[142] We must also accept the possibility that Carson and his bosses have no FKD but are intentionally ignoring information for self and group (corporate) profit. Whether a FKD stems from a true deficit in knowledge or from intentional reasons, from a societal perspective, the FKD still exists.

Carson could also argue that he is just meeting the customers' desires, offering options for the consumers. A counter-argument to this might be that advertisers are "convincing" consumers that they need power, status, and luxury that align with and fulfill their paradigms.

[143] A conspiracy theorist might offer that by not developing fuel-efficient vehicles, the auto industry and Big Oil were working together to increase the demand for and price of oil, and therefore the profits generated.

examine the interrelationships among the various fields of knowledge. Functional knowledge therefore facilitates access to the truth.

Earlier, the question arose, "Who decides what knowledge is worth knowing?" No specific person or group should have this authority. By separating fact from fiction and applying disciplined methods of examination, the answer should become self-evident. In any era, the functional knowledge necessary to achieve a communal oneness should be the priority, thereby indicating what is worth knowing. Of course, our paradigms must shift if we ever expect to attain societal bliss. Later, we will introduce other dominant paradigms which can help us reach this goal.

Consider another situation where a person has Big Picture knowledge of climate change but has not acquired an in-depth knowledge of the science behind climate change. She has, however, learned the basic driving forces behind global warming. When presented with new (to her) information about climate change, she can determine whether the new knowledge aligns with what she already knows. Her cognitive processing skills give her the ability to question herself and others about the validity of the new information. Her interrogatives fulfill the function of Socratic questions or act as a simplified and personalized version of the scientific method.

Yet another example involving climate change will serve to illustrate the application of functional knowledge and the manner in which functional knowledge minimizes ignorance. Concerned citizen and secretary, Jane Q. Public, is trying to decide which of two candidates she favors in an upcoming election. The candidates have similar positions on all issues but one. They differ on the selection of a fuel for a power plant that will serve their district. One favors "clean" coal plants, and the other natural gas (methane). The natural gas candidate maintains that his fuel of choice is much superior to coal because it produces much less carbon dioxide. Jane has read a little about global warming and its causes and has doubts about the veracity of the natural gas candidate's claim. She uses Internet search engines to find further information about the effects of coal and natural gas and learns that natural gas does produce less carbon dioxide, but through processing and incomplete combustion releases significant quantities of methane, a more potent greenhouse gas. From a global warming perspective, the two plants are effectively equivalent. Jane does further research and learns that coal companies often employ strip-mining practices that pose significantly greater risks to the environment than the installation of natural gas pipelines. Jane supports the natural gas candidate in the election, but also sends him a letter voicing her concerns about his continued support for fossil-fuel solutions to the nation's energy needs instead of developing alternative energy options.

In the preceding example, Citizen Jane had limited knowledge of climate change, but she possessed the initiative to seek out amplifying information. From Garnett's perspective, Jane is politically free and capably engaged in the democratic process. Her questioning attitude, open-mindedness, and logical approaches to assess the candidates' positions exemplify the cognitive-processing skills component of functional knowledge. She has exhibited the critical skills set that support informed decision-making. For the decision-making process to be nationally and globally beneficial, however, the Jane's of the world must become a majority.

Since the hunter-gatherer epoch, every era of history has confronted a similar scenario: How to apply functional knowledge to make the best possible decisions to improve the individual's and group's probability of survival. Humans must *figure out* how to *survive* and *thrive* with others and within the environments that support them; they must acquire a requisite level of functional knowledge. FKDs could lead to disastrous consequences for a society. Culture, religion, the system of authority, and ego can impede a society in its efforts to acquire important knowledge. For example, inhabitants of island ecosystems must quickly learn that they cannot consume their critical resources without a plan to sustain them at an appropriate level. Otherwise, they threaten their own survival.

In *Collapse: How Societies Choose to Fail and Succeed*, Jared Diamond provides numerous examples of FKDs that inadvertently forced ecosystem collapse for the local humans.[144] One example included the residents of Rapa Nui (Easter Island) who depleted their island resources through deforestation and overharvesting.[145]

Easter Islanders' FKDs stemmed in large part from the lack of a fundamental cognitive processing skill; they lacked a questioning attitude. They failed to question their deforestation practices and to consider the impact of their actions until it was too late. The residents of Rapa Nui lived in a spiritual-supernatural-social class paradigm that

---

[144] Diamond did not use the term FKD explicitly but implicitly did.

[145] Diamond, *Collapse*, 102-111.

impeded the development of intellectual practices. None of their cognitive skill sets approximated either the Socratic or scientific method. Other hunter-gatherer societies shared similar fates, but the results were not as devastating since they lived on continents rather than islands. Most continental ecosystems are more forgiving due to their expanse or, at the very least, offer easy access to suitable nearby environments. For most of human history, early continental societies with FKDs had little need to balance their wants with their neighbors and with the resources available in their local environments. They could become nomadic or warlike to find or acquire other food and material resources to survive and thrive.

As agricultural civilizations became the norm, the division of labor within society allowed some group members to pursue cognitive activities. Some societies, such as the ancient Greeks and Romans, formulated questioning methodologies. While FKDs still prevailed on whole, they were able to answer the question, "What knowledge is worth knowing," to a level well above most of their contemporaries. Unfortunately for the Greeks and many other ancient civilizations, the power elite had FKDs that kept ignorance in their societies at a high level. Survive and thrive they did—until ignorance eventually undermined their continued success. Societies that fail to shift their dominant paradigms to counter internal and external threats are destined for failure. Their cognitive processing skills will stagnate and decline and their decision-making suffer.

In the present, FKDs have accumulated to create gross ignorance—collectively, the Age of Ignorance. The reason FKDs persist in an era when information is readily available to all is much the same for the reason it persisted through much of human history: a lack of holistic education. Holistic educational systems would minimize most FKDs and reduce overall ignorance. They would embrace the Scientific paradigm to ensure each member of society had the opportunity to acquire the cognitive ability to think scientifically and logically and to filter out the noise created by the other dominant paradigms. Applied without the distractions of other paradigms, the Scientific paradigm could alleviate the significant social chaos created by FKDs.

Certainly, the complexities of today's society require a formal educational system to impart specialized and general knowledge, but formal education was not a necessity in the past. Hunter-gatherers had an effective informal system of education that helped their groups survive and thrive. We should acknowledge hunter-gatherer efforts to develop effective cognitive processing skills and questioning attitudes, often with more positive outcomes than improperly labeled "advanced civilizations" of the ancient world that enslaved their own and other peoples. Consider, for example, how Native American societies developed the Medicine Wheel process to complete the education of their youth.[146] By moving about a symbolic wheel depicting the reality one confronted—the flora, fauna, other tribes, weather, hunting and gathering practices, and more—they could gain new, broadened perspectives of life. The Medicine Wheel approach complemented the important knowledge of their day (e.g., shelter construction) and the Big Picture knowledge of the human relationships with other peoples and the environment—all for the good of the whole.

The ecological and cultural history of Easter Islanders underscores the importance of formal education. Like most societies, islanders sought the communal Good Life but lacked a system of education that would adequately reduce their ignorance. Human development has reduced the Earth to the equivalent of an Easter Island, but attaining any semblance of the communal Good Life has become inordinately difficult. The modern era contains an entangled and disorderly network of interconnected issues that have dramatically increased with the "shrinking globe." Yet, for those who are fortunate to receive an education today, the curricula generally fail to develop critical thinking abilities—such as the cognitive processing skills inherent in the Socratic and scientific methods and even the wisdom of the Medicine Wheel. For the world's populations, FKDs are the rule rather than the exception. Poor educational systems also reduce the probability that a person will compile enough of the right experiences to negate his FKDs.

Today's educational systems serve two chief purposes: to ensure an adequate number of technically proficient individuals to sustain the productive efficiency of the supply side of capitalism and to ensure a critical mass of capricious consumers to fuel the materialistic demand side of capitalism. Stuff matters, more so than people and the environment. One could imagine a conspiratorial core of corporate capitalists engineering the modern educational systems to feed their power fancies, but capitalists too have to live in the ignorant

---

[146] Storm, "The Teaching of the Medicine Wheel," from the introduction to *Seven Arrows.*

world they've fashioned. They cannot possibly want such a world for their children as the one they have helped create. Hardcore capitalists and other power elite do what they do because their formal and informal education has kept them as ignorant as the rest of the people the educational systems serve. They are victims of their own Self, Group, Power, and Economic paradigms, who have consciously aligned themselves with those influenced by a specific Religious paradigm (Christianity, Judaism, etc.) and allied themselves with similarly-minded Ideological paradigms. They enter the adult phase of their lives with FKDs. Stuck in their paradigms, their two greatest deficit areas are a lack of emotional connectedness to others through Big Picture knowledge and an inability to perform cognitive processing using inquiry and questioning methodologies.

The transition from the Age of Ignorance to a New Enlightenment will depend on a paradigm shift within the formal education systems of all nations. The process will take time and must consider the intellectual and emotional development stages of children. The initial phases must focus on developing cognitive processing skills and the personal relationships conducive to building an emotional connectedness to others. Important and Big Picture knowledge will follow. By implanting these skills and knowledge in the youth of the world, future generations will have a minority of people with FKDs and a plurality capable of engaging with the rest of society in achieving a communal Good Life.

To kick-start the paradigm shift in education, the United Nations must step up and take the lead, with key nations backing the effort. Recently, UNESCO (the United Nations Educational, Scientific, and Cultural Organization) attempted to generate initiatives to improve the quality of education worldwide, but to date, the effort is struggling to make headway under shrinking budgets. The organization has evaluated numerous curricula proposals as a way of "Rethinking Education" and has encouraged nations to focus on creativity as a way to spark innovations.[147] Although creative skill sets contain many of the cognitive processing skills required to erase many FKDs, the skill

[147] Taddei, paper for the Economic Cooperation and Development (OECD) Innovation Strategy, 2009.

sets outlined in UNESCO documents are incomplete.[148] They omit, for example, the cognitive processes for examining Big Picture interrelationships and interdependencies. Still, UNESCO could easily remedy these basic deficiencies and should be the lead organization to advance a global paradigm shift in education.[149]

As for those who have completed their formal education, UNESCO should consider using audiovisual media to encourage attitudinal shifts. The initiative may spawn adult education classes that help adults to think holistically. UNESCO should also develop film specials that challenge existing paradigms so parents are open-minded both to changes in their children's education and to forward-thinking policies. By shining the light on education, UNESCO can help penetrate the many cultural caves of the modern era.

---

[148] Taddei, 33-34.

[149] UNESCO does strongly encourage curricula that develop scientific knowledge and methodologies so the organization's current educational initiatives, if followed by nations, would contribute to a decline of ignorance; however, until a comprehensive package of cognitive processing and interpersonal skills are incorporated into the general education of the world's youth, ignorance will persist.

Chapter 6: Paradigm-Ignorance Thought Experiments

The true sign of intelligence is not knowledge but imagination. – Albert Einstein

Albert Einstein's quest for knowledge about the universe stemmed from an acquired curiosity. His successes relied on an active imagination—an ability to view situations from different perspectives. To clarify those perspectives, he sometimes devised and conducted a *Gedankenerfahrung* or a thought experiment. Such mental expeditions helped him to understand what his mathematical analyses and what the experiments of others were indicating about the nature of the universe. We shall follow his example. It's time to create some thought experiments that you, the reader, can examine in terms of paradigms and ignorance. It's time for you to imagine yourself living a much different life than you're accustomed to.

Picture yourself living on the Italian peninsula in the year 90 ACE. What would occupy your thoughts? How would your daily actions differ from today? This is a difficult but not impossible task if you conduct a thought experiment. First, you must gather more information about the era and yourself. What is your sex? Where precisely do you live—in Rome, a small village on the coast, a hill town? Are you a Roman citizen, slave, or foreigner? What is your economic status? Are you part of a family unit or group, an orphan, or a loner?

For sure, your personal history matters—all the factors that make you *you*. Armed with the knowledge you've acquired in this book, more refined and expansive information would lead you to conclude that your thoughts and actions would strongly align with one or more of the dominant paradigms of the ancient era. Your composite paradigm would be very first-century-like for your local environs.

If you learned that you are male and a foot soldier in a Roman legion, you'd have a better idea of the paradigms that dominate your thoughts and behaviors. You'd likely accept the hierarchal authority structure typically associated with military organizations. You'd carry out your orders to fulfill your sense of duty to the empire, your Caesar, and your Senate (Power paradigm), but you also feel a strong bond to your comrades in arms—a tribal loyalty to preserve your unit (Group paradigm). In battle, you are merciless and ready to kill, maim, rape, and pillage those who would oppose the empire (Self and Ideological paradigms). You became a soldier, in part, because you needed money to survive; you also wanted to improve your social status (Self and Economic paradigms). You weakly believe in the gods and the harm they can inflict on you through divine intervention (Religious paradigm). You often cynically scoff at the gods due to your exposure to the many divinities of the era, including the slowly blossoming Christian religion.

As you reflect, you think that you're immune to any and all of these paradigms, that you can rise above them and be the person you want to be despite the influences to which you've been subjected. But the fact is you wouldn't think like you do today as a citizen of the twenty-first century. In this *gedanken* experiment, you're not who you are today, but who would have been back then. As a soldier, maybe you wouldn't rape and maim the conquered, but remember that the paradigms of your era align strongly with the notion of "to the victors go the spoils." Sorry, but you're probably not a very caring individual and your ignorance level typifies that of an uneducated foot soldier of the late first century.

You can set up thought experiments however you want, but if you adhere to scientific methods, logic, and historically accurate and relevant data, the outcome will be the same. You will inevitably think and behave according to the set of paradigms that existed at a particular time in history, including those passed onto you from childhood via parents, family, and friends. Your ignorance aligns with your paradigms. Of course, your behavior may vary from what I've described, but statistically you'll likely fall within the norms for thoughts and behaviors associated with the specific set of dominant paradigms that have influenced your life. In a sense, we are all slaves to our own paradigms. They are difficult to shift once they become firmly established.

Imagining the past as part of a thought experiment is relatively easy if you are true to the process of identifying the then-existing composite paradigm that would influence your thoughts and behaviors (which film makers rarely adopt to help audiences relate). However, one type of thought experiment is extremely difficult to conduct—one in which you imagine that your composite paradigm in the present suddenly shifts. For example, let's say you are a pro-life Christian (Baptist) and a political conservative who believes government should have a minimal footprint in the daily lives of citizens. Now, conduct a thought experiment where you shift your paradigms to that of a pro-choice, secular agnostic who believes government must play a significant role in the daily lives of citizens to ensure an egalitarian society. What could possibly motivate such a dramatic shift in perspective? What could possibly motivate even a small paradigm shift?

One answer to the last two questions is, "Crises." When we feel threatened by outside forces, either from nature or other humans, we'll set aside our paradigms for the greater good, or more often, our mutual benefit. Why focus our attention on fetal rights when flood waters threaten our neighborhoods, a pandemic infiltrates our locality, or a foreign army is massing at our borders? We largely put our differences aside and address the crisis. So, yes, there are times when our paradigms have minimal influence upon our thoughts and behaviors. When the crises are over, however, the status quo returns. Some small shifts in perspectives may occur as a result of the crises. If certain individuals or groups proved helpful during the calamities, attitudes toward these people and groups could shift slightly. However, the nature of some crises could reinforce existing dominant paradigms, including strengthening biases toward certain racial, religious, and ethnic groups (e.g., perspectives related to Middle Easterners and their religious affiliations after the 9-11 attacks).

The passage of time can also stimulate paradigm shifts, but the process is generally slow—usually measured in years, centuries, and even millennia. The Christian religion slowly morphed from secretive groups holding clandestine meetings to discuss the teachings of Jesus to an immense state-driven religion under Rome, later bolstered by a missionary presence in far-off places. The Protestant Reformation followed about a millennium later, and subsequently, the formation of denominations and sects. It's taken about two thousand years to get to where we are today. The Christian paradigm has changed incrementally—for example, the ordination of female clergy in certain religious divisions. What will the Christian paradigm be in another two thousand years? The answer awaits those in the future. We, today, cannot say. For sure, the strength of other dominant paradigms will play a major role in determining the status of Christianity and other religions. The interconnections among the dominant paradigms will likely persist. As such, the Religious paradigm will likewise play a role in the future construct of the other dominant paradigms. Then again, one or more dominant paradigms may completely overwhelm the other dominant paradigms. Perhaps, for example, two thousand years from now, people will come to rely on AI (Artificial Intelligence) mentors who guide them through life, each tailored to individual capabilities and potentials. Family and religious ties could be dramatically minimized under such tutelage. With a logical and intellectually honest AI mentor assisting every person, ignorance *could* drastically decline.

In the near future, however, there are many other influences that can stimulate paradigm shifts. Education is one, but as the studies of Chapter 5 highlighted (e.g., changes in voter knowledge over a forty-year span), perspectives don't change readily. One would assume that individuals who intently and rigorously study academic topics should acquire evidence that alters their views. For example, if one actually dissects the history of racism in the United States with academic rigor, he or she will find a litany of data in laws and actions that provide proof of longstanding racist attitudes.[150] These racist mindsets concerned African-Americans, Native Americans, and immigrant Americans (Asians, Irish, Jewish, etc.). We're collectively better today but the roots of racism and xenophobia remain hibernating in the wintering consciousness of many Americans. They are as dormant seeds, imbedded in our neural terrain, awaiting the conditions

[150] A recent book, *These Truths*, by Jill Lepore documents the many policies and acts of racism in U.S. history. See References.

to sprout anew like weeds, ready to choke the fields of progress made in improving race relations. In the United States in 2020, we have catalogued numerous examples of institutionalized racism.

Based on our racist past alone, Americans should cringe whenever they hear slogans to "return to the good old days" of American greatness. References to America's prominence are just a mythological paradigm manufactured to manipulate group cohesion among whites. It promotes exclusivity, not inclusivity. Such posturing, while feigning ignorance of our past miscues, belittles the truly immense role *all* Americans played in saving the world from Nazism and fascism.

By dwelling on myths and disregarding ideology, we fail to comprehend the true meaning of greatness. I maintain that America has been and still is great, not because of its actions, but because of the potential within its ideals, specifically those embodied in our amended Constitution. Our Constitution provides a blueprint for greatness and goodness despite its need for additional amendments to align it with twenty-first century realities. Many brave but ordinary citizens have sacrificed their lives to ensure that the promise of a better nation will one day be fulfilled. They found Constitutional ideology a powerful and meaningful paradigm, one they could relate to—even if their understanding of the Constitution was elementary.

For certain, the Constitution had and still has flaws, but corrective amendments have improved its internal content. The Constitution is the one Great American Paradigm, a vision and mental model to which we must all subscribe. That vision is summarized simply in the Constitution's Preamble.

The Constitution should have a greater influence on the dominant paradigms of the present—Self, Group, Power, Economic, Ideological, Religious, and Scientific. Unfortunately, it does not. Our legislators and Presidents have overstepped and/or neglected their Constitutional mandates. Instead of fulfilling the Constitutional vision to "Promote the General Welfare," too many laws have passed that "Support the Special Interests." Manufactured mythological paradigms clutter our brain—from "trickle-down economics" to "expanding the middle class" to "restoring the American dream." These perspectives are a small part of the War of Paradigms to which I referred earlier in this book.

The War wages within our borders and on distant shores. We live in a paradigmatically fractured world; contrasting dominant paradigms are vying for control. The Haves want more and manipulate circumstances to increase their coffers; the Have-nots lack and struggle as the victims of circumstance, getting proportionally less. Radical religious elements are attempting to drive a wedge between Islam and Christianity. MCI is ever-present in daily human life, asking us to consume and possess. Scientific and technical innovations are feeding global capitalism to create a highly materialistic lifestyle and to steer our Self and Group paradigms. Win-win is an infrequent outcome.

Since the current political agenda persists as a polarization of paradigms, humanity collectively faces a lose-lose future. For example, with the richness of Earth's ecosystems in decline, the Haves won't have as many options in experiencing the natural beauty of our planet. They lose with the rest of us. Their ignorance is caused by the short-term luxuries achievable by maintaining their narrow, self-serving outlook on life. Is there a thought experiment that could convince the economic top one-to-five percent of the folly of their ways? Perhaps, but note that documentaries, science fiction novels, and films about a dystopian future have failed to resonate with the super-rich. They are entrenched in their paradigms and chained in their caves. It's not their wealth that threatens the future but their paradigms—the very paradigms that keep us entrenched in mental models that marginalize our collective lives.

The problem with thought experiments is that they largely lack emotional components and true-to-life experiences. They have utility in examining the past and understanding the present, but rarely in projecting the future. Still, it is instructive to attempt to do so.

The easiest projection for the future is a paradigm status quo; or more precisely, the world's nations maintain their specific blend of dominant paradigms. Very minor shifts would occur in each dominant paradigm. Consumerism, globalism, MCI, political tribalism, weak regulatory policies, entrenched religious perspectives, and racism, among many other local and worldviews, will persist in most nations. Since the current set of composite paradigms have persisted for decades, we can project their impact on the future with reasonable confidence. A list of outcomes resulting from our projected paradigmatic stagnation through the 21st century follows:

(1) Rising human population accompanied by rapidly declining species diversity;
(2) World and regional demographic shifts due to different rates of population growth among religious, cultural, ethnic, and racial groups;
(3) Wretched poverty for well over a billion people due to a continuing growth in the disparity between the wealthiest and poorest;
(4) A warming Earth, with its slow but steady impact on, weather, climate, sea level, and resources;
(5) A world dominated by materialism, consumerism, and self-indulgences;
(6) Continued pollution of the Earth's water resources, particularly from plastics and other waste products entering the oceans;
(7) Continuing globalization amid political tensions, tribalism, and regionalism, spurred by MCI and techno-capitalistic colonialism;
(8) Ideological and religious absolutism;
(9) A continuing blend of technocratic and scientific rationalism, empiricism, skepticism, and positivism (as applied to social systems); and
(10) A large segment of the world's population burdened by FKDs and afflicted with widespread ignorance.

The outcomes listed illustrate the need for dramatic shifts in the paradigms that evoke our current thoughts and behavior. Item (10) in the preceding paragraph is the author's assessment that the Age of Ignorance will easily persist into the next century. Our current set of dominant paradigms has reinforced the human grip on the planet such that we may want to refer to the coming geo-climatic era as the Hyper-Anthropocene Epoch. The ecological impact on Earth will continue unabated. Future geologists and historians may also choose to call this period, the Plasticene Age, to indicate the mass infusion of plastics into the Earth's ecosystems.

If we attempted to tweak this grim paradigmatic forecast, we might choose several *gedanken* experiments and imagine that one of more of the dominant paradigms shift dramatically. The goal would be to develop strategies for paradigmatic reengineering of the world's population. To make these experiments useful, we'd have to find evidence that several of the dominant paradigms are poised to shift. To date, the author has found no such evidence. In the next and future chapters, we will examine the nature of paradigm shifts and the mechanisms necessary to stimulate changes to our dominant and composite paradigms.

Chapter 7: The Nature of Paradigm Shifts

All significant breakthroughs are break -"withs" old ways of thinking. – Thomas Kuhn

In this chapter, we'll explore the mechanisms of the significant paradigm shifts in human history. We will learn that while some shifts occur dramatically and quickly, most occur gradually when compared to a human life span. We will find that tool-making, advances in science, and technological innovations have spurred most paradigm shifts. To a lesser extent, changes in religious and ideological perspectives contributed to gradual shifts in worldviews.

The Self, Group, Religious, Economic, Ideological, and Power paradigms, either individually or in combinations, have largely steered the course of history for the past ten millennia. Only relatively recently has the Scientific paradigm become a major influence upon events. During humanity's civilized existence, the other six dominant paradigms have basically been recycled and reflect minor shifts in perspectives. For example, throughout human history, ego has significantly defined the core characteristic of the Self paradigm. An egotistical leader of a hunter-gatherer tribe, ancient kingdom, or present-day nation-state shares the same, basic Self paradigm. Where ego is involved, we can summarize the paradigm as "the world revolves around me." As history has shown, when the Self paradigm dominates a group or society, the results are typically disastrous for those external and, eventually, internal to the group.

The Economic paradigm of capitalism has similar characteristics of simple bartering systems of the past, especially after profit motive became an integral component of negotiated exchange. At their core, these changes do not represent radical shifts in perspectives. Whether a laborer is earning monetary wages, receiving valuables, or accepting food and shelter for her services is irrelevant. Individuals and groups had capitalistic tendencies in early civilizations through informal application of supply and demand bartering. Under modern capitalism, however, the owner (individual or corporation) seeks to maximize profits for its shareholders even if by doing so, there are negative impacts upon society or the employees. In this regard, incorporation reflects a significant shift in the Economic paradigm structure.

To alter the present corporate-driven Economic paradigm, we'd need to experience something truly transformational. One highly unlikely revolution would be a shift to a purely communistic paradigm. No such system has ever thrived or survived. One could also imagine, with great difficulty, that all corporations would migrate into nonprofit conglomerates. Their primary goal would be to serve the best interests of society by providing products and services that satisfy consumers' needs *and* that pose the least harm to the local and extended environs. Again, the probability of "nonprofit capitalism" becoming the new economics is effectively zero. One telling aspect about capitalism's grip upon the economic perspective is the nature of today's socialism. American capitalism has shifted the socialist paradigm. Socialist nations now either operate as capitalistic socialist states or socialistic capitalist states, depending on specific national policies. Further discussion will follow in Chapter 8.

The Power and Group paradigms have also undergone minor shifts but only over the civilized portion of human history. The qualities which characterize most Power paradigms are control and authority—over people, over circumstances, or over a person's or group's environment. Group paradigms typically contain perspectives that will favor outcomes for a specific group—even at the expense of other groups.

The Ideological paradigm consists mostly of non-theological and noneconomic isms. Numerous shifts in ideology have occurred over the span of human history. Interactions between and among groups helped to disperse ideas and ways of life. Ideological perspectives necessarily changed as civilized life advanced, with some benefits for the general populations. Eventually, the challenges of urban and rural living stimulated an awakening of social consciousness from which new philosophies sprung. For example, industrialism added a step increase in complexity to human existence. To Karl Marx, the factory became a symbol of alienated labor, where people lost their individuality by being forced to perform repetitive, dehumanizing tasks on assembly lines. Under the direction of industrial capitalists, factory workers became a new, subordinate class of citizens. Marx's perspectives helped to advance ideological nuances that expanded the meaning of classism and contributed substance to the Economic paradigm of communism. In the modern era, Ideological paradigms have become so numerous and so interconnected that most fail to elevate to dominant status. The ones that have gained dominance are typically those dealing with human rights and freedoms.

Only relatively recently has the Scientific paradigm become a major influence upon events. Science and technology have contributed to or catalyzed the most significant paradigm shifts in our history. Some have occurred very slowly; others dramatically. We have briefly touched upon a few instances. In the following sections, we will examine several more.

Advances in Cosmology

The worldview describing our place in the cosmos has matured very slowly until recent times. Religious paradigms largely dominated over scientific observations, stymieing shifts in perspectives of our place in the universe. The early and long-held Christian perspective maintained that humankind existed on the Earth, which is at the center of a universe created by God in six days. Spheres of "realms" surrounded the Earth ending in the heavenly realm, a paradise for the afterlife.

Because scientific and technological advances were beginning to have significant payoffs for societies—particularly improving the quality of human life—the cosmological worldview gradually began to shift. Science gained credibility through its utility and the efforts of trailblazers such as Copernicus and Galileo. Then along came Isaac Newton and his ideas of a mechanistic world that aligned with certain universal laws. Newton's laws could predict the future with mathematical certainty—including the path of moving objects and even the date and time of the next lunar and solar eclipses.

Technological leaps occurred as a result. The Scientific paradigm had inserted itself into everyday life, albeit still much less prominent than other established dominant paradigms.

While Newton's ideas would later be refined by Albert Einstein and a host of quantum physics pioneers, his methods became a catalyst in permanently shifting the cosmological perspective. Newton made it possible to take abstract mathematical relationships and convert them into a concrete essence. His mathematical "engines" became real-world engines—steam, internal combustion, jet, and rocket.

As described in an earlier chapter, the shift in cosmological perspective to today's Big Bang theory marked a paradigmatic turning point. Religions could no longer ignore the *new* truths revealed about the universe. Yes, intransigents still exist, wallowing in ignorance within their paradigmatic caves. Most religions have adapted and incorporated the new revelations in the Scientific paradigm into the Religious paradigm. Creation stories are now often portrayed as metaphorical representations of reality passed from God to humans. "Let there be light" is the Big Bang. Six days represents the much more extensive transitional evolution of the universe. Eve emanating from Adam's rib is a crude representation of the biological mechanisms of life and reproduction. Such shifts within Religious paradigms have not undermined the core tenets upon which religions operate, but they threaten to further erode existing religious perspectives.

Advances in Transportation and Communication

We rightly should marvel at human advances in mobility. For most of its existence, humankind relied on its legs. The domestication of animals enhanced human mobility on land. Human ingenuity led to the development of floating structures used for water transport. Muscle, simple machines (e.g., oars), and wind power improved the speed of transport on water. The wheel, sail, and other simple devices further increased the speed and capacity of what and who could be transported. It remained that way for centuries. Enter Isaac Newton. The abstract became concrete in the form of James Watt's steam engine. Rail transport and steamships followed.

Soon thereafter, James Clerk Maxwell entered the mix and became another catalyst for a major shift in the Scientific paradigm.

Maxwell did for electromagnetism what Newton had done for mass and motion. Electricity was no longer static or dependent upon chemical reactions from batteries. By marrying Newton's and Maxwell's ideas, mechanical and electromagnetic phenomena could complement each other. The internal combustion engine and electric motors and generators became reality. These inventions produced a step increase in human mobility. Eventually, they would lead to flight and an even faster means of transporting people and material.

The dramatic increase in human mobility resulted in a significant increase in the magnitude and speed at which shifts in dominant paradigms *could* occur. Increased human mobility meant increased interactions among individuals and groups on a grand terrestrial scale. Ideologies and cultures confronted each other with more frequency and intensity. Wars were fought, goods exchanged, languages translated, ideas shared, and cultures intertwined. The exchange of material and technology affected the ways in which humans spent their time. As routines and lifestyles shifted under technological pressures, not only did individual composite paradigms drift but so did interrelationships among individuals and groups. As micro-shifts in the prevailing perspectives accrued, many cultures experienced step changes. For example, private and public rapid transit allowed the subcultures of the suburbs and inner city to blossom.

As with advances in human mobility, advances in communications have had similar influences on our paradigm structure. The loss of "lesser" languages is one notable shift even as English and Mandarin have spread internationally, the latter mostly within China's Asian sphere of influence. Money talks, and the dollar and yuan are among the most vocal. As a result, many Western and several Asian languages have infiltrated numerous societies as secondary languages, creating cultural undercurrents. Languages help shape paradigms through the meanings invoked by the acquired symbolism of words and the circumstances under which they are learned. Words may summon emotional or rationalized responses through their historical, cultural, racial, or ethnic context. Foreign terminology adds another dimension to Group and Ideological paradigms, in particular.

Lesser languages refer to those belonging to small populations and subject to assimilation and socioeconomic pressures. These languages are struggling to remain vital. The native peoples of Africa and the North, Central, and South Americas are among the many societies whose tribal languages have withered since the onset of

European colonialism. Dominant national languages permeated and displaced these languages under colonial rule, in part for economic activity to flourish. European colonialism ravaged these native societies, eroding the diverse language base that once existed throughout the New World and sub-Saharan Africa. Many languages, cultures, and paradigms have been lost forever.

Technology has also increased the quantity of communications within and among societies. As we learned earlier in discussing the impact of the cell phone on modern life, these far-reaching communications are not always constructive. A smorgasbord of dialogue feverishly occurs daily on or via the internet or cell phones, much of which rarely expresses well-considered positions.[151] Simultaneously, perspectives are constantly under assault as the noösphere explodes with information and misinformation. As we saw in Chapter 5, however, significant shifts in the existing paradigm structure rarely develop. Most people feel safe and secure in the caves of their past. Experience and genetics have hardwired their neural networks.

Pendular Paradigms

Some paradigm shifts are transient and oscillatory, similar to the motion of a pendulum. Events can temporarily shift perspectives. World War II created paranoia within the United States of foreign nationals, resident aliens, and even citizens who had or might have connections to the Axis powers through their race, national origin, and/or ethnicity. The government took measures to isolate some of these groups through internment camps and deportations. The attack on Pearl Harbor directed the greatest animus and fear toward those of Japanese descent. After the war, the paradigm gradually swung back to the old normal and more recently to a state of healthy collaboration and competition with former Axis powers. After the attacks on September 11, 2001, a similar but more muted hostility developed in the United States toward those of Muslim and Arab origin.

Pendular paradigms typically undergo small amplitude changes. The dominant paradigms of our neural networks are difficult to alter. The shifts are largely situational and short-lived. For example, an

[151] This is not to imply that the conversations do not have utility. Much of the dialogue adds value to the routines of life—setting up meeting times, coordinating efforts, reviewing shopping lists, etc.

American who held strong biases against those of Asian descent *prior to* World War II would find it difficult to transcend those prejudices after the war. We'd expect the person to remain inwardly or overtly hostile to Japanese even though Japan developed into a staunch ally in the post-war era. Similarly, when encountering difficult times, we shouldn't expect a devoutly religious person to deviate significantly from the core tenets of her religion nor should we expect an egoist to consider the needs of others over his own self-interest. Only individuals with weakly held dominant paradigms will experience significant pendular paradigms shifts.

Chapter 8: The Present – Deeper into the Abyss

It was the best of times. It was the worst of times.

- Charles Dickens, *A Tale of Two Cities* (opening)

It is the most enlightened of times. It is the most ignorant of times. Yes, Charles Dickens could have used these words to describe his own era and found justifications for them. Today, the words ring true once again, but there's a significant difference. While we know a lot more now than in Dickens' day, we have fallen much deeper into an abyss of ignorance. The collective effort required to escape from our paradigmatic caves has unnecessarily multiplied. The sooner we break free from the chains confining us, the more likely our future will improve.

Let's start in the United States, where, as of this writing, we are a nation crippled by polarizing perspectives. Right or left, conservative or liberal, Red, Blue, and Purple—these worldviews have created a paralysis in government operations. Driven by an almost maniacal allegiance to specific dominant paradigms, democracy has suffered considerably as opposing camps invoke a win-lose mentality.[152] A closer look at each dominant paradigm in the present will prove instructive.

The Self and Group paradigms have grown in prominence in recent years as personalities in positions of power seek self-aggrandizement and groups maneuver to steer resources and policies to fulfill their tribal objectives. The win-lose scenarios and dramas that play out in American politics on almost a daily basis exemplify the dismal state of affairs. The continuing battles over healthcare, head-in-the-sand thinking on human contributions to climate change, and a host of differing perspectives on international and domestic issues are clear indicators that the engines of democratic governance are stalling. We are well into the presidency of Donald Trump, and unfortunately, the Self paradigm, specifically the element of ego, seems to be dominating the President's thoughts and actions. A paradigm shift to a "shepherd" mindset, that is, finding ways to benefit the entire "flock," would better serve the People.

But Congress has many who similarly strongly adhere to their ego-driven Self paradigms, reinforced by highly prejudicial Group and Ideological paradigms. The way that many Republican Party members treated former President Barrack Obama clearly indicated racial bias. These mostly white men could not tolerate the idea of an African-American steering the course of the American future. For example, when President Obama nominated an individual to fill a vacancy in the Supreme Court in his last year in office, the Republicans ganged together to say they would not consider any nominee from the president. One might argue that the ploy was simply political strategizing, but it went much deeper than that. The Republicans had the votes to block any nominee who could not demonstrate alignment with their party's ideologies. The Senators ignored their constitutional responsibility to vet the president's nominee. Why? The nomination was made by an African American. Ego and emotion (hatred and acquired biases) dictated many of the senators' Self paradigms. Their behavior is just another case illustrating the power and perils of

---

[152] For a more in-depth history and analysis of the paradigms that drive American society, see Woodard, *American Nations*. His descriptions focus on the subcultures that have blossomed in North America as a result of European colonization. Here, we are exploring this topic from a more global, Big Picture perspective by keeping our focus on the dominant paradigms.

paradigms in influencing human thought and behavior.[153] Ironically, when President Trump nominated an individual to the Supreme Court after assuming the presidency, Democrats in the Senate tried to use the filibuster to thwart the nomination proceedings. In true "theater of the absurd" style, the same Republican Senators who would not even consider Obama's nominee called the Democratic action obstructionist and disgraceful.

Another recent trend is the growing tribalism within the political party systems. Over the past several decades, Republicans and Democrats have become increasing myopic and clannish as they see the world through party lenses only. Any presumption of optimism for an era of open-mindedness by either party is clearly misguided.

None of these trends, tendencies, or behaviors is unique to the United States or to our times. Paradigms have and always will control the human mind and therefore dictate human actions. The frustrations for those alive today is enduring the daily darkness of dysfunctional governance. To reduce the tiring and exasperating circumstances, we must collectively shift to an all-inclusive, nonviolent, and intellectually honest mindset. The barriers to achieve this "Paradigm Paradise" are formidable. It won't happen any time soon. The studies in Chapter 5 illustrated the inclination of people to become entrenched in their paradigms when confronted with the truth or contrary theses. Typically, to overcome these deep-rooted tendencies, small shifts in perspectives must take place first—ones that build trust among those holding conflicting paradigms. However, trust must always be earned. In the case of paradigms, it could take decades or centuries.

A relatively quick shift occurred, however, in Eastern Europe and some former Soviet republics when the Soviet Union collapsed in 1989. East Germany, which had morphed into a police state as a Soviet puppet, had to undergo a significant shift in perspectives and political structures to accomplish reunification with West Germany. West Germany was highly motivated and determined to help its former brethren to escape from their totalitarian caves. The West Germans poured resources into the reunification process, seeking win-win for

---

[153] There are more cases indicating racial prejudice toward President Obama by public officials and notable personalities, such as the Birther movement to discredit the president's citizenship and the blatant vocal outbursts against the president in public forums (e.g., "You lie!" at an address to Congress).

the former republics in forging a new, greater republic. West Germany's goodwill built trust with the East.

The same cannot be said for Russia. Russia was on its own, steered by those invested in the paradigms held during the glory days of the Soviet Union. There was little help from the international community to instigate shifts away from the corrupt, personality-driven, and hierarchal power structures within the former Soviet Union. Russia's aggressive posture on the world stage today exemplifies the Power paradigm of its Soviet past.

The paradigm reality of the present era stems, in part, from the political transformations occurring after the end of the Cold War as reflected in the weighted combination of the seven dominant paradigms (see Chapter 4, Present Era, Figure 7 and Table 7). However, the existence of majority perspectives within a given society doesn't mean a specific set of dominant paradigms will prevail and align with the majority. Recall the previous discussions on global warming, for example. In the U.S., there is *now* a growing acceptance that human-induced climate change contributes significantly to global warming.[154] Unfortunately, the Power paradigm has negated the impact of this new prevailing perspective, once again exemplifying how one dominant paradigm can affect the scope and influence of other dominant perspectives. Figure 7 illustrated how both the Power and Scientific paradigms have similar strengths of influence over present-day thoughts and actions in the modern era. However, under the Trump administration, politically, economically, and ideologically motivated policies have temporarily enlarged the wedge for the Power paradigm and thinned the slice for the Scientific paradigm (not reflected in Figure 7). For example, our new environmental policies would make us seem to overtly deny the scientific consensus on climate change and take us back to an earlier industrial era when economics topped ecological ethics. Yet the majority of Americans, bolstered by the young, have had a real paradigm shift with respect to environmental consciousness and global warming. To the dismay of the new majority, the Power and Group (political party) paradigms have taken hold of the legal structures that dictate policy rather than determining policy through logical and scientific methods. In this regard, Republicans and Democrats share responsibility.

---

[154] Meyer, title page.

Thus, politics and power often dictate the paradigms the populace must endure. Whether righteous or not, when paradigms are forced upon people, especially those with a significant impact on lifestyle, societies experience conflict among individuals and/or groups. For example, after the American Civil War, the North passed laws and dictated policies in an effort to change long-held paradigms in the South. The brute force approach may have been just in its intention, but it lead to well over a century of social and political discord. Few today would argue against the necessity of the acts and edicts carried out to curb the mistreatment of African Americans, but the approach might have differed. Paradigm shifts had to occur to ensure African American civil rights. The shifts are still incomplete because little was done by the victors to educate and demonstrate the benefits of a cohesive society. The defeated in war rarely rapidly accept new paradigms.

An important takeaway, however, is that not all forced paradigm shifts are just. Consider those of the European colonial era and twentieth-century totalitarian regimes. Physical and political power can have a profound effect on the paradigms in play. The group in power can legally and illegally shape the effective paradigm funnel and alter the content and mix of a society's dominant paradigms. Native populations in the New World, Africa, Asia, Australia, and Polynesia suffered under the paradigmatic pressures imposed by European colonists. Societies underwent significant structural shifts. In the twentieth century, Nazi Germany and the Soviet Union forced social reengineering upon their populations in an attempt to alter the content and scope of their dominant paradigms (e.g., Hitler Youth and commune system, respectively). The limited perspectives of these societies allowed ignorance to mushroom. They instigated laws to serve their purposes and to control the narrative.

The response to forced paradigms may be muted and measured initially. Those holding opposing views may retreat and find shelter in "underground" mental caves, perhaps to emerge only when expedient. Failure to expose and counter regressive policies can have dire consequences. Patience and apathy under such circumstances can allow societies to drift toward totalitarian rule. If the opposition waits too long to take constructive and peaceful action to stop the escalating ignorance, there are two likely outcomes. Either violence will ensue or people will have to endure repressive rule. If the latter occurs, we can conclude that the neural structure of opposition paradigms provided insufficient motivation for action.[155] For example, after the Bolshevik Revolution in Russia, a bloody civil war ensued with the Bolsheviks the victors. However, in Germany, the transition to Nazism occurred in gradual, sinister steps that fostered blind, misguided, or indifferent acceptance of the regime's paradigms.

Yet greater dangers lurk than those created by the ebb and flow of political ideologies and power shifts. An insidious Economic paradigm now exerts undue influence on human affairs: global, capitalistic, mega-corporate imperialism or MCI. We introduced this phenomenon earlier and expand our previous discussion below.

In the 21st century, capitalism has acquired prominence as the dominant Economic paradigm, enabling MCI to gain a foothold in most nations. Socialism has become a second-tier Economic paradigm despite its ascendancy in the European Union (EU) and its pseudo-existence in China. In fact, the EU has a hybridized economy, which one could characterize as capitalistic socialism. Once a communist stronghold, China has ascended to socialistic capitalism, a government-sponsored and supported system of mildly fettered, free enterprise designed to gain a competitive edge over other nations. China's disregard for intellectual property rights and its acquisition of trade secrets through espionage have been newsworthy stories for decades. Yet China's Economic paradigm and its rise as a techno-industrial giant have their roots in MCI.

U.S. corporations have had a significant hand in enabling the capitalist way of life worldwide. Cheap labor and new, expansive markets have always whetted the appetite of capitalists. Western corporations looked to Asia, South America, and Africa and cut deals with many nations on these continents for cheap labor and resources. As a result, multinational corporations from the U.S. and other nations now operate worldwide. They are having a growing influence upon socioeconomic perspectives and the routines of life almost everywhere on the planet. When people rely on food, transportation, and other necessities produced by a dwindling source of suppliers, they gradually become to see their worldview collapse into a narrow producer-consumer relationship. To survive and prosper as a Modern,

[155] Climate change policy has no noticeable effect on lifestyle in the short term so we shouldn't expect individuals, groups, or states to take up arms in support of the scientific perspectives on the causes of climate change. The best we can expect are large and vocal protests.

one must eat the foods and utilize the goods and services provided in large part by mega-corporations. And let's not forget the onslaught of advertising, a paradigm-shaping form of propaganda and psychological manipulation to impel the consumer to the Promised Land of products and services. This is the primary reason Figure 7 shows the Economic paradigm occupying the greatest wedge of the funnel. Our minds have become conditioned to materialistic and consumeristic ways of life. Paradigms have led us to this present, and the future promises more of the same.[156]

Why has this economic system evolved into a form of imperialism? It boils down to two simple factors: control and exclusivity. Corporations have charters configured to realize the best possible financial outcomes for their shareholders, often over national priorities. Profits are the bottom line. Shareholders are happy when profits are high and scatter when they fail to receive a decent return on investment or incur losses. In the early days of industrialism, few corporations had a social conscience. They created air, water, and other forms of pollution, passing on the cost of cleanup to the general public. The few benefited at the expense of the many. Wages and other benefits were minimal to ensure a substantial profit margin.

The new elites are not of royal blood, but of corporate blood, creating an upper-upper class that uses some of its profits to influence laws and statutes in its favor. Our current form of corporate capitalism parallels that of an exclusive club which exerts control on the political environment to further its wealth objectives. Similar to the European nations whose imperialistic mandates controlled the lives and minimized the resources available to their colonial subjects, mega-corporate imperialists have infiltrated world markets to influence the lives and politics of most nations and to siphon wealth into their coffers, often at the expense of their (foreign) employee base.

In the United States, the Great Depression resulted in some gains for the poor and middle classes. Socialism was on the rise as the capitalism bubble had burst. Socialistic legislation (New Deal) preserved a relative status quo via regulations, graduated income taxes, the enactment of social security benefits, and public projects such as

---

[156] Paradigms have evolved to create our current way of life. Many lives are better. Many are worse. What we need to ask is whether there are paradigmatic shifts that would maximize those with better lives and minimize those with worse lives.

the Civilian Conservation Corps, Tennessee Valley Authority, and the Hoover Dam.

With the advent of World War II and the subsequent Cold War, the pendular Economic paradigm swung back to a less bridled capitalism. What followed was a reinvigorated economic globalism, driven initially from the United States. Soon the flood gates opened for mega-multinational enterprises.[157] With the near-geometric growth rate in technological advances, mega-corporate imperialists are establishing financial empires and shaping our paradigmatic future. This is not science fiction, but likely the actual dystopian future that awaits humanity. We will be at the mercy not of artificial intelligence but of the paradigms manufactured for us by MCI elites.

In the post-World War II era, there has been significant fear-mongering over socialism in the United States. The perpetrators are naturally the capitalists and their politicos and other agents who describe socialism as a great evil. The evil they speak of is actually a more egalitarian society with a more equitable distribution of wealth. They warn that socialism will bring about widespread unemployment and runaway inflation. Of course, the alarmists are stuck in their paradigms, unable to consider other hybridized economic systems. The fact is we are already a hybrid system that the elite are trying to dismantle. The U.S. has social security, military, federal, and state retirement systems, Medicare, Medicaid, welfare, and food stamps. Even in this environment, the rich appear wary of losing the great wealth they have amassed and continue to accumulate. Meanwhile, we insanely borrow money to keep the tax rate low on those who can easily afford it. The anti-socialism crowds cite the American Dream as a foundational element of our democracy even though it is unavailable to most and only serves as a pseudo-paradigm to maintain the status quo.

A recent example of psychological warfare waged to ensure the current state of the capitalist Economic paradigm in the U.S. occurred during the 2019 State of the Union address. President Trump vowed that America would never adopt socialism to the resounding cheers of his party and others. End of debate—apparently. This spectacle highlights yet again the subtle and menacing nature of paradigms, and

---

[157] Lest we forget, the U.S. modeled itself after Europe, in particular the economic imperialism of Great Britain and the Netherlands. The British East India Tea Company is an example of a forerunner of today's MCI.

the extremism which accompanies the mental and physical wars waged on their behalf.

Can we ever expect to escape the demons within our own paradigms?

Chapter 9: A Possible Way Ahead

"Where ignorance is our master, there is no possibility of real peace." – Dalai Lama

As we stated from the beginning, humans will always exist at some level of ignorance about their surroundings, about their relationships, about the universe at large, and even about themselves. A person or group's composite paradigm largely determines the degree of ignorance. Humans tend to be prisoners of their own paradigms. We may escape our caves and gain enlightenment, but many of our experiences in the cave still reside within our neural networks. Few if any of us have the wherewithal to extract ourselves from those experiences completely. Accordingly, the future of humanity, and to some degree the planet, will rely on whatever future shifts occur in the dominant paradigms within the global community.[158] If the shifts are

[158] Since we've only been despoiling the planet for 10 millennia at best, it is admittedly anthropocentric of me to assume humans will have sufficient impact on the planet to change the course of long-term Earth history. Species come and go as a result of other species, asteroid strikes, continental drift, and instabilities in the Earth's mantle. However, we are (likely) the first species that know we are dramatically influencing the biosphere: the flora, fauna, air, soil, and water. Short-term, irreversible impact has occurred, particularly to the diversity of species. Even then, a massive, extended Ice Age in the not-too-distant future could reboot the planet and erase many of the ills we've caused. Like the dinosaurs, there would be some evidence we once existed.

minor, world societies will continue on the courses dictated by existing dominant paradigms.

History tells us that most of these governing paradigms create friction and conflict among nations, within nations, and among groups and individuals. Though present trends indicate a more peaceful planet in the twenty-first century, we can attribute these developments to a period of great abundance where quality of life, on average, is improving. However, the paradigms that led to the bloodiest century in human history have not shifted significantly, meaning we should expect a repeat of many of the ills of the past, particularly if resources (food, potable water, energy) decline. If resource crises occur, major paradigmatic shifts would have to occur to avert conflict. The challenges that lie ahead for humanity, particularly those associated with a warming planet, will require a dominant paradigm structure that fosters a cooperative spirit. Thus, we should seek to develop and adopt a "best set" of dominant paradigms that serves the greater good. If we find such paradigms, we must determine how we can strengthen their presence in the noösphere.

To aid in this quest, we must look at history and examine those circumstances where progress toward the greater good occurred. As we do, we must recognize that *sometimes* warfare and natural disasters were often the cause of temporary shifts in perspectives that moved humanity toward an optimal good for all. We should also note that history contains no grand reeducation or spiritual oneness that stimulated positive outcomes for humanity. Thus, we should be wary of history's messages. Although war sometimes spurred humanistic tendencies in its aftermath, shifting existing composite paradigms toward greater cooperation, war could also incite less humanistic trends, such as revenge. I am in no way suggesting we must wage war or hope for disasters to create the circumstances where constructive paradigm shifts occur. That would involve *real* suffering. Perhaps, however, legitimate, imminent threats of real suffering will incite the majority of humanity to change its ways. Major paradigm shifts *could* arise from perils global in nature, not local and isolated, but we can also learn from regional challenges as well. The 2020 coronavirus pandemic (COVID-19) has had devastating effects on rich and poor societies alike, being deadly, fast-acting, and widespread. As of this writing, however, the pandemic has done little to change the existing dominant paradigm structure. The suffering and threat apparently aren't calamitous enough. Catchphrases such as "We're all in this together," mean little, especially since the Haves and Have-nots are experiencing the effects of the pandemic in disparate ways. As for phenomena that are slow-acting, such as climate change, there's little hope that they will generate significant paradigmatic shifts. For most, climate change is not perceived as a real threat to life or quality of life, but rather a phenomenon we'll engineer ourselves through and around some time in the future.

Utopian Dominant Paradigms

Figure 8, Table 8, and Table J Overview

By dissecting history to determine the factors that promote global cooperation, such as almost occurred *immediately* following World War II, we would likely conclude that a composite paradigm dominated by secular-humanistic, ecological-holistic, and scientific perspectives would reduce worldwide ignorance. This composite would consist of what we might choose to call a Utopian collection of dominant paradigms.

Under such an amalgamated set of paradigms, egomania, clannish extremism, special interest policies and laws, and twisted ideologies and philosophies would significantly diminish. Institutionalized and organized religions would not dominate society's perspectives. Ideally, one's view of divinity would evolve to a strictly personal perspective, with the process of worship up to the individual and not according to institutional dogmas. This does not mean that a person could not believe in Allah, Jehovah, the Trinity, or any other theism, divine being, or Savior. It does mean, however, that the polarizing religious tribalism that exists would fade away and be replaced by the holistic perspective that all religious beliefs are worthy of respect—assuming, of course, they support humanistic principles, which most religions do. There would be no right or wrong God, and personalized religious paradigms would include atheism and agnosticism. In my ideal world, humans would make community-level decisions based on fact and moral nuances, not egoism, tribalism, fancy, or faith. The decisions would favor the greater good and stem from logical argument and the best available scientifically determined data.

In this paradigmatic paradise, beliefs in religion and the divine will likely undergo significant shifts. In their place, a complementary dominant Educational paradigm would emerge that promotes intellectual honesty.[159] Accordingly, perspectives such as creationism would devolve into metaphorical parallels of scientific theory. A well-structured Educational paradigm would make the learning of functional knowledge and analytic tools a priority. One mandatory element must be the study of logic, with emphasis on distinguishing fact from opinion and learning how to test for rightness (truths) and wrongness (falsehoods). By giving every human such capability, the conflicts between faith and reason should subside as convictions give way to provable theses.

How will people acquire functional knowledge and other skill sets to escape their caves? Education must become a priority as we briefly discussed in a previous chapter. A truly worldwide, United Nations-backed Educational paradigm must arise from our existing educational systems to help restructure the neural networks of as many children and adults as possible. One critical mission of the world's educational systems will be to provide the citizens of each nation the functional skills and cognitive processing proficiencies to succeed in their realms. Though most societies differ on what constitutes the communal Good Life, if utopian paradigms dominate, all people should be equipped with the functional knowledge and critical thinking skills to participate in and contribute to the advancement of their societies and to understand the paradigmatic variations of other societies.

In this paradigmatic utopia, capitalism would no longer dominate the Economic paradigm. We would dismantle MCI and blend elements of capitalism, socialism, and other holistic economic isms to ensure the best possible outcomes for humanity and the planet.[160] Wealth would not determine fame, though many would be

---

[159] Religious institutions may seem to some to be on the path to extinction. No one who has read this book should believe so.

[160] I have named this new economic paradigm "entropism" because it would combine the thermodynamic concept of entropy with holistic economic principles. Entropy, or the measure of disorder in the universe, increases naturally. We can't stop it. However, an entropic economic system would seek to minimize (social) disorder through integrated public-private partnerships that serve the greater good. "Entropreneurs" would find ways to optimize economic activity to limit the impact of waste streams upon human and ecological systems while providing increased opportunities for sharing wealth.

wealthy—just not obscenely wealthy. Financial inequalities will remain, but they won't affect each person's or family unit's ability to pursue personal goals. Success and fame would stem from serving humanity's and the Earth's best interests, not the interests of individuals, select groups, corporations, or financiers.

In keeping with humanistic principles, the Self paradigm would become an Others paradigm and the Group paradigm would shift from competitive to cooperative. Specifically, to achieve utopian goals, the Group paradigm would necessarily shift dramatically to an Interconnectedness (ICN) paradigm. The difference between the Others and ICN paradigms is in the structure of the neural networks. The Others paradigm is inward looking, relating to the individual's self-perception of his or her connection to the greater human community. The ICN paradigm is outward looking, relating to the modes of interactions and communications necessary for cooperative engagement with others. These perspectives would not eliminate conflict but would reduce ignorance-driven human turmoil. We would come to better understand how cultures, races, ethnicities, genders, sexual preferences, and ideologies interrelate. The ICN paradigm would extend holistic principles to include not only the varieties and richness of humanity's many subcultures but also Nature's diversity. The ICN paradigm would also include spiritual streamlining to open communication pathways that eventually minimize religious differences and focus on the common elements of religious doctrines.

The Holistic paradigm means we identify ourselves first, and foremost, as members of the broader human family, respecting our differences and collaborating to improve the human condition. It wouldn't stop there, however. We would also recognize ourselves as just one species in a complex web of living and inanimate environments in an effort to achieve an ecological oneness for planet Earth. In effect, the Holistic paradigm will meld together and restructure diverging ideologies into a narrow set of core tenets. Ecology would become a major facet of the Scientific paradigm.

Figure 8 shows the utopian set of dominant paradigms using the funnel model. The seven dominant paradigms of past and present periods have morphed into the five dominant paradigms of the future: Others, ICN, Educational, Holistic, and Scientific. Self, group, economic, ideological, and power paradigms will still exist (with the religious paradigm shifting to a spiritual one within the ICN), but they will no longer dominate human affairs. Utopian paradigms will mute "old world" paradigms, rewriting neural networks. Humans will think and act under a revised set of paradigms or a composite paradigm of utopian perspectives. Table 8 summarizes the major filters of utopian dominant paradigms, described in general terms in the preceding paragraphs. Table J provides justification for a low ignorance level under utopian paradigms. The reader should easily recognize the reasoning applied to arrive at this determination.

Now, I know what you're thinking. The author has gone off the deep end and is attempting to draw the reader into an improbable dream world with mystical visions of Shangri-La. You're right, of course, but I had to put it out there, as ignorant of reality as it sounds. Such a world is not impossible but certainly unlikely. If we've learned anything about the paradigms that drive human behavior, it's that we don't like other people's paradigms, especially if we're invested in a group's paradigm and if our established paradigms serve our personal and group interests. Group paradigmatic unity reinforces and bolsters us—makes us think our reality is the right reality and our life meaningful.

Unfortunately, many existing paradigms represent "wrong" realities, which threaten our survival and make us uneasy. What's wrong depends on the paradigms we subscribe to. Ours are right. Theirs are wrong. In fact, we go to great efforts to contain opposition paradigms, if not entirely eliminate them, as highlighted in numerous examples in this book. And thus has human history progressed: a repeated and incessant conflict of paradigms. Ignorance, therefore, reigns supreme, but we shouldn't accept this as the status quo. Anything we can do to minimize ignorance will have a (small) positive impact on humanity's future. Utopia may be a fantasy, but that doesn't mean we should remain victims of our own stupidity. Instead, we must jump-start our efforts to change our neural networks and strive for a new enlightenment.

Figure 8: The Utopian Composite Paradigm

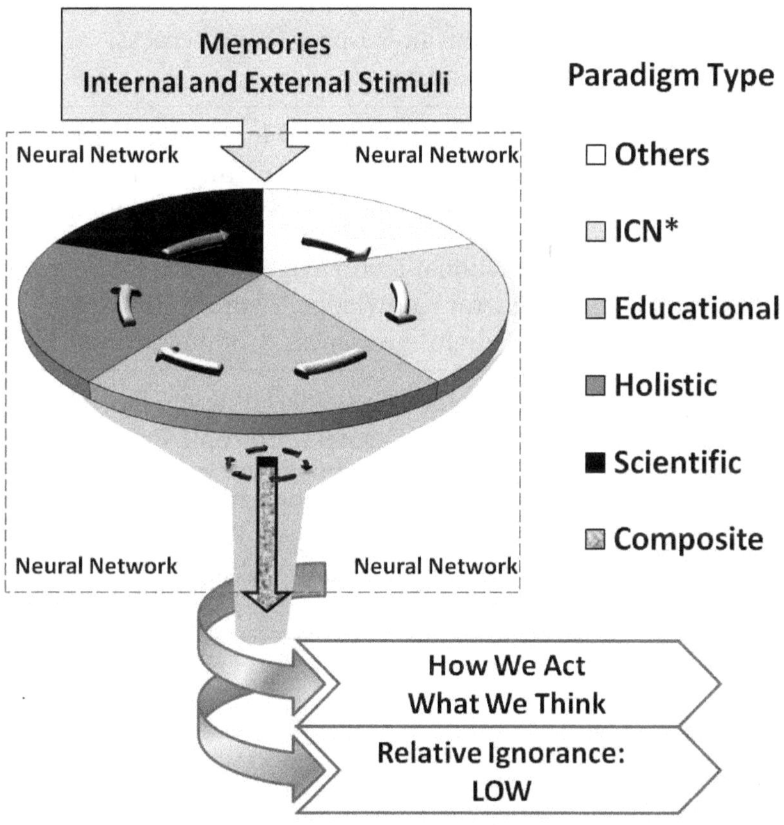

Table 8: Utopian Dominant Paradigm Neural Filters

Dominant Paradigm	Major Filters Affecting Thoughts and Actions
Others	Humanism, Respect, Togetherness, Philanthropy
Interconnectedness	Individual and Group Interdependence, Spiritual Unity, Mutualism, Reciprocity, Ecological Oneness, Systems Thinking
Educational	Functional Knowledge, Logical Discourse, General Knowledge, Critical Thinking, Paradigm Awareness, Communication Skills
Holistic	Big Picture, Systems Thinking, Synergy, Ecological Oneness, Entropic Principle
Scientific	Rigorous Observations and Data Collection; Formal Methodologies, Processes, Analysis, and Synthesis; Tool-Making

Table J: Utopian Ignorance Determination

Complements Figure 8 and Table 8

Ignorance Type	Era Score	Explanation
Known Unknowns	**2**	The Others and Educational paradigms provide a foundation for holistic scientific pursuits that collaboratively solve relevant problems, reducing the scope and effect of unknowns.
Unknown Unknowns	**3**	The ICN paradigm fosters the cooperative pursuit of knowledge that reduces uncertainty, unidentified risk, and unjustifiable assumptions.
Errors	**2**	With the support of other utopian dominant paradigms, the Scientific paradigm is able to reduce the number of errors and their effects.
Unknown Knowns	**2**	The Scientific and Education paradigms together strongly stimulate the search for new knowledge.
Taboos (Knowledge Avoidance)	**1**	Taboos decline to low levels as a result of holistic, Big Picture themes dominating daily life.
Denials	**1**	The Interconnectedness paradigm improves communication within and among groups, reducing the tribal thinking that fosters denial mentality.
Total Score	**11**	The composite paradigm leverages science, fosters interpersonal and inter/intra group communications, and drives Big Picture approaches to achieve ecological oneness.
Average Ignorance Level	**1.83**	**Era Assessment = Low Ignorance**

Paradigm Shifts: Free Will and Paths to Enlightenment

One aspect of my paradigmatic thesis is probably troubling the reader. It troubled me as well. What happened to free will? Why can't people decide not to think and behave in accordance with their dominant paradigms? Why can't we readily shift our paradigms and escape their hold over us? What's stopping us from readily adopting utopian perspectives? The answers lie in the definition of paradigms and their biological foundations (i.e., neural networks). As described very early in this book, paradigms are mental models of the information processed by our senses. Incorporated into these models are genetically evolved physiological survival responses to stimuli and a rich, experiential memory database. We know that as a person matures, neurological patterns form in the human brain via its interconnected nervous system. Bolstered by language and other symbolic communications tools, the human brain will strengthen its neural networks to include abstract content—reinforcing the bio-electrical patterns or paradigms held by the individual. A person's belief and value systems effectively become hardwired within the brain. Whatever free will we think we have actually stems from our composite paradigm, a direct reflection of our personal belief and value systems. This is the primary reason paradigm shifts occur slowly unless a dramatic event or trauma occurs. In a sense, we are addicted to our own paradigms and therefore have a low probability of exercising free will. Sure, we may neurologically be chocoholics and situationally stray to eat vanilla ice cream; however, statistically, we think and act as if chocolate was our only flavor choice.

To illustrate further, imagine you are having a conversation with a co-worker about national policies. She believes in conservative Christian values. She supports pro-life policies, a strong national defense, and trickle-down economics, among others. She also opposes liberal social trends, such as same-sex marriage. You take a more secular view, support socialistic programs such as graduated taxes to redistribute wealth, and donate heavily to environmental causes. She is really irritating you today because she's harping on her position that society is undergoing moral decay because of the gay rights movement and the federal government's rulings in favor of same-sex relationships. Both you and your co-worker are heavily invested in your individual composite paradigms. In your conversation, she paints you into an ideological corner regarding same-sex relationships, from which you find no escape. You reluctantly tell your co-worker that she's made valid points. You think you are exercising free will in stepping out of your paradigm and acquiescing to her arguments, but you're fooling yourself. You failed to develop a reasonable counterargument to her position at the time.

Yet it doesn't really matter whether or not a rationale counterargument exists. During your conversation and subsequent mental review of what had transpired in your discussion, no physiological changes occurred in your mental patterns that would affect your paradigms. This is a case of what I call false free will, a passing, situational phenomenon. Nothing your co-worker said will have a lasting impact on you *unless* you dwell on her words for a considerable time (days) and carefully and deliberately mull her ideas over, researching and dissecting arguments and counterarguments.

Maybe something else was at work. Perhaps you became frustrated with yourself for failing to find a cogent opposition view. So, you conceded the point just to shut her up. Conversations such as these occur daily. Most are probably highly superficial in the sense that the speakers have sound-bite understanding of the issues and/or are emotionally invested in their paradigms. The notion that we can *easily* break free of our paradigms by drawing upon free will or by intellectual reasoning is purely wishful thinking.

Some people believe that meditation can help them attain a higher plane of abstract thought by tuning out stimuli, focusing on their breathing and quieting the brain. [161] The calmed brain subsequently is capable of clearer thinking—in theory, at least. Mindfulness is another meditative technique where people try to focus on the moment, dwelling in the present rather than anguishing about what lies ahead. These mental "great escapes," while useful, are fleeting. We are merely trying to avoid the perpetual mental clutter forced upon us by our paradigms. We must all eventually return to the reality of mental activity. We experience our drives (hunger, thirst, sex, ego) and respond to stimuli. And unless we opt for a hermit lifestyle or devote a significant portion of each day to meditative practices, we will inevitably have notable interactions with others. Each time we do

---

[161] One doesn't necessarily have to quiet the brain to escape paradigms. If, for example, a person were to engage in developing or exercising pure mathematical operations—ones related to idealized models of the world, one could have a fully engaged mind, effectively, in a (temporary) paradigm-free state.

so, our paradigms come into play. Others will detect our paradigmatic propensities through our words and actions.

Earlier in this chapter, I proposed a utopian blend of Scientific, Holistic, Others, Educational, and Interconnectedness paradigms as a salvation to unbridled human ignorance. They offer an opportunity for the impartial pursuit of the truth about human affairs, our surroundings, and most importantly, our selves. Unfortunately, most of us operate under paradigms that corrosively bias our thoughts and irrationally blind our senses, leading to win-lose scenarios. One group or individual will end up in the winner's circle while others may never make it to the finish line. Nature may be indifferently cruel, but humankind should not facilitate the distasteful and barbaric aspects of life possible in a Hobbesian world.[162] By chance, some groups and individuals have profited naturally from their genetics, geography, and resource-rich surroundings. They enjoy life under a paradigm of abundance. Many of the less fortunate live in a paradigm of dearth and misery. We could do more for the downtrodden, but tribal tendencies keep us entrenched in the paradigms of plenty, unable to shift to humanistic perspectives. And so our future awaits us.

Since a utopian restructuring of dominant paradigms appears improbable, are there any other viable approaches that reduce ignorance? Perhaps, but we need to tread lightly. A plethora of bad ideas will likely surface, such as adopting an overarching national isolationist paradigm on the assumption that doing so would better serve the greater human community. In other words, societies would agree not to interfere with each other's paradigms or way of life. Unfortunately, under such a scheme, ignorance would continue to thrive, and perhaps escalate. We could divide the world into sectors—such as Islam, Christianity, Hindu, and so on. We could overlay economic and power paradigms onto these societies as determined by the individual nation-state. Commerce and an exchange of services could continue among the nation-states, undoubtedly with a restriction on certain imports and exports. Nations would operate under a Golden Rule of Paradigms: "Do not interfere with other's paradigms as you would not want them to interfere with yours." No paradigmatic interference means just that, even if human rights violations exist. Nation-states might consider exchanging citizens under a controlled, phased system to accommodate a limited number of those who want to

[162] Hobbes, 64.

immigrate to a country where they could live under preferred paradigms.

You're probably already uncomfortable with this Golden Rule notion and the idea of selective emigration and immigration. You know that certain religiously dominated societies treat women differently than your society does, or promotes the division of people into classes or castes, or aligns a specific religion with a nation. You're concerned that racism, ethnicism, or religious biases would proliferate. These attitudes are "wrong" according to your paradigm and you don't like it. Even within the United States, there are widely disparate views on religion, science, government regulation, economics, healthcare, morality, and more. Regional politics have already created major internal rifts. [163] Isolationism among nations would spur similar divisions within nations, marked by ethnic, racial, political, and economic groupings.

There *are* other options. Under the leadership of the United Nations—and without invoking a utopian package of perspectives, we could educate the world's population on what paradigms are, why they exist, and how they shape our thoughts and behaviors. We could do this without trying to invoke a dominant Educational paradigm described earlier. Most people will easily grasp that human conflict stems from one or more of the seven dominant paradigms. They will understand which specific paradigms lead to turmoil: the economics of Haves and Have-nots, ideological divergences, religious biases, cultural-ethnic-racial partiality, and political party supremacy. They will learn that warfare and civil and personal strife are ultimately a clash of two or more of the seven dominant paradigms.

Even if the U.N. were to police an expansive education program of this nature, my glass-half-empty view is that nations will only reinforce their existing paradigms, thereby exacerbating change. My pessimism is based on the U.N.'s previous attempt to educate the world's peoples on the content of the Universal Declaration of Human Rights following World War II—a dismal failure, despite almost all nations ratifying the declaration and agreeing to explain those rights to their citizens.

I do offer one last "best option" to improve our chances for a better future. Clearly, among the seven dominant paradigms that have shaped human history, the Scientific paradigm, when purely and

---

[163] See References: Woodard.

sincerely applied, is the only viable option for a paradigmatic foundation for the future. We could try to replace other existing dominant paradigms as suggested earlier (Holistic, ICN, et al), but the Scientific paradigm already is a dominant paradigm in the present era. We should leverage this worldview while attempting to reduce the significance of the other dominant paradigms. The Scientific paradigm must come to supersede all others, even attain super-dominance. It's our best hope, but would it lead to a global New Enlightenment that Steven Pinker sees for us (see Chapter 1)?

For a New Enlightenment to occur, we should consider briefly what the original Enlightenment entailed. In the words of Ian Mortimer:

> Immanuel Kant described the Enlightenment as the ability to think for oneself, free from convention and dogma. Given such a broad definition, it is hardly surprising that it has been treated as an enormously elastic term. It is frequently taken to be a synonym for all the changes that distinguish the breezy, elegant world of Jane Austen's novels from the dark depths of the witch-burning seventeenth century. It is an intellectual bucket into which scientific concepts and rationalist theories are idly tossed, along with the rise of political economy and the decline of superstition. In that general sense, the Enlightenment started with Francis Bacon and Galileo in the early seventeenth century, incorporated the Scientific Revolution in its entirety, and did not come to an end until after the fall of Napoleon in 1815. This clearly is too vague a definition and too long a time span. …[164]

Considering the spectrum of paradigms during the era historians have labeled as The Enlightenment, we would stumble in any attempt to bring clarity to the concept of enlightenment. Mortimer's assessment seems grounded; Pinker's proposal that a New Enlightenment has arrived or has been building upon the original enduring Enlightenment seems, at best, premature. Could a Buddhist worldview solve this quandary?

---

[164] Mortimer, 170.

Previously, in our discussion of ignorance, we referred to a depiction of ignorance from a Buddhist perspective (awareness and acceptance of impermanence in our lives). Buddhists also consider that a path to enlightenment exists via meditation and mindfulness. Legend has it that the Buddha attained true enlightenment after a 49-day, solitary meditative session under a Bodhi (Fig) Tree. While such extreme measures are impractical for most, let us assume the Buddha was able to acquire his enlightened state through his extended meditative practices. We must then ask, "How would his neural networks have changed?" By answering this question, we can gain insights into practical avenues for the less ascetic of us to attain enlightenment.

Effectively, the Buddha would have had to reboot his mind, rewriting his neural networks so that he was open-minded, a paradigm in itself, gained by reflection, allowing him to overcome the paradigms of his experiences and genetics. In being open-minded, he would have been able to apply logic to examine situations. He would have conceived of ethical structures for dealing with human interactions. The Buddha would still not have had free will since his new paradigms would have driven him toward specific thoughts and actions consistent with his modified neural networks. His open-mindedness would simply prevent him from blindly adhering to the socio-cultural paradigms of his era.

The teachings of and methods employed by the Buddha could serve as a launching pad for developing informal and formal educational approaches for achieving an enlightened society. Yet, on whole, this appears a pipe dream. While his and other ancient and modern techniques to escape our paradigmatic caves hold promise, reality tells us that "… all the world does never gregariously advance to Truth, but only here and there some of its individuals do; and by advancing, leave the rest behind…."[165] To create a mass enlightenment movement, we would have to integrate Buddhist and similar methodologies with other approaches, such as including them within the Scientific paradigm or the global educational initiative recently mentioned. One thing is for sure. If we don't make a concerted effort as a planet to collectively effect holistic paradigm shifts, the drumbeat of our dominant paradigms will continue, echoing down the ages to remind us of our shortcomings.

---

[165] Melville, 232.

It's clearly time for us Moderns to unshackle ourselves, collectively, without leaving others behind, to emerge from the caves that for so long have withheld us from best truths, and to take the necessary steps to replace the paradigms that would otherwise sustain our ignorance.

The journey will be a long and difficult one. Let us begin.

Epilogue: Paradigms, Identity, and the Soul

"Man is born free; and everywhere he is in chains. One thinks himself the master of others, and still remains a greater slave than they." – Rousseau [166]

In this quote from *The Social Contract*, Jean Jacques Rousseau was referring to the relationship between humans and the nation-state into which they are born.[167] Rousseau could have easily been referring to our paradigms or neural networks. We are born essentially paradigm free, but eventually we become chained to the paradigms that befall us. We may have illusions of mastery over our paradigms, but rarely unfetter ourselves from our caves.

Certainly, a troubling question then arises, "If our neural networks define us, are we simply an amalgamation of genetic and experiential paradigms?" After all, our expressed thoughts and behaviors tell us and others who we are as individuals. And we see ourselves through our own paradigms, meaning our self-perception is also biased; others see us through their paradigms, affecting how they perceive us. Following this logic, we have little ability to affect our

[166] Rousseau, 5.

[167] Of course, Rousseau's paradigms would likely not have been inclusive, meaning women and others might not elevate to the role of master. Accordingly, I've replaced "man" with "humans" in this sentence.

perception of identity—that is, our paradigms tell us who we and others are. In a real sense, then, identity is merely another tool or convenience (mental construct) for categorizing and classifying personalities, thereby assisting in social interactions and in comprehending ourselves and others. Each person's paradigms establish his identity. Those same paradigms provide a means (capability) to identify individual purpose, allowing us to assign meaning to life consistent with those paradigms. Still, some of us never find a paradigm-inspired direction to fulfill our lives. Most would find such a conclusion a difficult reality to swallow—specifically that our integrated neural networks provide identity, purpose, and meaning. We want to believe we're something more than genetic wiring and action-reaction programming. We want to think we're in control—masters of ourselves and others, as Rousseau might put it.

A counterargument to the idea that individual humans lack a distinctive identity and are simply paradigm-induced, tool-leveraging hominids, is human achievement—the genius of scientific discovery, the creation of works of art and musical composition, and the development of ethical and moral standards. Don't such activities imply the existence of individual identity that goes beyond mere wiring and programming? Again, the answer is a definitive "No." We have merely acquired paradigms that revere creative and skillful people within our group(s), assigning them special categories with unique identities. We may see them as "gifted" or "special." We do this to add meaning to our social and individual lives.

The reality is that each human brain and its associated nervous system possesses some level of creativity and skill potential, meaning we are all capable of ingenuity even if we fail to act creatively. In general, we create to survive and thrive, fulfilling in many cases, paradigmatically induced needs. What we call individual creativity is merely a statistical component of our collective skills resulting from our symbolic and physical tool-making and stimulated by our composite paradigms. A few of us are highly creative, most of us are moderately creative, and a few are barely creative. In many cases, our ingenuity has little opportunity to blossom due to premature death, social strife, accidents, disease, uninspiring upbringings, or other circumstance.

We should also note the dualistic nature of our paradigms and our tool-making. They stimulate each other co-dependently. The human brain has made us the consummate tool-makers among Earth's species, whether the tools be symbolic (e.g., mathematical equations and language) or physical (e.g., manipulation of materials and metallurgy). Our inventiveness is both a product of existing paradigms and a catalyst for new ones. Neural networks can change in substance and characteristic as a result of our creative endeavors. We addressed this effect in Chapter 7 while describing technology's impact in spurring paradigm shifts.

We must also acknowledge that tool-making is truly a social phenomenon, accomplished by cooperative engagement with others and/or by building upon the work of others. Einstein, Newton, da Vinci, ancient pyramid architects, Great Wall constructors, et al accomplished what they did by examining the work of contemporaries or those who preceded them; or through collaboration with others; and/or through the direct or indirect support of others provided by a societal division of labor. Social interaction, needs, and context stimulate the brain's tool-making ability, and conversely, tool-making inspires social networks and neural changes. Recognizing the social character of tool-making does not alter our conclusion about the source of our identities. The stimulation of our tool-making abilities facilitates the creation of identities. A person versed in woodworking calls himself a carpenter; the carpenter's identity symbolically originates in his woodworking paradigm, a subset of his composite paradigm. Accordingly, we assign uniquely skilled individuals symbolic identities—giants and geniuses among us. We label Newton and Einstein "Great Minds," Leonardo da Vinci an "Inventor and Artist Extraordinaire," pyramid designers and constructors "masterminds and master builders," and so on. Most of us have "everyday normal" identities, persevering through moments of genius and ineptitude.

While our paradigms provide us identities, they also help determine our level of ignorance. Our ignorance exposes our character traits to others. Similar to creative ability, ignorance has a statistical dispersion. Some of us are grossly ignorant, others moderately ignorant, and still others modestly ignorant. Although life without ignorance is impossible, a person can live a minimally ignorant life. Attaining this state is a long and difficult journey except when catastrophes, tragedies, and other significant experiences lead to major paradigm shifts of enlightenment. The prolonged path to enlightenment requires the individual to gradually restructure many paradigms of his youth and early adulthood, to possess the functional knowledge and mindset to critically analyze all paradigms, to overcome social and economic impediments, and to actively view paradigm shifts as an opportunity to improve one's self. Success in shifting one's paradigms affects how others see us and we see ourselves. Paradigm shifts equate to a change in identity—the only means to do so once reaching adulthood.

Unfortunately, as we've discussed on numerous occasions, the human mind naturally resists changing the imprinting experienced in early childhood and other periods of life. If one's experiences are negative, such as physical and mental abuse, the task of changing neural networks will be even more difficult. Since the brain's inherent genetic neural networks are wired for survival, our brains will do what they can to protect us, both from ourselves (e.g., bad memories) and the obstacles faced in the immediate environment. In the extreme, as in cases of abuse, the paradigms that form are subject to severe corruptions, but they serve as a means for the mind to sustain the individual (e.g., wives staying with abusive husbands because the alternatives seem bleak). The effect on identity can be devastating.

The tendency to behave and to think according to many early-in-life experiences is common throughout nature. Ducklings line up behind mother because of their genetic programming, a way to increase their probability of survival. The "hatch paradigm" is a pre-birth neural network causing the duckling to exhibit follow-the-leader behavior even if a substitute mother is present upon hatching (even a human substitute mother!). As the duckling grows, this paradigm will fade. Other experiential paradigms begin to dominate. These new networks integrate with other genetically induced paradigms such as nesting. As discussed previously, similar effects occur in humans in the formation of infant paradigms.

The rewiring process depends upon a host of factors, such as age, health, external environment, and the condition (robustness or weakness) of existing neural networks. Formal education provides one means to restructure paradigms in a constructive manner. The new perspectives *may* develop and strengthen one's neural networks, *possibly* reducing ignorance level. However, a caustic social environment during the education process could defeat the effects of educational enlightenment and increase an individual's or group's ignorance. A classic example in academia is the bullying of students by their peers. Bullying and other abusive behavior largely stem from negative stereotyping (paradigms), which often shapes ignorant perspectives regarding the intellectual, physical, racial, ethnic, religious, and economic backgrounds of others.

Do the preceding discussions on identity and the difficulty of lifting our individual veil of ignorance provide any insights into the concept of the human soul? Perhaps, but Religious paradigms already provide many their perspectives of a spiritual soul. However, we've also seen how dominant paradigms can overlap, meaning religious perspectives can easily intertwine with a person's Self paradigm. Accordingly, a person's identity paradigm(s) could meld with his religious paradigm(s) to create a spiritual individuality, a MC that equates to a soul. The merger of self, spiritual, emotional, and informational neural networks, therefore, would effectively define the soul—who we inherently are at a given time in our lives. This fusion of paradigms, however, introduces a time dependency into the essence of the soul, clouding our perspective. Thus, the soul remains a leap of human faith. Also, as done in many religions, special circumstances would have to apply to the souls of infants and others who die prematurely and never acquire a definitive paradigmatic identity.

Despite the aforementioned shortcomings, I will suggest a context for relating the idea of a soul to an individual's paradigm structure. In this book, we've seen that each person develops a unique composite paradigm, even if an individual is genetically identical to another at birth, such as with identical twins. This is so because composite paradigms form under distinct genetic and environmental influences. Even well-controlled environments for identical twins do not guarantee similar experiences (e.g., the position from which we view a half-blue and half-yellow sphere). Recall that a person's composite paradigm represents his composite neural network. It dictates his thoughts and behaviors. Is this not the person's soul—what makes him or her "tick?" Is this not how others judge us, and for those of faith, how a divine being would evaluate our worthiness for paradise?

Viewing the soul as a distinctive amalgamation of paradigms aligns, in one sense, with religious conceptions of good and evil. Our paradigms provide a foundation for defining good and evil. Goodness is the product of what religious doctrine would designate a worthy neural network (e.g., charitable); evil stems from an unworthy one (e.g., selfish).[168] An objective of many religions is to convert evil or sinful souls to good ones. The good news is that composite paradigms *can* change. Thus, we should find solace in knowing that, by shifting our paradigms to the good, we can save our souls, either with or without the assistance of others.

As for me, I'm comfortable dispensing with the idea that I have a soul. I'm satisfied knowing I can develop a more holistic composite paradigm and become less ignorant. I acknowledge it won't be easy. I'll need help from others. I'm confident my paradigmatic equivalent of a soul will shift to the good, making me a better person, but I'll aim much higher—for enlightenment.

---

[168] This sentence is highly contestable as it is a mental construct poorly linked to objective reality. However, it aligns with the assumptions associated with the characterization of a spiritual soul.

Glossary of Paradigm and Ignorance Terminology
(in alphabetical order)

Dominant and Special-Case Paradigms

Economic paradigm: The system of thought and behavior delineating the manner in which humans interact to barter goods and services.

Educational paradigm: The holistic system of thought and behavior, focused on functional knowledge and analytical skills, which facilitates the logical and scientific acquisition of knowledge about self, others, and the immediate and distant environs.

Group paradigm: The system of thought and behavior delineating the manner in which humans interact within, among, and between members of their own group(s) and with members of other groups.

Holistic paradigm: The system of thought and behavior stemming from open and logical inquiry into the causal relationships governing human affairs and the universe at large.

Ideological paradigm: The system of thoughts and behaviors, developed from the abstractions stimulated by experience, delineating how humans should live and interact.

Interconnectedness paradigm: The holistic system of thought and behavior by which humans cooperatively interact individually with each other and collectively within, between, and among groups, recognizing not only the varieties and richness of humanity's subcultures but also Nature's diversity.

Others paradigm: The system of thought and behavior stemming from the concern for the welfare of the local and greater human community.

Pendular Paradigm: A system of thought and behavior that shifts over time as a result of short-term experiences, eventually returning to its original characteristics, on whole alternating about a norm.

Power paradigm: The system of thought and behavior delineating the manner in which humans interact to control others, their circumstances, and their environment.

Religious paradigm: The system of thought and behavior stemming from the divinization of events within human experience, leading to belief in a spiritual existence that governs human affairs and the universe at large.

Scientific paradigm: The system of thought and behavior stemming from the diligent and disciplined examination of organic and inorganic environments, local and distant.

Self paradigm: The system of thought, behavior, and instinct delineating the manner in which humans experience themselves, whether in private thought or interacting with others.

Situational Paradigm: A neural network response that may override a dominant paradigm due to specific circumstances confronting a person or group, most typically affecting an individual's Self and Group paradigms.

Ignorance-Related Terms

Belief Perseverance: The persistence of a belief system, even in the presence of contrary factual evidence.

Factual Ignorance: The collective misperceptions stemming from the misinformation a person accepts as factual, often indicative of the political preferences of an individual or group.

Functional Knowledge: Acquired knowledge (and skills) that allows an individual to successfully function within his/her group, tribe, and society and which in the modern era, generally includes basic arithmetic, language proficiency, manual dexterity, and sufficient knowledge of the local environment.

Genetically Induced Ignorance: The selective rejection of sensory information resulting from species-inherited or parentally inherited genes.

Interpretational or Dependency Ignorance: An individual's or group's failure to pursue knowledge due to the intricacies of the situation(s) confronted, naively interpreting (or justifying) the complexities involved and depending instead on the systems that are in place to deal with the issues.

Rational Closed-Mindedness: The mental state in which a person dismisses certain types of information or limits his exposure to specific ideas because he finds the content too difficult to grasp or insufficiently rewarding to pursue, generally deeming the information or ideas irrelevant to his life and/or lifestyle.

Rational Ignorance: A quality exhibited by an individual when he justifies or rationalizes incongruent thoughts and actions based on personal comfort or benefit, thereby ignoring facts, trends, and other relevant information.

Rational Irrationality: A quality exhibited by an individual when he rationalizes his thoughts and actions based on unjustifiable or emotional premises, including the desire to belong to a group. Malice, whimsy, and a yearning to be accepted are among the factors which may motivate such behaviors.

Simulative Eco-Politics: Political posturing that promotes ideas in the abstract with no intention to act on them or with the specific intention of trivializing the effort required to implement them.

Veil of ignorance: A genetic influence on neural networks that suppresses competitive behaviors within a species and facilitates group cohesion.

Willful ignorance: The intentional perpetuation of nonfactual information, ideas, and perceptions in order to control or manipulate outcomes or to avoid learning a meaningful truth. Political and socioeconomic narratives often convey willfully ignorant messages.

References

Aliber, Robert Z. *The Multinational Paradigm.* The MIT Press, Cambridge, MA (1993).

Baldwin, James. *No Name in the Street.* The Dial Press, New York (1972).

Bayern, Shawn J. (2009). Rational ignorance, rational closed-mindedness, and modem economic formalism in contract law. *California Law Review,* Vol. 97: 943-973. Retrieved October 29, 2012 from University of Hawaii Library's Academic Search Premier.

Becker, Adam. *What is Real? The Unfinished Quest for the Meaning of Quantum Physics.* Basic Books, New York (2018).

Bertoldi, Paolo et al. "Standby Power Use: How Big is the Problem? What Policies and Technical Solutions Can Address It?" Lawrence Berkeley National Laboratory report (online) at https://escholarship.org/uc/item/6xm6k7wg, posted 05 Jun 2002.

Carpini, Michael X. Delli and Keeter, Scott (1991). Stability and change in the U.S. public's knowledge of politics. *Public Opinion Quarterly Volume 55*:583-612. Retrieved October 22, 2012 from University of Hawaii Library's Academic Search Premier.

Cavendish, Richard (ed.). *Mythology: An Illustrated Encyclopedia.* Barnes & Noble Books, New York (1992).

Diamond, Jared. *Collapse: How Societies Choose to Fail and Succeed.* Penguin Books, New York (2005).

Diamond, Jared. *The Third Chimpanzee: The Evolution and Future of the Human Animal.* Harper Perennial, New York (1992).

Firestein, Stuart. *Ignorance: How It Drives Science*, Oxford University Press, New York (2012).

Garnett, Michael (2007). Ignorance, incompetence and the concept of liberty. *The Journal of Political Philosophy:* Volume 15, Number 4: 428–446. Retrieved September 2, 2012 from University of Hawaii Library's Academic Search Premier.

Gilens, Martin (2001). Political ignorance and collective policy preferences. *American Political Science Review*, 95: 379–96. Retrieved October 25, 2012 from University of Hawaii Library's Academic Search Premier.

Goldberg, Harold J. (2007). *D-Day in the Pacific: The Battle of Saipan.* Indiana University Press, Bloomington, Indiana (e-book).

Goldstein, Joseph. "The Four Foundations of Mindfulness, *Lion's Roar*, November 12, 2013. Accessed 21 Jan 2017 at http://www.lionsroar.com/the-four-foundations-of-mindfulness-2/.

Green, Emma. "Islam Could Become the World's Largest Religion After 2070." *The Atlantic* (online), April 2, 2015.

Harari, Yuval Noah. *Homo Deus: A Brief History of Tomorrow.* Vintage (Penguin Random House, UK), London: 2015.

Harari, Yuval Noah. *Sapiens: A Brief History of Humankind.* HarperCollins Publishers, New York: 2015.

Harris S, Kaplan JT, Curiel A, Bookheimer SY, Iacoboni M, et al. (2009). "The Neural Correlates of Religious and Nonreligious Belief." Refer to PLoS ONE 4(10): e0007272. doi: 10.1371/journal.pone.0007272.

Herman, Louis. Lectures and readings from Political Science courses: Global Futures, Science and the Modern Prospect, and Political Philosophy courses, University of Hawaii West Oahu, 2010-2011. Major concepts: Socratic Method, Medicine Wheel, Truth Quest, and Good Life.

Hitler, Adolf. *Mein Kampf (My Struggle)*. Originally published 1925. Obtained online via the Internet Archive at www.archive.org. Translation by James Murphy. Published by Hurst and Blackett, Ltd., London (1939).

Hobbes, Thomas (1651). *Leviathan or the Matter, Form, & Power of a Commonwealth, Ecclesiastical and Civil*. George Routledge and Sons, London (Third Edition, 1887).

Hughes, Matthew. "When Soldiers Kill Civilians." History Today, Feb. 2010, Vol. 60, Issue 2, pp. 42-48.

Humphrey, Matthew (2009). Rational irrationality and simulation in environmental politics: The example of climate change. *Government and Opposition*, Vol. 44, No. 2, pp. 146–166. Retrieved September 9, 2012 from University of Hawaii Library's Academic Search Premier.

Johnson, Susan C. and Chen, Frances S.' "Socioemotional Information Processing in Human Infants: From Genes to Subjective Construals." *Emotion Review*, Vol. 3, No. 2 (April 2011), 169-178.

Johnson, Susan C., Dweck, Carol S., and Chen, Frances S., "Evidence for Infants' Internal Working Models of Attachment." *Psychological Science*, Vol. 18, No. 6 (June 2007), 501-502.

Kuhn, Thomas S. *The Structure of Scientific Revolutions (Second Edition)*. The University of Chicago Press, Chicago (1962, 1970).

Lepore, Jill. *These Truths: A History of the United States*. W.W. Norton and Company, New York (2018).

Levitin, Daniel J. *The Organized Mind: Thinking Straight in the Age of Information Overload*. Dutton (Penguin Group), New York (2014).

Lynch, Kevin. "Willful Ignorance and Self-Deception," Philosophical Studies: An International Journal for Philosophy in the Analytic Tradition, Vol. 173, No. 2 (February 2016).

Mejias, Jorge. *Sensory competition (1): A clash of odors.* Accessed October 17, 2019 and posted December 27, 2013 from https://mappingignorance.org/2013/12/27/sensory-competition-1-a-clash-of-odors/.

Melville, Herman. *Pierre or, The Ambiguities.* London: Constable and Company Ltd, 1923.

Meyer, Robinson. "The Unprecedented Surge in Fear About Climate Change," *The Atlantic* (online), January 23, 2019.

Mortimer, Ian. *Millennium: From Religion to Revolution: How Civilization Has Changed Over a Thousand Years*. Pegasus Books, New York (2016). Kindle Edition.

Nyhan, Brendan & Reifler, Jason (2010). "When corrections fail: The persistence of political misperceptions," *Political Behavior,* 32: 303–330. Retrieved September 2, 2012 from University of Hawaii Library's Academic Search Premier.

Pinker, Steven. *Enlightenment Now: The Case for Reason, Science, Humanism, and Progress*. Viking, New York (2018).

Plato. *The Republic*. From http://www.gutenberg.org/ebooks/1497. Project Gutenberg EBook #1497, August 27, 2008. Translated by B. Jowett.

Queller, David C. and Strassman, Joan E. "The veil of ignorance can favour biological cooperation." Downloaded from http://rsbl.royalsocietypublishing.org/ on January 18, 2016 from Biology Letters (Evolutionary Biology) 9: 20130365. http://dx.doi.org/10.1098/rsbl.2013.0365.

Rose, Lydia and Bartoli, Teresa. "Agnotology and the Epistemology of Ignorance: a Framework for the Propagation of Ignorance as a Consequence of Technology in a Balkanized Media

Ecosystem," Postdigital Science and Education (2020) 2:184–201. Refer to https://doi.org/10.1007/s42438-019-00084-5. Published online: 10 December 2019, © Springer Nature Switzerland AG 201.

Rousseau, Jean Jaques. *The Social Contract*. J. M. Dent & Sons Ltd., London (1938). Edited by Ernest Rhys. Originally published 1762.

Schwartz, Stephan A. (2008). Willful ignorance. *EXPLORE,* Vol. 4, No. 4, 232-234. Retrieved September 14, 2012 from University of Hawaii Library's Academic Search Premier.

Schwartz, Stephan A. (2010). The denier movements critique evolution, climate change, and nonlocal consciousness. *EXPLORE*, Vol. 6, No. 3: 135-142. Retrieved September 14, 2012 from University of Hawaii Library's Academic Search Premier.

Schwartz, Stephan A. (2012). Climate change and willful ignorance. *EXPLORE*, Vol. 8, No. 5: 268-270. Retrieved September 14, 2012 from University of Hawaii Library's Academic Search Premier.

Shepherd, Steven & Kay, Aaron C. (2012). On the perpetuation of ignorance: System dependence, system justification, and the motivated avoidance of sociopolitical information. *Journal of Personality and Social Psychology, Vol. 102, No. 2*, 264–280. Retrieved September 2, 2012 from University of Hawaii Library's Academic Search Premier.

Shermer, Michael. *Why People Believe Weird Things: Pseudoscience, Superstition, and Other Confusions of Our Time*. W. H. Freeman and Company, New York (1997).

Smith, Adam. *An Inquiry into the Nature and Causes of the Wealth of Nations*. Metal.ibri, New York (2007) available through the Internet Archive, at www.archive.org.

Somin, Ilya, Deliberative Democracy and Political Ignorance. *Critical Review*, Vol. 22, Nos. 2-3, 2010, pp. 253-279.

Storm, Heyemeyohsts. *Seven Arrows*. Harper & Row Publishers, New York (1972).

Taddei, François (2009). "Training creative and collaborative knowledge-builders: a major challenge for 21st century education." United Nations Educational, Scientific, and Cultural Organization (UNESCO) paper prepared for OECD Innovation Strategy. Retrieved November 28, 2012 from http://www.cri-paris.org/docs/ocde-francois-taddei-fev2009.pdf.

Teilhard de Chardin, Pierre. *The Phenomenon of Man*. Harper Perennial, New York (2008).

The Holy Bible - Revised Standard Edition. Boston, MA: Whittemore Associates, Inc., 1952.

Toland, John. *The Rising Sun: The Decline and Fall of the Japanese Empire, 1935-1945.* The Modern Library, New York (1970, 1998).

Ungar, Sheldon (2008). Ignorance as an under-identified social problem. *The British Journal of Sociology, Volume 59 Issue 2*. Retrieved September 14, 2012 from University of Hawaii Library's Academic Search Premier.

Witte, Marlys; Crown, Peter; Bernas, Michael; and Witte Charles: Chapter Title: "Lessons Learned from Ignorance: The Curriculum on Medical (and Other) Ignorance" from Vitek, Bill and Jackson Wes, editors of *The Virtues of Ignorance: Complexity, Sustainability, and the Limits of Knowledge,* University Press of Kentucky (2008), 251-272. Accessed via http://www.jstor.org/stable/j.ctt2jcj0d.19.

Woodard, Colin. *American Nations: A History of the Eleven Rival Regional Cultures of North America*. Viking (Penguin Group), New York (2011).

Index

www.ingramcontent.com/pod-product-compliance
Lightning Source LLC
LaVergne TN
LVHW010544160826
845677LV00013B/2991
* 9 7 9 8 5 5 2 8 9 3 8 5 0 *